T0354825

STEPPING FORWARD

On The Sidewalk

CAROL LUCAS

STEPPING FORWARD
ON THE SIDEWALK

iUniverse books may be ordered through booksellers or by contacting:

iUniverse
1663 Liberty Drive
Bloomington, IN 47403
www.iuniverse.com
844-349-9409

ISBN: 978-1-6632-5488-7 (sc)
ISBN: 978-1-6632-5489-4 (e)

Library of Congress Control Number: 2023913743

Print information available on the last page.

iUniverse rev. date: 04/05/2024

STEPPING FORWARD

On The Sidewalk

Real Healing

As I stated in my book *Fostered Adult Children on the Bridge to Healing*, telling my story is well worth it if it helps other former foster children. I will be as honest and real in the telling as I possibly can, as I believe that *revealing and feeling is healing.* The only way for me to truly heal from my childhood trauma was to be real, not sugar coating anything. I will reveal even the most traumatic parts of my past, not only to free myself, but to free others to also share their past. I am a true believer that *the truth will set you free.* Out of respect for my siblings and other family members I am only sharing the truth about me. And the truth is I had a very traumatic childhood, one that led to further trauma as an adult, living much my youth living on the fringes of life, very uncertain of who I was or what I wanted, mostly preferring to numb out through alcohol and drugs, which I did quite well for seven years. I have been suicidal, almost succeeding three times, and I have been in and out of therapy numerous times, preferring to run from it in my early years, as the truth was just too painful. I have also been a frequent visitor to AA, ACOA, sexual abuse support groups, grief support groups, and of course the **FACT** support group for former foster children. And let me not forget to say that I was also a frequent visitor to grocery stores, looking for boxes to help me pack my belongings in because I was moving, again. I was always on the move and running from my past, but I couldn't get away from until I faced it.

What was so painful about my childhood that drove me to escape from the memory of it? As I sat thinking about what to say that would adequately express my thoughts and feelings, was at a loss for words, but what came to mind was a woman who shared her story in my first book. Since I probably can't express it any better than she did, I will share what a woman wrote in her story about being a foster child:

What is it like being a foster child?

We are helpless, afraid, and alone. We are the foster children. For some of us our lives began in turmoil, and for some the turmoil started like a menacing flame and burst into a terrible flame. Our childhood is ripped from us. Then comes foster care. We start out in foster care already broken. Why are the foster parents so amazed when we don't act like normal children? What are the foster parents thinking? We have been taken away from everything familiar and thrust toward people we don't know. It was the behavior of adults that caused us to be taken in the first place, and now we are given to other adults. What are we supposed to do? We don't trust anymore, and we are given like property to strangers? The fear is unbearable. The loneliness is a black void. The insecurity is a dark cloud that follows us from home to home, from adult to adult. We have no place to call our own, no real beginnings, no hope, we are not loved, and we are so aware of that. There is really no way to describe what it is really like to be a foster child and have no control of what is happening to you. It is a horror beyond words. You are not alive; you are merely existing. Your feel nothing, you become numb, you trust no one, and you completely withdraw from the world. Some children become enraged, some become severely timid, some become dependent on anything that provides any semblance of comfort, and some children are completely destroyed. The few who flourish are those who have had the wise and understanding foster parents who grow to love 'their child.' These are the angels in the system, but they are far and few between. Imagine taking a broken child and placing them with foster parents who are abusive; how do they measure their self-worth? If you are a foster parent, please be good to us. We need to be loved and understood. We need patience and kindness. We are already broken...do not shatter us.

She went on to describe herself as a ***throwaway child,*** which is a perfect description of what many foster children feel like. Trash. Something to just be thrown away and forgotten about. In a book about foster care that I used years ago for a college class, a young foster boy was found hiding in a trash can, and when asked why he was there he replied, "because that's what I feel like—trash. You might as well just throw me away." A throwaway child. How sad. Whoever that little boy was, I sure hope that somewhere on his journey through this life he realized he was more than just a piece of trash.

As for me, it has been a long, hard journey in healing from my past, a journey I did not look forward to and resisted with all my might until I finally had to give up the fight. It was either do or die for me, as the path I was on was destroying me. I simply HAD to surrender to the *FACT* that I was messed up and needed help. What held me back for so many years? Shame. It was my enemy for a long time, until I realized shame can only be healed by bringing it out of the dark it lives in and into the light where it could no longer hurt me. An even bigger enemy for me than shame though was my fear of the emotional pain involved in *going back there*. It just hurt too much. My journey has been wrought with many anguished tears, tears that left me feeling so vulnerable and alone that I went in search for a support group for former foster children, only to discover there weren't any, so decided to form one myself.

I poured my whole heart and soul into forming FACT and I pray it will touch the many lives who need and/or want it, as I have seen the healing in my own life and wish it for others. As painful as it was for me to 'go back there,' it was only by doing so that I was finally able to begin a journey On the Bridge to Healing. As I look over my shoulder it is clear to me that God, my Heavenly Father, has been guiding me on my journey and healing me toward a greater truth. And the truth is He was able to take me, a broken child, and mend me. It is with this truth that I share my story.

In the Beginning was Innocence

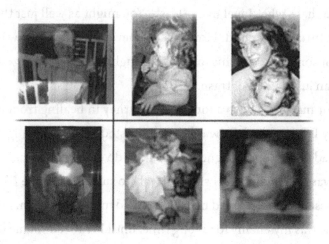

I came into this world on July 24, 1955, in Mattoon, Illinois. I am the seventh out of ten children who were all supposedly wanted by both of our parents, though I question my mother's desire for motherhood. Her attitude and behavior did not seem indicative of a woman who truly had a strong desire and love for children, but she was Catholic and obviously very fertile, so just kept popping us out one after the other. She looked content in pictures of her holding me and my siblings as babies, but not so much so as we got older. I believe my mother was at least a borderline narcissist who was mostly concerned about what her children could give to her rather than what she could give to her children. My father was the nurturing parent, not my mother. The fact that my mother later gave up custody of two more children she had to their father is also very telling. It appears none of us were that important to her, at least not as important as we should have been.

My father was the nurturing parent, not my mother. The fact that my mother later gave up custody of two more children she had to their father is also very telling. It appears none of us were that important to her, at least not as important as we should have been. What is even more telling of my mother's narcissism was the fact that she would never take any responsibility for abandoning her children, blaming my dad for everything.

My Father

As for my father, I only found out recently from a brother that my dad was around me when I was a young child. I always thought I didn't know my dad until I was ten years old, but I did; I was just too young to remember him. Other than one memory of him giving me candy, and another one of him coming home and making us hamburgers when he found out we hadn't been fed properly by our mom, I have no memories of him. But even though I don't have vivid memories of him, I do have a strong feeling in my heart and soul that he loved me as a young child and that is why I was so comfortable with him when I met him as a young girl.

I never knew all the facts about his time in the VA hospital while recovering from WW11, only fragments and rumors. I know he had malaria and that he suffered from PTSD, but I also heard he had amnesia for seven years, which would explain why he was gone so long from our family. My sister just recently told me that our dad was found on the side of the road in the Coca Cola truck he drove, not knowing who or where he was, which makes sense since he had PTSD. Who knows for sure? I will never know all the facts about either of my parents and I have long given up on it; at this point it would be a futile attempt at something that isn't that important to me anymore.

What is important to me is the fact of the few years I had the privilege of spending with my dad before he died. After hearing so many stories of other foster children who never even knew their fathers, I feel grateful I was blessed with at least a few years with him. My dad was the sunshine and rock in my otherwise insecure and unstable childhood. When my life went down the toilet in my young years, it was the years I spent with my dad that gave me a firm foundation to build my life on. If not for the love he showed me, I hate to think how much worse my life would have been.

Before I begin writing about my traumatic childhood, it is important that I share some happy memories, as my childhood was not all bad. I do recall some pleasant memories, which I believe is largely why foster care was so painful for me. I intuitively sense that I knew love as a young child and losing that was why I hurt so much when I was abandoned to foster care. I believe that losing love is the hardest thing for anyone of any age, but especially for a child who needs the love and nurturing in order to grow emotionally healthy. I also believe we are all born from pure love, and when children are abused and/or neglected we lose that connection, which hurts us to our core, to our heart and soul. I am a very sensitive soul who understands this deeply, and it is why I have cried deeply over my own issues and feel so much empathy for other foster children. Here is what my brother wrote so eloquently at the end of the FACT book about foster children:

We are the lost and abandoned children of this world. We do not wish to come *before the bar of man as yet another voice clamoring*

for rights. We make no claim in any earthly court for our birthrights which have been taken. We come from many lands and speak many languages, but our stories are remarkably the same. Our journeys have been through the darkest streets of the soul you can imagine. Often there was little light, neither from man who injured us, nor from God who seemed to stand by in divine indifference to our suffering. The petitions of our hearts fell on what seemed the deaf ears of a callous universe that had cast us away. For us the ties of blood and family were severed. For us, home was no longer a present place of safety and a loving refuge, but rather a hoped-for destination we might find some day. Like so many tiny boats adrift on the ocean, we have looked long for the lighthouse of our homeland.

What impressed me the most about this passage were the sentences, *Our journeys have been through the darkest streets of the soul you can imagine* and *For us, home was no longer a place of safety and a loving refuge, but rather a hoped for destination we might find some day. Like so many tiny boats adrift on the ocean, we have looked long for the lighthouse of our homeland.* Try explaining this to someone who has not experienced foster care and you won't find the understanding, which only serves to make you feel more isolated and unloved. I have come to the realization through my own interactions with the general population that they are mostly indifferent to my experience, which is why I don't care to share much about my past or my work with foster children. It is senseless and a waste of time trying to convey my experience to people who don't understand and/or care. It is like going to an empty well. I can't draw water from an empty well, and I can't get real understanding or empathy from people who haven't had my experience. They simply don't have it to give. The ones who will understand and give me empathy are the ones who have gone through it, and that is why *FACT* was formed.

It was an act of love on my part, one that will hopefully and God willing have a ripple effect throughout the foster care community. I can't change a thing that any of them have gone through, but I can offer some love and support. More than anything I want to give them hope. Hopefully I can at least do that with my words.

Happy Childhood Memories

As for my happy childhood memories, the most pleasant ones are of birthday parties, playing with a doll buggy, rocking on a play horse, and sitting outside in a washtub with a sun suit on that my mom made for me, occasionally getting outside the tub to make delicious mud pies. Toys were not so abundant back then, but my siblings and I entertained ourselves with what little we had. One of my favorite things was a little red wagon we used to take turns pushing and driving, no doubt bickering over who would get to drive next! Another very pleasant and vivid memory I have is the sound of the ice cream truck coming down our street. I don't recall getting any ice cream, but just the sound of it coming was anticipating. According to some film that surfaced in my mom's belongings after her death, we also had a television for entertainment, though I have no memories of watching it. There were also pictures of us doing the locomotion, which I vaguely remember. I don't remember the dog, but we had one because there are two pictures of me with him. I also vaguely remember my mom holding me. I also felt loved by her and I believe there was a strong bond between us like she told me years later when we reunited. Yes, at one time we were a happy family.

Of course, we had dysfunction, but what family doesn't, especially a large one? Perfect families only exist on Hallmark movies!

The only bad memories I have as a young child are of me running and jumping over a fence to escape from a dog chasing me, and there was the time I got my little arm caught in the old wringer washing machine roller, but the worst one was of me getting my hair caught on fire when my sister was playing around with matches. When my oldest sister began using a broom to fan the flames my brother came to the rescue and poured a bucket of water over my head, saving my life and at least part of my hair! I can envision this with humor now, me with my hair caught on fire and my siblings coming to the rescue! I remember being upset over my long and beautiful curly hair having to be cut to get the frizzled ends. As a young child not understanding the severity of the fire, I was more upset over my hair being burned than of me burning up alive! These were some of the good memories, but then came the bad memories...

Me on right at a birthday party! I want that cake!

A Storm Brewing

Due to my dad's absence my mom was forced into employment when I was about four years old, which created more chaos and dysfunction in the home. A home with ten children is bound to create chaos and dysfunction, but with no father and only a part time mother around, the chaos escalated beyond control. I recall watching my oldest sister having an epileptic fit, not understanding what was happening, and one of my older siblings fetching my mom from her job nearby. I remember standing on a stool by our stove trying to make my own oatmeal, feeling very frustrated and hungry. I can laugh about this now, but it was not funny then! I had no idea how to make my own oatmeal, but I sure was trying! My brother told me that him and our other brother used to steal hot dogs from the grocery store to feed the family. I remember eating a lot of peanut butter sandwiches and sandwich cookies, which I loved. I do recall eating cake and ice cream some, which of course I loved, but that was probably only on special occasions like birthdays.

I was eating a sandwich cookie here! Can I please have another one? I vividly recall sitting on the couch and rocking myself, no doubt to comfort myself. To this day I love rocking chairs.

I'm hungry. I so well remember eating a lot of sandwich cookies as a young child, that and peanut butter sandwiches. And I remember having ice cream and cake and loved mixing the two together. Yummmy.

With my mom gone I was left feeling more vulnerable and insecure, especially since some of my older siblings picked on me. My mother supposedly favored me, and my siblings took their jealousy out on me when she was not around to protect me, which only created a vicious cycle of her favoring and protecting me more, and them acting out their jealousy more. This is not just conjecture; it was written in my state file. I was right smack dab in the middle of a sibling war that I wanted out of! I asked my mom when I met her if she favored me and she said, "I didn't love you any more than the others; it's just that you were very sweet and sensitive and seemed to need more attention than the others." All I wanted was to love everyone, to have peace and harmony, but I guess I was in the wrong family for that! Today I can laugh about the sibling war, but as a child it was not funny! Being such a sweet and sensitive soul, it was terrifying to be around all that noise, chaos and drama with siblings who were not always kind to me.

As things became more dysfunctional and out of control, wild got wilder. I remember walking the streets barefooted, walking over to the Coca-Cola company where my dad's ex co-workers took pity on us and gave us free cokes. Here comes the Woodard clan again…. I get a silly vision of this now, imagining ten kids trying to survive on their own, running around like hoodlums, the older ones doing their best to care for the younger ones, but it was not funny then; I felt very insecure.

My older sister was more of a mother to me at this point than my own mom. When I got older and asked my sister to share some things she remembered about me, one of the things she said was that I used to carry a security blanket around the house with me. I felt insecure, and the blanket made me feel more secure. That is easy for me to imagine, since I still love soft blankets around me. She also told me that when she took me to kindergarten, I would cry for my mom and want to go home. I was definitely a sensitive child who needed a lot of nurturing. I still am a sensitive child at heart.

A Child's Trust Destroyed

I would love to skip over this traumatic part of my childhood and pretend it never happened, and just fast forward to entering foster care, but to do so would not be truthful and real, which is what I am all about. I am very real. *The truth will set you free* is a motto I live by. It is absolutely necessary to be truthful with yourself to truly heal. If I overlooked this *dirty secret* in my past, I would be overlooking a major chunk of my childhood trauma that ultimately was the final straw that forced our family into foster care.

When I was about four years old and my mom was no longer around much, our family fell prey to an unsuspecting friend of our mom's, a sexual predator who abused me. Out of respect for my siblings I am only speaking about my own experience. This man was the owner of a candy store my mom worked at. My deceased sister told me that he took me into the kitchenette area in the back of the store and did things to me with a wooden spoon. I have a gut feeling that he could have also forced me to do things with him, but I am not sure, as I have no memory of this abuse at all. I do not know what or how much the abuse happened, and I do not really want to know. I was no doubt disassociating like I did throughout my childhood with other traumas. One thing I DO know is that I have had panic attacks in the past when I was in kitchens that had wooden spoons, which is very telling. I will not even keep a wooden spoon in my kitchen because of this. I will never know the full truth of what happened; I only know what I have been told by my sisters and by what my state file said. I hate even thinking about it, let alone remembering it. It was very traumatic for me, and my young mind coped by blocking it out. *Thank God for defense mechanisms!* The only thing I do recall is being terrified of an older man who came to our house one day, and me hiding behind a couch in the corner to get away from him in order to feel safe. I would certainly much rather believe the abuse never happened, but aside from the doctor's confirmation of the abuse when I went into foster care, my gut tells me it did happen. I believe it happened a few times.

My file stated, *"to what extent Carol has been damaged by the sexual perversion of the older man is difficult to state. Carol does not mention these incidents and it is unknown to what extent Carol was molested."* Yeah right, like a six-year-old child can make sense of sexual abuse and go around talking about it even if they could make sense of it! "Oh, guess what happened to me today...I was sexually molested by a pervert. How was your day?" Like I even knew what sex was as a six-year-old girl! My God, how moronic to even say this in my file. Who were these people who said such stupid things? I sure hope psychology has advanced since that time!

I had so much rage at this man after reading it in my file, if he had still been alive, I would have made a special trip to Illinois to tell him off in a big way! I wanted to sue the state of Illinois for not prosecuting him but was told, "It's too late now." Then I went from being angry at the pervert to being angry at the neglect of our family for never pursuing prosecution, including my own mother, who not only knew about the abuse but continued working for the pervert after we were put in foster care. My uncle, the one who turned our family in to social services after discovering two siblings sexually acting out, was fully aware of the abuse and did nothing! The only ones who seemed to care were his own two daughters, who turned him in when we spent the night at his home during the summer of 1961. That monster should have been prosecuted but wasn't. Talk about injustice.

My mom denied it ever happened to me when I confronted her about the abuse. I went off on my mom that day; it was just too much! It is one thing to not know, but to deny the truth that you know is the truth is another thing. She knew it happened and denied it. She never attempted to apologize to me for this horrible abuse. She never said, "I'm so sorry that happened to you." When she realized that I caught her in a lie, her response was, "well, you know that happens to a lot of children." No big deal. What an insensitive thing to say. Maybe she was sexually abused herself, and so thought it was no big deal. Well, it was a huge deal to me! I was an innocent child, who was violated in the worst way possible. If I had been her, I think I would be looking for another job and visiting my children in foster care.

I believe my mom knew about the abuse and allowed it because she was working for the man and needed the money. I always thought she knew about the abuse deep down, but she just turned a blind eye. I do not believe she would purposely hurt me. I know my mom loved me, but it doesn't mean I wasn't hurt and angry about it. But more than anything, I am just so sad for that innocent four-year-old girl. When I look at pictures of myself as a young child and see the sweetness and innocence, I feel so sad.

I have never worked so hard on forgiveness for anyone like I have for this pervert who sexually abused me. I have never hated anyone like him.

He took advantage of a young child's trust and destroyed it. I believe God has mercy for child molester, but I don't believe many people do. Even hardcore criminals in prisons detest them. The resentment I had toward this man was so overwhelming that while writing the FACT book, I decided with the encouragement of my late husband to go through a spiritual process called *Healing of the Memories* to help me heal the hurt from my childhood. I did not want the burden of hate and unforgiveness anymore. It was hurting ME too much. I wanted peace. Today I am at peace with this abuser, but there will always be a scar on my soul from what happened to me when I was an innocent child. Today I can forgive the abuser because I understand he was probably abused and wounded himself as a child. I can even have some compassion for him, which is amazing. *By the Grace of God, the wound has been healed. I cannot live with an open wound, but I can live with a scar.*

Whenever I am around young children, I feel appalled and very saddened that anyone could harm a child like that and destroy their trust, which is the foundation for children to grow on. I have cried a lot about what happened to me. A friend of mine told me years ago that sexual abuse is considered a soul destroyer, which I understand so completely now. The hurt went very deep, but I no longer feel the deep hurt and pain today, only a lingering sadness. *We can heal from sexual abuse, thank God, but I only healed by facing the truth and letting it set me free.* There is a saying in AA, *we are only as sick as our secrets,* which I believe is so true. The shame associated with sexual abuse would continue to eat at my soul had I not faced the truth. And the truth is, the shame does not belong to me; it belongs to the perpetrator who abused me, which I gladly gave back to him! Shame on that perverted man who abused me! I faced this shameful secret because I do not want to be sick; I want to be free! *Though it took time, God set me free from the shame.*

I have said in the past that God will have to forgive me for not forgiving the perpetrator, but today I can honestly say that I do forgive him, but I did it more for myself than him. I want to be free.

Entering Foster Care

If I could remember my entry into foster care, I would write about it from my memory, but since I can't remember, I can only write about what I don't remember, which was told to me later by my mom and an aunt. All I can say about the day I entered foster care is that it was a total blank to me. I have absolutely no recall of it at all. Like the sexual abuse, my young mind coped by blocking it out. It was just too traumatic for me to deal with any other way. What my mom told me years later when I met her, was that I was hysterical. I wonder why? Knowing how sensitive and emotional I am, it is easy to imagine me being frozen with fear, confused, and terrified beyond words. What is happening? Where am I going? Why am I leaving my home and my mom? As a women stated in her story, *"it is a horror beyond words."* Not only do you not have any control over what is happening to you, but you also have no understanding of why it is happening. I was told by a therapist that as a six-year child being separated from my mother, I experienced it as an actual threat to my survival, that I would die. My mother told me I was hysterical the day I was removed from our home. My aunt told me that my me and my siblings were all a pitiful sight, each of us clutching a brown paper bag filled with our meager belongings. I can imagine all of us lined up, ready to march out into the unknown wild. ***How sad and terrifying! What the hell is going on?! Where are we going? Oh my God, what is happening?!***

According to my state file I entered foster care on August 3, 1961, shortly after my sixth birthday. I only have a very vague memory of my first foster home. I was only there for a few days due to my baby brother's crying so much.

From there I went to another foster home for about a month, which was horrible. I do not remember leaving this foster home or going to the next one. It is a total blank to me, just like leaving my home to go to the first foster home. What I was doing is called dissociation, which is real normal for a child in trauma. This was a constant in my childhood, of dissociating while I was being moved from one home to another.

As an adult I now realize just how traumatic it was for me to be placed in foster care. Like a woman who shared her story said, *"there is no way to describe it."* The fear is unbearable. To be taken away from your home and family is without a doubt the most traumatic thing that could ever happen to a child, and it happened to me.

Rose Hill Foster Home

Although I can't remember leaving the first foster home and arriving at this foster home, I do remember the home somewhat. It was in the country around a small town called Rose Hill, but I can tell you the home was no rose. It was a terrible foster home. It would have been better if I blocked this home out of my memory like I did the sexual abuse, but unfortunately, I do remember at least some of my time there.

I was put there with two or three of my siblings. I am certain I was there with my two older brothers, and I believe there might have another sister with me, but I am not sure. My file stated, "Carol did not seem to be too happy in this home. She was very quiet and shy on the days the social worker visited." Really?? What a surprise! What did this woman think, that I would be all smiles and sunshine after being yanked away from my home and family? How dumb could this social worker be? What did she expect, for me to be filled with delight, dancing around like a fairy singing, "I am so happy to be here!" It is astonishing how ignorant this woman was, to have no emotional understanding of the trauma I was going through. One of the biggest issues I have with my foster care experience is the lack of emotional care I received, especially in the beginning when I was so traumatized.

I did not ask or care to be put in this strange foster home. I was forced. I had no way to make sense of what was happening to me, no one to help me through the trauma, to console me, to reassure me I would be all right, that my life was not actually falling apart, when in fact it was. All this woman could say was that I was shy. Maybe, just maybe, her time would have been better spent being compassionate toward me! When she asked me if I were happy there and I said, "no," she could have asked why I wasn't happy, and I would tell her, "I am hungry." Then she might ask me, "Oh, what are you eating honey?" "A little white rice, with some bread and butter," I would reply. She might then ask me further questions about why I was not happy there, and I would tell her I did not like being yanked out of bed at 4:00 in the morning, with no food, and thrown outside in the dark to do farm chores. I especially did not like feeding farm animals that chased me! I will never forget being chased by a pig there and how fast I ran to get away from it! You would think I was in a marathon! It is funny now, but it was not then! I was terrified of that pig! And I especially did not like being thrown out in the dark! I became the *queen of disassociation* when this happened.

Thrown Out in the Dark

Years later, I asked a therapist if being thrown out in the dark was abusive, and he just looked at me with disbelief that I was asking the question and said, "Carol, of course that is abuse. You would never throw a young child out in the dark like that!" I replied, "No, of course I wouldn't." The only way I knew how to cope with that particular trauma was by what psychologists call *dissociation.* I vaguely remember being outside in the dark and looking up at the beautiful stars to escape from the ugly situation I was in. I was at the age when children are very imaginative, so it was only natural for me to do this. We all have our ways of coping with trauma, and I found mine.

Thankfully, God was watching over me. This place was only a temporary placement until a more permanent one could be found. I was at Rose Hill a little over a month, but a day would have been too long in that wretched place. That place left lasting scars. I would call this place a foster home, but it was not deserving of even that! The foster parents wanted farm hands, not foster children who needed love.

I remember watching a true movie about a woman who had a similar experience in foster care. The movie showed her having flashbacks of being locked out of her house and thrown outside in the dark. I remember crying uncontrollably when I watched the movie, but I was not in touch with my childhood issues enough in early sobriety yet to understand why I was crying. I remember thinking to myself, why are you crying so much? Once I got in some serious therapy, I totally understood why I cried while watching that movie. And I'm sure if I watched this movie today I would cry some and feel very sad for the both of us.

It is amazing to me how much I stuffed as a child, how I blocked out all the trauma and the feelings attached to the trauma. As a child, all I knew was that I had to cope somehow, and of course it was all unconscious coping. I did not consciously say, "I will disassociate," or "I will numb out my feelings," or "I will block this out." I just did it without any understanding of how or why. ***Thank God I could do this!*** The coping mechanisms I learned at this foster placement would continue to serve me well throughout foster care. Children do what they must do to cope, and I was no exception to this rule. And I was exceptionally good at it!

As I am in EMDR therapy now, I understand all this much more today.

Courtroom Drama and Trauma

On September 12, 1961, I left Rose Hill and was taken to a family gathering in a court room. Again, although I vaguely remember getting in a car at Rose Hill to go somewhere, I have no recall of the trip to the courthouse. Not being able to remember going from one place to another was a constant throughout my foster care experience. I was frozen in terror again, not understanding where I was going or what was happening. I only vaguely recall the court room drama/trauma. On a scale of 1-10, my recall is only about a 2-3. All I remember is having a vague sense of being confused, and sensing something important happening in our family, but I did not understand what. I did not understand a thing about anything. I was too young to make sense out of anything that was happening. The only thing that made sense was that it did not make sense! Mostly what I remember is the feelings I had at the time—confusion and fear. A lot of fear, like, ***oh my God, what is happening?!***

Whatever was happening, I didn't have any control over it. None. I was at the mercy of the court to decide my fate.

A Family Shattered and Scattered

In my file it states that the court declared me and my siblings *neglected children,* and we were officially made *wards of the state of Illinois.* As my brother so eloquently stated, *we were thrown to the winds.* After all this time, I am still gathering bits of information from various siblings about things that happened with me in our home and about various things that happened in their foster care experience. It is bad enough if it involved two or three children, but a family of ten is overwhelming. So much happened to all of us. There were times when some of were together, then separated again. The whirlwind of chaos in our home did not compare to the whirlwind of chaos of foster care.

As I reflect on the day I was removed from my home, I wonder what everyone was thinking. I did not even understand what was happening, or where we were going. How do you say goodbye to your mom and siblings, your whole family? Will I ever see you again? When? Where? Why can't we all be together? Where are we going? The idea of not being a family was foreign to me; we had always been a family up to this point, so why would I think we would not be one now? I am sure I felt like screaming, "What the hell is happening to us?!"

What was happening is that we were all scattered to the winds, wherever the wind took us. Our lives became as unstable as the wind blowing. That is the most perfect definition of what it was like for our family, and unfortunately the winds left a lot of irreparable damage in our family. Our family was gone with the wind.

As I stated in my first book, what happened in my family is something that should never happen to any family. It was tragic beyond words, which I will always feel sad about. But I can live with sadness.

GONE WITH THE WIND

I have wondered if the right thing was for us to be put in foster care, but still I hate to ponder how much more damage might have been done to our family had we stayed together. It was a stormy mess at home, and it was a stormy mess in foster care. *Only God really knows what was best, but I like to think God was watching our family by putting us in foster care.*

Another Strange Place

The wind blew me to anther strange place on September 12, 1961. Again, I do not remember leaving the courtroom, but according to my sister, we left with our mom holding our hands, me on one side, and her on the other. And again, I do not remember the trip from the courthouse to my new *home* in Normal, Illinois, ISSCS (Illinois Soldiers and Sailors Children School). *God does have a sense of humor!* Normal? There was not anything normal about me having to be put there, but the home did provide some normalcy for me that I so desperately needed.

I remember when I first arrived at the children's home. I was given a meal, with some buttermilk, which I did not want. This really sticks out in my memory for some reason, probably because it was the first good meal I had eaten since August 3rd when I was first put in care, or even long before then. According to my state file, three older sisters went there also,

CAROL LUCAS

but I only remember my two older brothers. My younger sister told me that she was put in the baby fold for a short time before they placed her in a foster home. I spent the first six months in a receiving cottage, with no family contact. I was isolated.

I believe there was a lot of emotional damage done during those six months alone without any family. This is where my strong fear of abandonment came from. I felt completely abandoned, alone, and forgotten. My file stated, *"on the days the worker came to take Carol's sisters on pre-placement and placement, Carol seemed to ignore the worker to a great extent, perhaps fearing the day she would have to go, or feeling hurt that she was not the first one chosen for placement."* How incredibly off was this worker? Dumb and dumber. Really? Why would she think I was eager to be moved to another home? I was on home number three at the children's home, and I can hardly wait to be moved again?! Could she not figure out that the reason I was ignoring her was because I was afraid of being separated from my sisters? My file states, "Carol took the separation from her sisters very hard," like that was noteworthy, some great revelation! Of course I missed my sisters, you idiot! What child wouldn't?! I especially missed my older sister Mary, who took care of me so much at home. Children from dysfunctional homes like ours cling together for dear life. With our dad gone absent from the home and our mom mostly absent, we siblings were all we had! I am shocked at the lack of emotional understanding these social workers had about me and my family.

Normal?

As for this home in Normal, Illinois, the most *normal* thing about this home was my emotional responses to being there. Overall, it was a decent and caring children's home that really tried to provide some normalcy for me and other children there, but for all the normalcy they provided for me, I still DID NOT want to be there! I wanted to be home with my mom and siblings, not with a bunch of strange kids, who no doubt felt the same way I did. I missed my family terribly. All I wanted was to be with them.

What a women said in her story perfectly describes how I felt about being thrust to strangers. *How can you expect us to be grateful? We're thrown to you. We were ripped away from everything and everyone we know, and you want us to be grateful? We are helpless, our lives lay in pieces around us. We are damaged, broken, shattered. How can you expect us to be grateful?* As an adult I can be grateful that I was given some *normalcy* in this children's home, but as a child I was NOT GRATEFUL!

I missed my family SO much that I got on my knees by my bedside every night and prayed to God for each one of them. I thought nothing of it at the time; it just seemed like the natural thing to do, but now as an adult, I think it was amazing that I did this on my own. It was simply done out of pure love and concern for my family. I also believe that my young imaginative mind thought if I prayed for them, our family would magically reunite. People who know me well say I have a magical quality about me. Maybe I am still like that six-year-old girl with the magical mind! *I am glad God gave me a magical mind and spirit!*

Imagine being a young child and not only missing your family but wondering where they are and if they are all right, if you will ever see them again. What a heavy burden that is for a young child who does not even have the reasoning ability to comprehend what is happening. None of it made any sense to me at all. It was all so confusing. All I knew was that my family was gone, and there was no one to support me emotionally and help me through the loss. I believe a lot of my trauma was due to the lack of understanding I had about everything. Why am I here? How long will I be here? Will I ever see my family again? I spent a lot of time wondering. I wonder if…I wonder when…I wonder what…I wonder…

A therapist described my foster care experience as *having my world turned upside down,* so much so that I really felt like I did not know if, when, or where the sun came up. I agree with that. It was disorienting and confusing, to say the least.

Not only was my world turned upside down, but I didn't have any way of even understanding that it was upside down. All I knew was that I was scared and insecure. Like Debra Cruz said, *"there is really no way to describe what it's like to be foster child and have no control over what is happening to you."*

Family Visits

For the first six months at the children's home, I was not allowed any visits with any family. I was all alone, with no explanation why, which only served to make me feel more abandoned than ever. After six months I was finally allowed family visits with my aunt, uncle, and my paternal grandma, which brought me some comfort and security while I was with them, but I hated going back to the children's home after being with them. I remember riding in the car and dreading going back to the children's home. I especially loved visiting with my grandma, who was a very loving woman. I remember one special night alone with her, when she said prayers with me and tucked me into her soft feather bed. I felt so safe and loved with her. I could have stayed with her forever! But back to the children's home I went, feeling sad, and wondering when I would get to visit her again. It hurt so much.

There is so much I do not remember about being at the children's home, partly due to my age, and largely due to the emotional trauma I was in. I am sure I felt very insecure, and that I was extremely shy and withdrawn. My file stated that my shyness was appealing to the adults there, that they felt drawn to care for me, so at least I had that going for me! I now envision myself as a sweet looking puppy in the animal shelter with sad eyes, looking for a home, and love from someone, anyone. Please love me, please! my eyes pleaded. I remember the house mother being a nice woman. She would sit at the piano playing *The Old Rugged Cross*, with me singing along as she played. What I do not remember though, is any emotional support. I do not recall getting any hugs, etc. All my basic physical needs were met, such as food, clothing, school, church, play activities, but I so longed for hugs and comfort that I never received, and I was much too shy to approach her for it.

I remember wetting the bed a lot and being forced to wash and hang out my own sheets on the clothesline, even in the winter when the sheets got stiff. I get a funny picture of this now, of me trying to fold frozen sheets! When I needed to be emotionally understood for my insecurities, I felt like I was being shamed and punished. I know from Child Psychology that children usually pee the bed because they are insecure and angry about not receiving love. That certainly makes sense to me! Piss on you!

Flunking First Grade

According to my state file, I had a difficult time in school. I went into first grade when I entered the children's home and did so poorly that I

CAROL LUCAS

had to take it over. I flunked first grade! Boy, talk about starting out on the wrong foot! My file stated that, *"Carol has a slight speech difficulty and is inattentive, has difficulty concentrating, and is always daydreaming."* My file also stated that, *"Carol's innate intelligence is higher than her present test scores indicate. This is due to her emotional deprivation. She used withdrawal as a defense mechanism. She is considered a sick little girl. Carol would not see any of the men who planned to interview and test her. She needs affection, love, and support. She has suffered much deprivation during her first six years. It was felt that she has the ability to relate, but she is afraid of men because of her past experiences. If Carol is left at ISSCS she will probably become more withdrawn. She is at present emotionally emaciated. It would be difficult to find a mother for Carol who could be too protective. The foster father would need to be a quiet, in the background type. Since Carol is disturbed, she needs to be treated for the disturbance. This would not mean custodial care. Therapy will be to find her a good foster mother."*

Upon reading this I thought, well at least someone knew what they were talking about. It was especially nice to know they thought I wasn't stupid like I thought I was growing up because I flunked first grade! Throughout my file I was impressed by many of the comments, like it was such a surprise to them that I withdrew and daydreamed. Really? What did they expect, for me to be all happy and well adjusted? Oh, it's no big deal that I am in this strange home without my mom and family. It's fine. My definition of fine is f'd up, insecure, neurotic, and emotionally unstable. I'm pretty sure I was just fine! What child who has been yanked away from her home and family, and thrown into a strange home, wouldn't be traumatized and try to find some comfort and safety somehow to escape the horrible reality? I found mine by daydreaming, spacing out, and disassociating. I just wanted to crawl in my shell where I felt safe. As an adult I still use withdrawal as a defense mechanism if I am emotionally overwhelmed. I will withdraw into my safe shell, and I will not come out until I am good and ready, which may be a long while, and I usually crawl out, not walk.

A Foster Home Visit

I remember going for an overnight visit to a foster home once, and I believe they wanted to keep me. I remember eating a whole bunch of peanut brittles while I was there, and I remember them teaching me how to blow my nose. My file stated that I was taken there on January 4, 1962. Even though the foster parents loved me and probably would have been great parents and even adopted me, I did not want to stay there because I wanted to be with my own family, and I think I believed in my heart of hearts that I would be reunited with them. Even as a young child I was tenacious with my loved ones. This happened only a few months into my time at ISSCS, when I still had a lot of hope of returning home to my family.

A Playaholic

CAROL LUCAS

There are many different coping mechanisms for children, and I believe another one I used besides withdrawal, was playing. Of course I didn't know this at the time, but in retrospect I can see that I stayed busy playing as a way to escape my painful emotions. As a child I became a *playaholic*. I know all children love to play, but I was like a whirlwind of activity, never stopping. I was a high energy child and never tired of playing. I bicycled, jumped rope (I loved that!), played hopscotch, golfed, played on swings, slides, merry-go-round, monkey bars, anything and everything on the playground, but my two favorite play activities were swinging around on the maypole and swimming in the indoor pool. I loved the water! I was not afraid of the water at all and loved jumping off into the deep end of the pool. I remember a time when me and some other little girls did a swim show, parading around in the water. I still love water!

One fond memory of ISSCS was *Legionaire's Day*, otherwise known there as *Children's Day*. We were all treated special on that day by the surrounding community. I remember how thrilled I was to receive a package of toiletries, goodies, sweet treats, and have a ride on a fire truck. I will never forget the Girl Scout cookies I received that day; I wanted the peanut butter ones, so I talked a girl into trading with me. To this day I still love the peanut butter Girl Scout cookies!

As I sit writing today, it is June 7th, 2023, and after being in EMDR therapy for ten months I understand what I was actually doing by being a playaholic. My therapist explained to me that I was dissociating, which is normal for children going through trauma. I am sure I was a high energy child, but a lot of my playing was a way of escaping from my painful feelings. I was coping the only way I knew how to as a child in trauma. Wow, after all these years I finally found out what was actually happening! No wonder I loved the Maypole so much!

I was initially upset when informed of my dissociation, but now I understand it was my brain's way of coping. I was normal.

Family Returning to Me

Although I was not returned to my family like I longed for, part of my family came to me. My file stated that in February 1962, my older sister came to ISSCS. This was shortly after my foster home visit, so I guess my tenacity paid off! I remember very well the day she appeared at the home. I was sitting on the floor in the living room watching the movie *The Wizard of Oz when* she came walking in the front door. I said, "aren't you my sister?" and she said, "yes," and of course I was thrilled to have her with me again!

While in therapy years later, Frank asked me what my favorite was, and when I told him *The Wizard of Oz* he replied, "of course, Carol. There's no place like home." Wow. I was so spellbound by the movie! What a perfect, magical movie for a six-year-old girl who desperately wants to return home! My file stated, *"Carol seems quite dependent upon her sister. They are very close."* My file also said that we got in trouble for riding our bicycles out in the line of traffic. We also got sent up to bed numerous times without any dinner because we made too much noise. To this day I cannot go to bed hungry. It makes me feel insecure. I also remember being in a *Snow White* play, in which my sister got to be Snow White because her hair was darker than mine, and I had to be the mirror! At the time I thought it was strange being a mirror, but now I think it is funny! I also remember dressing up as a Scottish girl for Halloween.

Decent Memories of ISSCS

I have some good memories of ISSCS, which I am grateful for now. Was I grateful then? NO! Am I grateful now? YES! It could have so much worse! At least I was not in a terrible foster home like at Rose Hill, or in bad foster homes like some of my siblings, but oh how I longed for my own home and family. *I really do believe that God was watching over me when I was placed in this home and when he brought my sister to me.*

Me on the left with my sister

I still remember that dress; it had a brown checkered pattern. I think it was the only dress I had there. It is no wonder clothes are so important to me today! I hated having my hair chopped off but had no choice. This is one example of not having any control.

One thing I repeatedly heard from foster children who shared their stories in the FACT book was their lack of control over anything that was happening while they were in foster care. You just do whatever people tell you to. You have no choice. And if you are moved around a lot, as many are, then you are constantly having to adjust to different things. There is no stability.

One outstanding memory I have, was of having my *first communion* with my sister and older brother. I did not understand a thing about communion, but I loved the white dress, veil, and shoes I got! We attended a Catholic Church, but since I was a typical restless child and didn't understand Latin, my sister and I ran down the church aisles getting attention from people.

While coming back to ISSCS one Sunday on the bus, my three siblings decided to play a prank on me and told me they were all leaving the children's home, but I had to stay there all alone. They were only teasing, but I believed them and got terribly upset! Talk about a hysterical little girl! I started crying and screaming, "you guys can't leave me here all alone; please don't leave me here all alone!" I just remember how terrified I was of the prospect of being left there all alone by myself. They reassured me they were only kidding, and they never pulled that prank on me again! I was such a sensitive little girl who was SO terrified of abandonment.

What a sensitive little girl I was. The thought of being there alone without any of my family was so terrifying to me! At least I had the comfort of knowing some of my family was with me, especially my brother Glen and my sister Kathy.

My sister and I are pretty close today and have talked about some of our past in foster care and agree we didn't have a normal childhood.

We were talking one day and my sister said, "if there was a contest for dysfunctional families, ours would be runner up!" I said, "I think we'd win!" "I could use the money!" I think part of the reason for so much dysfunction in my family is due to the largeness. I have no doubt how dysfunctional it was in our original home, and it just kept getting more dysfunctional due to all the emotional baggage we all carried. Seriously, if a movie was made about our family, it would be a big hit!

Hospital Trauma

Where is my mommy? I need her! I want
my mommy now! Please!!!!!!!

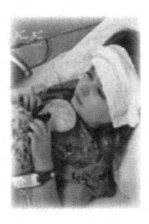

My fear of abandonment surfaced big time when I had to be hospitalized for whooping cough. This was a very traumatic experience for me. I did not want to go in the hospital! I remember crying and screaming, "I can't go in the hospital; I have to go to school!" I remember a cough drop falling out of my mouth as the personnel were pulling me up the stairs, and me doing my best to fight them off. I was forced in the hospital, where I believe I stayed for a week in a bubble, coughing and crying. It was so terrifying for me. I thought I was dying. This took place within a few months of me being at the home, which made it even worse. I wanted my mom so much then. I felt like screaming, "Where is my mommy? I need her now!" To this day I HATE hospitals! This experience was another example of me not getting the emotional comfort I so much needed. Really, why couldn't they have been more humane and gentle with me? I was a tiny girl, so why couldn't someone have carried me up the stairs, instead of dragging me up the stairs like I was bag of garbage? If they had been gentle with me in the first place, they would not have had to drag me up the stairs! They could have said something like, "I know you are afraid honey, but you have to go in the hospital. You are going to ok. You will be taken very good care of, and you will get out in a few days. We're here for you." What I ended up feeling was that nobody was there for me. They made an already traumatized child even more traumatized. Did they really have to drag me up the stairs like they did? Why couldn't they understand how traumatized I was by the prospect of being hospitalized? To this day, whenever I am ill, I tend to regress to that six-year girl old girl who felt insecure. My husband understood this about me and pampered me when I was sick. The only good thing I got out of that experience was a little windup doll that I kept, which I wound up every night to lull myself off to sleep. I took the doll with me and continued to sleep with it when I finally left the home. Children will do what they can to find love and comfort, and that little doll gave me some love, comfort, and security. I am assuming it was probably after this hospital stay that I started giving up on my mom. Seriously, if she couldn't even come to see me when I was sick, there probably wasn't any hope of her ever coming to see me. Hope for returning to my mom was waning. I believe I probably started stepping on the sidewalk a lot after this, saying, "step on a crack, you break your mother's back."

No wonder I was so mesmerized by *The Wizard of Oz* movie so much. Maybe I could magically go back home with the help of the good witch? I remember so well watching the movie. Of course I didn't understand then why I was so spellbound by the movie, but I do now. It took some therapy to figure that out. What a perfect way for a six-year-old girl to use her imagination for a happy ending.

I had the opportunity to see a play of The Wizard of Oz with my husband, which was both awesome and sad. When Dorothy said, "there's no place like home," Larry looked over at me with such compassion.

There's No Place Like HOME...

As I already mentioned, a therapist I had years ago made a comment about me liking *The Wizard of Oz*. As a child I never understood why, but I sure do now. I was dreaming about going back home. I wanted some hope, and the way my young magical mind found it was by fantasizing about Glenda the good witch helping to get back there.

It is amazing to me how children cope with trauma. I so desperately wanted to be back home with my mom and family and found a way to make it happen!

Me as Glinda for Halloween 2021

On the Sidewalks

Although I do not remember consciously feeling angry and hurt over my mom's abandonment, I believe my unconscious was busy trying to work it out somehow, which it repeatedly did on the sidewalks. I certainly did not talk to anyone about my mom, not even my siblings, but I did talk to the sidewalks often, saying, *"step on a crack, you break your mother's back."* I would look at the sidewalk crack for maybe ten seconds, trying to decide if I should step on it. My ambivalence toward my mom was evident in my behavior on the sidewalks, as I could not make up my mind about what to do. If I stepped on a crack, it would mean I hated my mom and wanted to hurt her, and if I hurt her, she'd never be able to, or even want to come visit me, so I always declined stepping on a crack, but I came very close sometimes. I guess I felt that if I did not hurt her, there was still hope. This might seem illogical to an adult mind, but it made perfect sense to a six-year-old child with a very magical mind. After being in the home for a good while, I think I just became apathetic about her, having the attitude of *out of sight, out of mind.* Toward the end of my time at the home, I don't believe I did the sidewalk ritual much. I had pretty much given up hope about of me returning to her. Hope was dying, and almost completely dead. As hope died for returning to my mom, so did my love for her.

CAROL LUCAS

My reaction to my mom's abandonment was a very normal one. I was a child who needed and wanted my mother's love, but she was no longer with me, which I was very hurt and angry about.

Love/Hate Relationship with My Mom

I went from hope to a love/hate relationship with my mom, which is pretty much how it remained until after her death, when I finally decided to let the resentment go and forgive her, but only after working through my anger and hurt in therapy. Honestly though, I did not completely let go of my resentment toward her until I went through **Healing of the Memories** in 2011. How could a mother abandon her own children when they needed her love and reassurance the most? It will always baffle me. I simply cannot understand a mother doing what my mother did. My file stated, *"the mother has stated that she doubts very much whether she will be able to visit due to the fact that she works on Sundays and has no transportation facilities."* Yes, it was true, she was too busy working for the sex pervert who abused me. The truth is, she just did not care enough to visit any of her children, including me. I believe it was easier and less painful for her to just walk away from the whole mess. When I asked my mom years later why she did not visit us, she told me she thought it was for the best, that it would only cause us more pain. Really? You mean it is better to completely abandon us than see us sometimes? That is like saying it is better to only have half a sandwich than a whole sandwich when you are hungry. I will take the half sandwich, thank you so much!

It is now 2023 and I have since realized things at a deeper level. Today, I honestly do understand that my mom really did do what she thought was right. But it doesn't make it right and it doesn't mean the hurt will ever completely go away, as my therapist told me.

I Hope...I Hope...I Hope.......

Although I did not have much hope of returning to my mom, hope was still the underlying feeling while I was at the home...I hope I see my mom and siblings, I hope I see my relatives, my aunt, uncle, and grandma, I hope my brother comes to visit me today, I hope I don't wet the bed again tonight, I hope I get supper tonight, I hope I get to go to camp (I was denied once because I wet the bed too much and was left all alone at the cottage by myself while the other children were having fun), and the biggest hope of all was that I would get to leave this place soon. To this day I am still a hopeful person about everything, always looking for the bright side of everything, for the hope. Hope was all I had as a child, and now with my husband gone and so much uncertainty in my life, hope is all I am hanging onto. *There is always HOPE!*

Hope is Here!

Hope finally came to me one day when I received a white ticket to leave ISSCS for good. A pink ticket meant I was leaving for a visit and a white one meant I was leaving permanently. WOW! I had been visiting with relatives for about a year and was hoping I could stay with them for good, and the day finally came! *Again, though my mom abandoned me, God did not.* He made sure I was taken care of, and although I was not reunited with my whole family, I was at least going to be with some of them now, which was a huge comfort to me. Though this was yet another change for me, it was one I looked forward to, as I was leaving the children's home to be with family, which gave me a sense of security I so longed for. I was going to live with my aunt and uncle, who I had already been visiting with on a regular basis. My older brother was going with me, which was also a comfort. I left ISSCS on June 12, 1963, which meant I had spent almost two years there, which was way too long for me! *But Thank God I finally got to leave to be with some family!*

A Relative Foster Home

Again, I cannot remember the trip to my new home, nor do I recall much of my initial time there. Even though I was happy to be with some family, it was still another change for me, which was scary. I had some time before school started, and I do recall going with my aunt when she cleaned a doctor's office. I was like her shadow at first, just wanting the security of her presence. My aunt understood my insecurity and was very nurturing to me. She was what I needed at the time, and I am thankful to her for taking me in and caring for me. I really did feel like she sincerely cared about me. She even told me years later that she wished I would have stayed with her and not gone to live with my dad, which was both flattering and rather disturbing to me. If she truly cared about me, wouldn't she want was best for me? Apparently not if she wanted me for her own selfish reasons. I explained to her that I wanted to be with my dad, which is only natural. What child wouldn't want to be with their natural parents? Of course I wanted to go live with my daddy. He was my daddy!

The Teacher's Pet

What I do remember very well is my first day of school when I entered 2nd grade. I was so afraid of going into this new classroom that the teacher had to take me by the hand and walk me gently in, while I was crying. I was terrified of this strange environment, but that teacher was an Angel! I loved that teacher! She was so nice to me! Everyone probably thought I was the teacher's pet because she took special care of me. She knew my situation and understood my insecurity, that I needed extra nurturing. I did well in school there and got along well with the other children, playing with them during recess. I was an easy child to get along with and loved all the other children. I was rather shy at first but warmed up to the other children once I knew they liked me and accepted me. I hated rejection more than anything, but once I knew I was accepted I was fine. I still hate rejection!

Good Memories of My Relative Foster Home

Although I knew I was not my aunt and uncle's child, that their three children were naturally favored over me, I did feel loved and accepted by them, especially by my aunt. I was her little kitchen helper, always asking her if I could help her in the kitchen. Even as a young girl I wanted to learn how to keep house and cook. I also helped in the garden and recall shelling peas on her back porch. She also had a walnut tree and I recall cracking walnuts and eating them. I remember watching chickens running around without their heads, and her hanging them on a clothesline. To this day

I will never really enjoy eating chicken because of this. I have often felt like them chickens! I loved anything to do with the home, and still do. I LOVE my home! I also loved being a *Brownie Scout* while I was there, and the best part was eating the brownies we made! Brownies are still my favorite!

I tend to love the things from my childhood that brought me happiness and comfort, being grateful for them instead of focusing on the negative things that caused me pain. I am a born optimist, always looking on the bright side. I want to be happy and joyful, and the only way to be that way is to be grateful. Another fond memory I have of my time there, is making snow forts and angels in the snow. I loved the snow as a child, and still do. It is a good memory that I like to hold onto. It is important to do that when you come from a traumatic childhood; otherwise, you might drown in the pity pot!

I was not around my uncle on a regular basis, as he was gone a lot as a truck driver, but I got along very well with him when he was home. I was not afraid of him as I had been of the other men like my state file stated. I felt safe with him. I remember very well sitting next to him and rubbing his feet, which he loved. I remember there were times when I would wake up from nightmares and go crawl into bed with my aunt and uncle, snuggling between them, which they seemed to love as much as I did. I felt so safe and secure like that. The only real problem I had with this relative foster home was my three cousins, especially the youngest one, who was around my age and was jealous of me and resented the attention I got from my aunt. The oldest cousin tried messing with me, and even chased me once with his pants down, which frightened me terribly, as he could have raped me. Luckily, my aunt heard me scream and put an end to that, but I never felt safe with him after that. *Again, I believe God was watching over me, as I left there not long after that incident. As I look over my shoulder, I see the Hand of God.*

Jesus Loves Me

I went to a Pentecostal Church regularly, which I liked a lot. *I always liked church, and particularly loved Sunday school and learning about Jesus.* I remember hearing the song *Jesus loves me, yes I know, for the Bible tells me so.* I also recall saying my goodnight prayer, *now I lay me down to sleep, I pray the Lord my soul to keep, if I should die before I wake, I pray the Lord my soul to take.* I said this prayer well into my late teens. I was always a very curious child, and I recall going up to the altar and asking the pastor how I could be *born again.* Maybe I wanted to start my life over? Maybe I was just curious about what he meant by somebody being born again spiritually? I wasn't shy at all about asking him this question. I don't remember what his reply was, or if he said anything, but I remember him looking at me rather strangely. Hmm...

Monkeying Around

One thing I recall very vividly is going to the playground, which I was allowed to do by myself since it was only a few blocks away from home. I loved going there and playing all by myself, especially on the monkey bars. I also have vague memories of being at the playground with my cousins.

One unhappy memory I have is coming home from the playground and having fainting spells, almost passing out. I talked with my therapist recently about this and realize now that this happened after my older cousin messed with me. Knowing what I know about trauma now, it makes perfect sense. The body keeps the score and my body was telling me I was anxious and angry, though I had no clue about any of this as a child. But I see it now.

Me on the right,
balancing myself on the monkey bar.

The most memorable day of all was when a monkey appeared at the playground when I was by myself and started swinging around on the monkey bars with me! This really happened! What amazes me now is that I was not afraid of this monkey; in fact, it seemed quite natural for me to be hanging around with him. He tried following me home, but he went back to the park after I told him he couldn't go home with me. When I returned home and told my aunt about the monkey, she accused me of lying, but then when the evening news said there was a monkey that got loose from a nearby zoo, she looked over at me and said, "you WEREN'T lying," and I said, "I told you so!" Knowing how she would wash my mouth out with soap for lying, I probably got a mouth full of bubbles that day, but I think she apologized once she knew the truth.

The Christmas Holidays

The Christmas holidays were especially memorable with my aunt. We had a real tree, and I recall singing Christmas Carol's. My aunt loved baking boxes of Christmas cookies, which I loved eating! I got a tea set one year, which my cousin and I loved having tea and cookies with. I also remember very well getting a barbie doll, which I loved dressing. Again, I took that fond memory and recreated it in my adult life. I love baking Christmas cookies today! I am a born optimist and love to look for the good in everything, even in my unstable childhood.

My Paternal Grandma

One of the greatest things about living with my aunt was visiting my paternal grandma who lived across the street. I was always visiting her. I remember her warning me about eating some Ex-Lax that I thought was chocolate! I remember how good a cook she was. I recall having some fun Easter egg hunts, and one year I even got a little chick for Easter! My grandma was a real sweet woman. I heard she was present for every one of her grandchildren's births. The sad day came though, when my aunt came to pick me up from school and informed me that my grandma died. Although I did not really understand death, I remember consoling my cousin, telling her, "Grandma is in Heaven." I find it amazing that I did this on my own. I also recall how natural it seemed to be saying this, like I had been in Heaven and understood it. Even as a young child I had some spiritual understanding, that seemed to just spring within me naturally. *God's Spirit was in me, even when I was so young.*

My Daddy!

It was during my time at this relative foster home, when I was about 10 years old, that my dad reentered my life. Since I could only have vague memories of him as a young child, really only two brief moments with him as a young child, I felt like I was meeting him for the first time. I was so thrilled to see my daddy! It seemed like he just magically appeared out of thin air, and he loved me, telling me how happy he was to see his sweet little girl. Though I was a bit shy around him at first, I quickly warmed up to his love. He gave me a bicycle for my tenth birthday, which was like a dream come true. Not only did I get to see him, but now he was showering me with love, and a new bicycle! *And he also gave me a birthday card! For a young girl who felt so insecure, this truly was like a miracle. Wow! My daddy loves me! I felt so blessed to have him back in my life. And I knew he truly loved me. Children intuitively know when they are loved, and I knew my dad really did care about me. God is so good!*

My dad was getting married, and he took me out alone one day shopping for a new outfit to wear for the wedding, which was so awesome and special! I got my daddy's undivided attention for the first time that I was aware of, and I loved it! He even took a picture of me that day wearing a wedding veil. That day will always stand out as a precious memory for me! I love you, daddy!

I realize that because I had a loving father, it has been natural and easy for me to believe in a loving Heavenly Father, who is my Big Daddy!

My Daddy for Good!

My dad was remarried on March 21, 1965, and it was only a few months later, right before my tenth birthday, that I went to live with him. *God was looking out for me again!* It came about because of my brother, who had been forewarned that another temper tantrum would land him on his dad's doorstep, did just that, getting angry and throwing things off the back porch, resulting in him being told by my aunt, "pack your bags; you're leaving." I'm not sure if he did this on purpose so he could go live with our dad, but I'm glad he did it. I was so shy then that I was afraid to come right out and ask my aunt if I could leave with him, so I kept following her around all day, until finally she asked me if I wanted to go to my dad's too, which of course I replied "yes" to. Years later while visiting my aunt, she admitted that she was hurt when I left, that she wanted me to stay there with her, and I told her to please understand that I wanted to be with my dad. I appreciated her caring for me, but my dad was my dad. I also did not want to be there alone without my brother, who had been my only constant sibling connection throughout my childhood, especially since I did not feel safe with my oldest cousin who tried raping me.

Although moving to live with my dad was another change for me, this one was one I wanted, even more than I had when I left ISSCS to go to my aunt's. And I remember this day! It was an incredibly happy and memorable day for me! The day I went to live with *my daddy* was indescribably the happiest day of my childhood! I was so thrilled to be with *my daddy*! It truly was like being lifted out of the darkness into the light. It was that profound for me. I always say my dad was like my knight in shining armor because he rescued me from foster care. After hearing other foster children's stories, I feel so humbled and grateful that I was blessed with six years with my dad, as many others never had that privilege; in fact, many do not even know who their fathers are. I was lucky. *God was caring for me again. I treasure the memories and thank God for every one of them!*

Years ago while talking with a friend, she said, "Carol, you were shown more love by your dad in six years than most people are ever shown in a lifetime, and from that point on I have nothing but gratitude for my daddy!

My dad gave me a sense of security and stability that I had never had in my childhood before. When I first started living with him and went into fourth grade, he made me a name tag, which may not seem like a lot to the average child, but I was not the average child; I was an emotionally damaged child with a shaky identity. Having that name tag made especially for me by my own dad gave me a sense of identity, of belonging. It gave me a sense of pride about myself that I had been lacking.

Me looking happier!

My dad made me feel incredibly special. He was always expressing and showing his love for me, both in person and in birthday cards he gave me. He would always say, *"I am so happy you're back in my life again; you're a very sweet girl."* I was very needy for his attention, and he was happy to shower it on me, but one thing I felt was that although my dad loved me, he never showed any favoritism toward any of his children. I think the younger ones seemed emotionally needier, which I believe my dad understood, but he never loved us anymore than the others. I was a sensitive child by nature, which my dad also understood, and he just wanted me to feel secure. He understood we were all emotionally damaged by foster care, and I am also sure he carried a lot of guilt about it. I was a *daddy's girl* all the way, which is apparent in a picture I have of me sitting on his lap. He had a look of pride, and I looked happy and contented.

He was a very nurturing dad. I always say he was the real mom because he was so loving. I had tonsillitis once, and he took care of me all day, coming into my bedroom and checking my temperature, giving me water, asking me how I felt, etc. I also remember the day I was not feeling well, and my brother called my dad while he was gone visiting with relatives to tell him about me, and he came home to be with me. I was a big baby, and still can be.

Happy Family Times

There were many fun family times with my dad. We had birthday parties with presents, cake and ice cream, and even hats, and whoever had a birthday was spared of any work. He made me incredibly special on my birthday! And we in turn made him special on his birthday, which he also loved. I think my dad had a lot of child in him, which made him a lot of fun. He loved playing Santa Claus and we always had a real Christmas tree, and even though he did not have a lot of money, he always managed to buy presents, and give each child a small amount to spend on siblings. My dad gave from his heart, and I appreciated everything he did for me, and he knew it. I am still like that today— grateful for what I have. It is very ingrained in me from growing up the way I did. My dad also liked playing the tooth fairy. I will never forget the time I found a dime under my pillow when I lost a tooth, and when I asked him where it came from, he said, "the tooth fairy," while I smiled. Knowing how innocent I was at that age, I probably believed him! My dad loving having cookouts in the summer. I remember one evening he told me it was time for me to go to dreamland, and I was innocently hoping it was a special park or something, but he said, "it's time for you to go to bed." I think my dad had a lot of fun with me because I was so innocent, but he also worried about me a lot because of it. I remember family outings to *Spitler Woods*, walking in the woods, and walking on logs across the creek. My Maiden name is *Woodard*, which means *hearty woodsmen*, so it natural for me to love the woods. He would also take me to the park to feed ducks, which I still love to do.

I walk in the woods around a lake near my home, and love to watch the ducks while I walk. It is so beautiful. ***One of the ways I connect with God is by being around nature. I always say, "if you want to fall in love with God, fall in love with His creation.***

His creation is so beautiful!

A Teenager Me on left with my best friend on 8th grade graduation day

As I grew from a young girl into a young teenager, I started calling my father *dad* instead of *daddy*, and he went from calling me *Annie*, to calling me *Carol Ann*. I will never forget how proud of me he was when I was in middle school. He used to help me with my math homework, and I remember him showing me his report card from college, that showed A's for math. I made the honor roll in 7th and 8th grade, and even though it was not easy for him to do, he managed to scrape the money together to pay for my cheerleading outfit when I was a cheerleader in 8th grade. He would watch me do cheers in the house and yard, and tease me, telling me I should be a dancer. I was so high energy! I still am high energy, and love dancing in my home! It was around this time he began encouraging me to go to college, telling me he thought I had the brains and ambition to do it. What brains I do have, I inherited from my dad! I would have loved to have had him there in the audience watching me get my diploma when I graduated from college. My dad always wanted better for his children than what he had, and he never had the chance to complete college, so I know he would have been so proud of me for graduating from the University of Michigan.

Part of the reason I wanted to complete college was to make him proud. It was my way of saying "thank you for all of your love and support while I was with you, dad." I am so thankful for the values and morals my dad instilled in me. I know if he could see me now I would make him proud. I know I am proud of me.

I also believe my dad would be proud of my work for foster children.

A Rebellious Teenager

As teenagers can often be, I become somewhat rebellious because I wanted more freedom than my dad would allow. A friend wanted me to go stay with her in California for the summer, and he forbid it. My dad did not even really approve of my friendship with this girl, let alone going to live with her for the whole summer. I remember when I told my dad about this girl, and him telling me he wanted to meet her before I had any sleepovers with her. He had good reason to be concerned about my friendship with her, as she was not a good influence on me, just as he suspected she would not be. She turned me on to cigarettes one night on a sleepover, and my dad was so upset when he found out I was smoking that he made me smoke a pipe until it made me sick, to hopefully make me quit smoking. Unfortunately, I continued smoking some, which he was smoking hot over it! My friend was on the wild side, and he did not want his daughter becoming wild. My dad understood the dangers involved in me going out to the wild land of CA and put his foot down. He told me, "No! You are not going!" I wanted more independence than I was ready for, and he knew it. He also knew how naïve I was and would have worried himself sick over me had I gone out there. *Thank God my dad had more sense than me!*

The End of Innocence

My rebellion got worse after this situation with my friend. Something happened shortly after this that changed the whole course of my young life. While walking around one early evening in the small town where I lived, an older man in a car stopped and offered me a beer, then invited me to go for a ride in his car, which was very stupid and naïve of me to do, but teenagers can be that way, and I was no exception to the rule. One beer turned into six beers, and apparently I got drunk, though I don't remember any of the evening past the first beer. I apparently had a problem with alcohol from the very beginning, as I blacked out and could not remember anything about that night. Although I didn't remember what happened that night, he did, and informed me that we had sex! I said, "What?!" One would think he would not want to tell me this, but he seemed more than willing to, as if he was proud of it. He may have been proud of it, but I was not! I had planned on being a virgin when I got married! He was 23 and I was only 15! This man was eight years older than me and was a bad influence on me. It was only recently that I fully realized that this man raped me! He took advantage of a very sweet and innocent young girl. How could I have been swayed so easily by this man? It is no wonder my dad worried about me. He had good reason to. One time my sister and I came home drunk with this man and his brother, and my dad threatened them with a rifle and told them, "stay away from my daughters." He made his point perfectly clear with me, and that was the end of that relationship, but I was still rebellious, sneaking out at night and running around with friends. There were stairs on the left side of this house that led to our bathroom window, which I snuck out of a few times! I will never forget getting in the old bathtub that was by the window and crawling out on the roof to get to the stairs. I might have thought I was being sneaky, but my dad was on to me. I always say that my dad had eyes in the back of his head!

This is the house I lived in from age 13-16. I loved this house and mostly have happy memories associated with it. It was overall a very wholesome time for me, a time of innocence and dreams. I remember sitting on the porch a lot and I also remember doing my homework on the step by the side of the house. My dad helped me with my math homework a lot. He told me he hoped I would consider going to college someday because I thought I had the brains and ambition to do it. Yes, this was a wholesome time for me, which I treasure.

A Runaway

My rebellious streak went to the extreme one time, and I ran away from home for a few days with my siblings. I do not think was my idea at all; I believe I was going along with my siblings, who also were not the best influence on me. We spent time on a farm with some friends, getting drunk and partying the whole time. I never will forget me and my siblings taking a bunch of pennies and driving into the city to buy *Burger Beer*, which was the cheapest beer available. I get a silly picture of us doing this now because of the lengths we went to for some cheap beer to get drunk on! It appears I was an alcoholic from the beginning!

When I got home from my runaway, my dad was so terribly upset that I ended up feeling as terrible as he did. I was as happy to be home as he was to have me home, but along with being happy about my return, he was also angry and threatened to put me in a girl's home if I did not straighten up. That was all it took for me to stop being rebellious. My stepsister tried getting me to run away again, this time to CA, and somehow my dad found out and begged me not to. It hurts me to think I caused him any grief. I loved my dad way too much to really want to hurt him. I will never forget him standing on our back porch and looking at me with tears in his eyes, saying, "honey, please don't leave. I worked so hard to get you back." I reassured my dad I would never run away again, and from that point on I was back to being a good girl. Having my dad's love and approval really meant everything to me. My little bout with rebelliousness was over for good. Of course I was the typical teenager and with a war between peer pressure and parent pressure, but my love for my dad and wanting to remain with him won.

My First Job

My dad was proud of me when I took my first job working in the soybean fields and encouraged me to take the money to buy new school clothes, which I did. I was thrilled to have some new clothes! That work ethic he instilled in me has stuck with me. I believe in earning what I own, maybe even to a fault. It is not easy for me to take something for nothing. I am a better giver than taker, but I am learning to accept graciously. My dad instilled strong morals and values in me, encouraging me to attend church, which I enjoyed. The little town I lived in had a church kitty cornered from me, and I used to love to lay on my bed and listen to the church bells ringing. I still love to listen to church bells. There is something otherworldly and magical about the sound of church bells ringing that I love. I have always had a spiritual longing in me, so attending church seemed natural to me. I can remember going to Sunday school as a young girl and loving it! I loved to learn about Jesus! *I have always had a love for Jesus, and I always will!*

I have always had a love for Jesus, and I always will!

Girlhood Dreams

I also loved to lay on my bed and daydream about the man I would marry someday. Interestingly, I do not recall ever daydreaming about having children, but I did daydream about my prince charming. I always had a very romantic, old fashioned, pure, and idealistic view of love and marriage, which is why my two failed marriages hurt me so much. Everything I had ever hoped for in my girlhood dreams were shattered. Maybe it sounds corny to some people, especially these days, but that is just who I am, and I am proud of it. I always say that I am 100% lady and I take a lot of pride in that! Friends of mine tell me that I am like a *Southern Belle,* which I take as a great compliment. My favorite movie is **Gone with the Wind!** I love the charm and romance, and I can also identify with the feeling of being **gone with the wind and with Scarlett being a strong survivor.**

My First Boyfriend

I will always remember my first boyfriend when I was fourteen years old. We liked each other a lot, and he carried my schoolbooks home for me while he held my hand. I am amazed at the innocence of it now, especially when I see the young people today. I will never forget the time he came up to my bedroom to do some homework with me and said, "someday I'm going to marry you," which I believe he was sincere about. I went to my first school dance with him, which was quite memorable. He had to ask for my dad's permission first, then he had to come pick me up at the door and have me back by 9:00. I got my first kiss that night! He walked me the door and gave me a sweet kiss on the lips, which was so sweet and romantic. I will always remember him, as he was my first love experience. I don't remember why we broke up, but I believe it had something to do with him thinking I was ashamed of him because I didn't want to dance on the edge of the dance floor, which was not the case, but teenagers can be so sensitive. I remember crying over the breakup. I was heartbroken. It seems so silly to me now, but as a teenager I was really crushed over the breakup.

The reason I am writing about this is to convey the innocence I had then. It saddens me to think of that sweet and innocent girl wandering down the dark path I did in my late teens and young adulthood. There was a song years ago that says, *"she's only an angel who lost her wings,"* which is how I felt during those dark years. ***I did lose my wings for a time, but they grew back again, praise God! He is the One Who grew back my Angel wings! And I never want to lose them again!*** When I speak of Angel wings, I am not talking of perfection; I am only speaking of Godliness, which I know today I have.

High School

As I entered high school, I started hanging around with a wild girl who was not a good influence any more than the one from CA, and although I wasn't really rebellious, peer pressure was on, and I didn't do as well in school as I had in middle school. I wanted to have fun more than I wanted to do homework. I remember her getting me in trouble in class one time because she had me throwing frogs around the classroom instead of dissecting them! A lot of my problem with peer pressure had to do with my fear of rejection, which is normal for any teen, but given the deep-seated fears of rejection from my childhood, I think it was a real struggle for me. I was made fun of in my family for being such a goodie two shoes, which hurt me. I was truly just a wholesome girl next door type but felt torn between being wholesome and getting along with my peers because of my fear of rejection. I remember my siblings teasing me when I told them I did not want to smoke, drink, and get in trouble, which hurt me. I could not seem to win then! Today *I am who I am*, and do not care if someone wants to ridicule me for being such a wholesome woman. I would much rather be thought of as wholesome woman than a tramp!

Sweet Sixteen

I remember my 16th birthday when my dad gave me a *Sweet 16* birthday card, expressing how he understood how hard it was to be a teenager and growing up, and that he loved me as always. He also gave me my first watch, a Timex, which I was thrilled to get! I loved my dad so much. I had compassion for him and took care of him toward the end of his life when he was forced to be on oxygen. My dad was a disabled veteran who suffered from PTSD, and even though I did not understand what PTSD was then, I knew something was wrong. I knew he was getting psychiatric care on a regular basis. One time I found him curled up by the bathtub crying in anguish, and my heart just went out to him. I remember asking him, "dad, are you all right?" He just looked at me like he was ashamed to have me see him like that.

Knowing what I know about PTSD today, and suffering from it some myself, it makes me feel sad about the way he suffered, and back then veterans did not get the support they do today, so he was suffering all alone. One thing I know for sure, is that my dad knew I loved him. I went out with him when he collected money for the DAV and passed out poppies. I just loved being with my dad, no matter what we were doing. I even dressed up for Halloween one year in grade school as him, with all his army attire. I'm sure my dad thought that was something! I remember so well being in a Halloween parade at school dressed like my dad.

It is now 2023 and I have a deeper understand of PTSD. I understand my own trauma and how I was affected, and that is why I am doing EMDR therapy now.

A Kiss on the Cheek

The most outstanding memory of all with my dad is of me kissing him on the cheek every day before going to school and every night before going to bed, telling him I loved him. I had a sweet and loving relationship with my dad that I will always remember and treasure. That sweet and loving relationship with my dad would serve me well later in life when I finally met my husband. I told my husband numerous times that the reason I was so loving with him was because I had such a loving relationship with my dad. I also told him that my dad would have loved him. He would never have approved of the first two, but for sure he would have loved Larry! He would have said, "I am happy to have you marry my daughter."

My Stepmom Jean

Although my dad was very loving, the woman he married, who I choose to only call *Jean* today, was not so loving. I eventually found out she was bi-polar and alcoholic, which would explain the blackouts and hospital visits. Back then it was hush hush, so I never knew what was wrong, and I do not think my dad wanted to burden his children with this dark secret. When I was about 15 years old, I came home one day to find my dad waiting for me at the back door, warning me to go stay with my sister down the road because I was not safe at home, that Jean had threatened to kill both me and my dad. I didn't question what my dad said, that she wanted to kill me and him. I know now she was jealous of my relationship with my dad, but I didn't know that then. I don't remember what I thought or felt about what he was saying, but I took his warning seriously and stayed with my sister that night. It didn't help that I was blossoming into a young woman who looked a lot like her beautiful mother, who my dad still loved.

I will never forget the time Jean came upstairs and yanked me off the bed and dragged me across the floor by the sponge rollers I had in my hair. I was laying on my bed daydreaming as usual, and didn't hear her because the fan was blowing, and what a psycho she was! She had tried abusing me some when I was younger, but this was much worse. She started beating me real hard and calling me nasty names, while I was trying to fight her off. I went flying down the stairs to where my dad was at in our living room and yelled, "you better keep that bitch away from me!" as I told him what she had done. I don't think my dad knew what to do, but I let him know that I was not happy about what happened!

Why he ever married her is beyond me, but I believe the main reason he did was to have a mother for his children. In that regard I am glad he married her, as I may not have had a chance to live with my dad if he had not, but oh Lord, he could have done so much better! The only issue I had with my dad is that he did not do more to prevent Jean's abuse, but I think he was afraid if he intervened too much it would get worse for everyone, including himself. He also wasn't always present when she was abusive, so he didn't even know the full extent of her abuse. I remember Jean had to be in the hospital numerous times, but I never understood why. He said something about her having blackouts, but I was too young to understand alcoholism, and it wasn't talked much about back then. I also think my dad wanted to protect us from the truth.

My dad had a lot to deal with—emotionally damaged children, a mentally ill and alcoholic wife, who was the stepmom for his children, along with his own issues with PTSD. He was also struggling just to put food on the table. I remember he went grocery shopping once a month, and filled the station wagon up, and we all helped him unload it. It got to the point that he had put a lock on our grocery pantry, so we didn't run out of food for the month. My dad did not have it easy, and neither did his children, but I would have taken a little hardship any day over not being with him. Being with my dad was what was most important to me. Considering all the obstacles in his path at the time, it is amazing to me now that he did as well as he did. He wanted a mom for his children and just made a bad choice. If I can forgive myself for making bad choices with men when I was younger, then I can also forgive my dad for making a bad choice. I can even forgive Jean today for abusive behavior toward me, but my dad would roll over in his grave if he knew the evil she did to my brother after he passed away!

Another Cruel Blow

I hate writing about this part of my story because it is so sad for me. I just wrote about the happiest times of my childhood, to now writing about the saddest time. Life threw me another cruel blow, one that changed the course of my young life and headed me down a path to disaster. Love and security were once again taken away from me. On November 11, 1971, just a few months after turning *sweet sixteen*, my dad passed away, which left me feeling abandoned all over again, and this time for good. There was no hope of him coming back to me. My precious daddy, the one who was like my knight in shining armor, the one who rescued me from foster care, the one who loved me and gave me stability I so longed for and needed, was gone from my life forever. I knew he had suffered a heart attack in March that year, but I never thought he would die at the young age of 49. It was a brutal blow to me.

I remember the day so well. I knew he was going to the hospital that day and gave him my very last kiss on the cheek before I went to school, and told him I would visit him later, but his sad eyes told me otherwise. He looked at me like he knew he would be gone from my life, that he would never see his little girl again. I never had the chance to visit him, as I was informed of his passing before I could. I was holding my infant niece when I was told the sad news, and almost dropped her on the floor because I was in so much shock. I reacted with shock and tears, devastated beyond words. I screamed, "How could this be? No! Not my dad!"

He received a military funeral. He died on Veteran's Day, which I do not believe was an accident. I always had respect for my dad's service to our country during WW11, and I always give to the DAV because I know the devastating effect of war firsthand from watching him suffer with PTSD. War was really the cause of our family breaking up, as it was why my dad was not around for so many years to care for his family. It was no fault of his; it simply was what it was.

I never understood his pain as a young girl, but I do now as an adult. I was so young and so happy to be living with my dad, that I never thought of what he went through to get his children back. It brings tears to my eyes now when I think of everything he went through in the war—the combat, watching his best buddy be killed right in front of him, being sick with Malaria, the PTSD, the amnesia, and yet he loved his children so much that he overcame all his obstacles to get us back. This was amazing, especially in the 1960's, when it was almost unheard for men to get custody of their children. My mom did not care enough to get us back, but my dad did. I have such a tremendous amount of respect for my dad for doing this. Just the fact that he did this speaks volumes of his love for his children. He could have walked away like my mom did and leave us stranded in foster care forever, but he made a choice to rise to the occasion and overcome his own demons enough to get his children back.

Wow. I love my dad so much for this. ***When I speak of Angels God put in my childhood, my dad was the best one of all!***

My mom bad mouthed my dad and blamed him for everything that happened with our family, which infuriated me. How dare her speak badly of my dad, who went through hell and high water to get us back! True to her narcissistic nature, she would never take any responsibility for anything, and instead blamed my dad. She apparently couldn't even be happy for me that I had some happy years with him. No, she abandoned me, and then tried to take away the happy years I had with my dad, resenting him for having custody of me. If she really wanted to have custody of me, she should have at least tried! She didn't even come visit me while I was in foster care, and she wants to criticize my dad?! How dare her! But I refused to let her badmouth my dad without speaking up about it. I told her that her criticism would not fly with me. Nobody can take away the happy years I had with my dad, or the loving memories of him. Nobody. They are in my heart forever. I believe I would have had a better relationship with my mom when she reentered my life, had she not had such a bitter attitude toward my dad. Had she been a genuinely loving mother, she would have only wanted the best for me, which she obviously did not.

It's YOUR Fault!

When my dad passed away, I was the oldest of three children left at home, trying my best to cope with my loss and be there for my siblings who were also grieving. I was 16, my sister was 15, and my younger brother was only 12. This was particularly difficult for my brother because he had only been with my dad for about a year when he passed away. None of really knew how to handle the loss, and it certainly didn't help that Jean blamed us for his death, telling us, "it's your fault because you caused him so much stress."

My sister and I both remember the day she sat us down at the dining room table and told us we were responsible for our dad's death. What an incredibly cruel and thoughtless thing to say to three grieving children. We needed emotional support, but instead we got emotionally beat up. I remember seeing a therapist once right after my dad passed, who explained to me that I was grieving, and suffering from guilt. I doubt if I told the therapist that guilt was being dumped on me by Jean, as I was too troubled and withdrawn at the time, and I probably had already convinced myself that Jean was right about it being my fault, just like it was my fault I ended up in foster care when I was.

Today I understand that none of this was my fault. I didn't cause his death. My dad would purposely abandon me or any of his children. And he would never want his children to carry any guilt about his death.

A few months after his death I had a spiritual experience with my dad. He called me to him and wrapped his arms around me and said, "I still love you." He was letting me know that I didn't do anything wrong to cause his death. I always knew my daddy loved me and I always will. And I will always love him.

In Withdrawal Again

I withdraw into my emotional shell after my dad's death, which was only natural for me since it is what I did as a young girl when I went into foster care. It was too painful for me to cope with. My main coping mechanism throughout my childhood was withdrawal, and I resorted right back to it when my dad passed away. I became very depressed and could barely function enough to even make it to school, but I managed somehow. There was an English teacher who really liked me, who was constantly drawing me back into the classroom because I was daydreaming again, just like I did when I was a little girl. I had to have a Tonsillectomy that year, and she was in the hospital at the same time and sent me a get-well card, which I thought was so sweet and thoughtful.

She was another Angel in my life, someone God put there to love me. All throughout my upbringing there was always someone there for me, a human Angel put there by God to love and nurture me. My state file said that there was something about me that drew adults to me, which seemed to be the case. There was always someone to nurture me when I needed it, which I am so grateful for. My report cards at school always remarked about my good nature. I was a sweet girl. I remember one time in English class the teacher had everyone write something about each person in the class, and everyone said, "Carol is a very nice girl." I was lovable, though I didn't think so. I look over my shoulder and see the Hand of God loving me. Thank You God, for putting so many Angels in my life!

Another Change

I have never liked change (I wonder why?), but another one came my way not long after my dad's death. Jean could not afford to keep us in the house we had been living in while my dad was alive, and moved us into a trailer in another town, which I hated. This took place right before my junior year of high school, which only further fed my insecurity. Not only did I not have my dad and had to put up with an abusive stepmom, (I will not even call her that today; I only call her Jean), but now I had to leave my school, my friends, and all the things familiar to me, and be forced into a dumpy trailer, and into a new school with new classmates.

The only familiar friend I had was my defense mechanism, withdrawal, which helped me cope. I had already been feeling insecure, but it got worse with all the new changes in my life, and I crawled deeper into my shell, withdrawing to the point where I was so shy that I would not even speak when spoken to by nice girls at school who were sincerely trying to be friendly and make me feel welcome. It is hard for people to believe that I was that shy at one time, but believe me, I was very, very shy. I started daydreaming even more in class than I had been right after my dad passed. *Somewhere over the Rainbow...*

Not a Normal Teenager

I remember so well walking home from school with my head down, feeling sad, depressed, lonely, and old. The teenage things I should have been interested did not have any appeal for me. I shuffled through my days feeling more like an old lady than a teenage girl. I never looked forward to coming home (why would I?), and when I did come home, I would go into my bedroom and read the Bible, especially Revelation. *I became a spiritual seeker. Whether or not I was consciously aware of what my longing was for, I know now that I was seeking love, comfort, and hope that I so desperately needed and wanted, so I turned to God. I felt as though everyone else had failed me, and I had nowhere else to turn to except God.* Nobody told me to read the Bible or become a seeker. I wasn't even going to church at this time; it just seemed like the natural thing for me to do. As Oswald Chambers said in his devotional book *My Utmost for His Highest*, we need to be humbled enough to want to seek Him. *I was humbled; there was nowhere else for me to turn to except God.*

Jean's Abuse

Jean became more abusive than ever after my dad passed, verbally abusing me a lot, telling me I would never amount to anything, that no man would ever want me. She hated me. I know now she was projecting her own hatred toward herself onto me, and was extremely jealous of me, but I took her abuse personally then. I was living with a woman who had already threatened to kill me when my dad was alive, and now with him gone I had no way to protect myself from her! Scary! I came home one day and found my bedroom a complete shambles, with all my belongings thrown all over the place. She had a fit one time and called me vile names when she found me making out with a boyfriend I had at the time. After what my younger brother told me years later, I think she should have been looking in the mirror calling herself those vile names, not me! Mirror, mirror, on the wall... She was projecting her own self-hatred onto me. Projection is a quite common thing for people to do; that is why when someone says something negative about me today, I do not take it personally. I pause, then tell myself, "that is their issue, not mine," and I give it back to them. Everyone has their issues, and I have learned that they are not mine to take responsibility for. How freeing!

Although I did not feel like a normal teenager, I decided to at least try to do some normal teenage things. I worked nights as a waitress in a truck stop the summer before my junior year, but I got so uncomfortable with men flirting with me and telling me what nice looking legs I had, that I asked to wash dishes instead. I was not a good flirt then, nor am I now. For me, flirting with men is flirting with disaster, which I never wanted or needed! I quit the job after about a month due to sleep deprivation. So much for being a normal teenager.

Falling Through the Cracks... Would somebody please help me!?

I wish I had gotten the emotional support I needed to help me deal with the loss of my dad. I am sure I would have fared so much better. I felt so alone. Knowing what I know about grief now, I realize I was grieving deeply back then, not only my dad, but the earlier grief as a young child in foster care. I know now that my unresolved grief led me down rocky roads as a young adult that I would have never traveled had I received the love and support I needed as a teenager. *I did not just stare at the cracks on the sidewalk as a young girl; I fell through them.* There was nobody supporting me.

My older brother would sometimes visit me, but he wasn't aware of Jean's abuse. I have often said that I am amazed that I didn't become another teenage suicide statistic. I have known teens who have attempted suicide in normal homes, and I was a teenage girl from an abnormal and traumatic past, trying to cope with yet more trauma in a very abusive home. The saying **what doesn't kill you makes you stronger** would certainly apply to my life then and throughout my young adult years.

I always say. "it's amazing I made it out of my late teens and twenties alive!" When I think of all the times I could have died when I was younger, I am utterly amazed and humbled. *God was watching over me, big time! Working overtime! Thank you, God, my Dearest Heavenly Father! Thank you for caring about me, even when I did not care about myself! Thank You for treating me like Your worthy and lovable child when I did not believe I was worth it! You are without a doubt, my Heavenly Father! I love You, Big Daddy!*

Copping Out to Cope

This is the perfect title for this phase of my life, as I truly was *copping out to cope.* I was searching for a way out of this mess I was in at home and school, and at least subconsciously thought that the only way out was to escape, where to I was not sure, but I had to do something because I was unhappy and depressed. When I had enough, I had enough, and I had had enough. I simply had to do something. I was on the run. I had to leave school, and I had to leave home. This time I truly was running away from home! And I was not coming back!

I did not make a sound and conscious decision in order to move forward to a better life; I was just reacting to an intolerable situation. At least I had enough sense to feel that I deserved a better life than the one

I had at home with Jean and all the abuse she was dumping on me, even though I was not clearly able to label it as abuse. All I knew was that I did not like her, and I did not feel safe with her. I wanted love and support from her and was angry and hurt that I was not getting it. I also believe I was angry at my dad for leaving me alone with this abusive woman. *I was an angry girl who felt like she was ready to crack up and fall through the cracks on the same sidewalk I stood staring at as a young girl. Please, somebody, help me! I feel SO alone! God, please help me!*

I was a very confused girl, and I believe a lot of my confusion was due to not being able to comprehend the abuse. There is no doubt in my mind today that it was abuse, but I did not see it as abuse then; I only knew something did not feel right. I was passive/aggressive in my reaction to Jean's abuse. I did not even try talking to her about the abuse, partly because I was afraid to, and partly because I did not understand what was happening. I do not remember her saying much about me leaving. If my memory serves me correctly, I do not think she even tried to encourage me to stay with her. If she were angry at all about me leaving, it was only because she would not be getting any money for me, not because she missed me. I am sure she was just as happy to see me gone as I was to leave. Good riddance!

My saving grace in leaving home, was knowing deep down that I deserved love. Maybe I didn't recognize the abuse for what it was, but I unconsciously knew I received love from my parents as a young child, and I knew for sure I received love from my dad, so I knew what I was experiencing with Jean was definitely not love. All I knew was that I wanted a mom like any other teenage girl. She was all I had at the time, and I did my best to live with her, but when I began to hate her as much as she hated me, I had to leave. I detested her

I have a sister who detests Jean so much that she spits and stomps on her grave when she visits our dad's grave. I think she would like to demolish her gravesite! Neither one of us likes the fact that she is buried next to our dad, but grave robbing is a crime! She deserves worse than spit and stomps after the way she treated my brother. *All I can say now is, God have mercy on her soul!*

When I went back to Jean's place to get my things, she got rid of everything that belonged to me. She got rid of my dolls, stuffed dog, etc. that were precious to me, but the worst thing she did was get rid of all the cards I kept that my dad gave me. She was an evil woman, but I have forgiven her today.

I Quit School!

Right before the third semester of my junior year in January 1973, I walked into the principal's office at school and said, "I am quitting school." Just like that. It was an impulsive decision, not something that was well thought out. I think I just woke up one day and said, "I have had enough! I don't care about school anymore." The counselor tried talking some sense into me, to no avail. I had made up my mind that I was done, and I doubt God himself could have changed my mind at that point. I was fed up, not with just school and my home life, but with life itself. I was going through severe depression and anxiety, feeling like I was ready to drown in a sea of hopelessness, with no one to bring me to shore. It was a very scary time for me.

In retrospect, I wonder why the school counselor did not dive a little deeper into my home life and try to figure out what was so wrong that I would just leave school. I suppose if she had, I would not have said much, as I was too shy and withdrawn then, but she should have at least tried. I do not remember anything being said about my home life. Shouldn't she have suspected abuse? Teenager do not typically just quit school for no reason. It seemed like the counselor made the whole issue about school, like she thought I just didn't like school. From my point of view now, it was a no brainer. If I had been the counselor, I would have probed gently until I opened up, and then maybe, just maybe, she might have confronted my guardian, the woman who called herself my stepmom, and found out the truth—that I wasn't coping well at home due to her emotional and verbal abuse. And let's not forget the whole issue of my dad passing, and the grief I was going through, and let's not forget about all the changes. And oh, last but not least, let's not overlook my traumatic childhood. *It is a good thing God was watching over me, because the counselor sure wasn't! When I think of Angels God put in my life, the school counselor was not one of them! Sadly, there did not seem to be any Angels in my life at that time.*

The counselor did not dive deep enough into the water to bring me shore; instead, she made it all about school, preaching to me what a big mistake I was making. I should have said, "well, counselor, give me a good reason to stay, other than saying it is a mistake because it will mess up my life. What life? As far as I am concerned, I have no real life." I guess I am coming across rather angry, and rightly so. Even if I couldn't express it, I was desperately seeking some love and understanding, not someone telling me, "you're making a mistake." I already felt like a mistake, and now she is telling I am making a mistake, just like Jean did. Teenagers often cannot express themselves well when they are hurting, and I was no exception, but a good counselor should know this. I was angry, hurt, and afraid, with no way to express it, except to leave, slam the door, and never look back, which I did. Bye! I am leaving school! And bye, Jean! I am not taking your crap anymore!

In retrospect, I only wish there had been somebody to really reach out to me and mentor me, but there wasn't. I felt so alone, but I had no way of expressing even that. I was SO depressed. As a therapist expressed to me, "you really did fall through the cracks, didn't you?" I replied, "yes, I guess I did." Without my dad's love I was lost and went searching for love in all the wrong places.

Meeting my First Husband

I needed help, and since my older brother had always been with me growing up, and was doing his best to fill our dad's shoes, I called him. I informed him of my situation and told him I wanted to leave home, so he offered to come get me and let me live with him. It just so happened that a previous roommate of his, who had left to reunite with his estranged wife, was now coming back to live with my brother again, and fate would have it that we arrived on the same day. Fate would also have it that we clicked. How our relationship started is still a mystery to me. It just did. He was a produce truck driver, and I went along with him on his routes, and we fell in love. He must have been in one of those cracks in the sidewalk! We were both in the cracks in the sidewalk, looking to each other to help each other out! But because we were both lost, we were never able to do that; instead we kept falling back into the cracks! We only knew each other a brief time before this happened, maybe two weeks at the most.

I know I missed my dad terribly, and was no doubt drawn to him because of my neediness, but he sure was a poor substitute for my dad! I know for sure that my dad would never have approved of him and would not have given me to Dale! "No way are you going to marry him," my dad would have yelled. He would have put his foot down hard. A drug addicted junkie with a prison record? Are you kidding?! Seriously, I was not raised like that, but it only goes to show you how lost I was that I would even consider getting involved with a man like that. I knew better, but I was so lost, alone, and vulnerable, that I got pulled right into him. I did not use my head at all; I acted purely on emotional neediness.

My brother told me years later how sorry he was that I ever got mixed up with him, as if he was responsible, which of course he wasn't. We both came from abandonment, though I did not know of his childhood until years later. Like attracts like, and we were attracted to each other because of our similar childhoods, though it was unconscious. I didn't consciously say, "gee, I really love him because he is so sick emotionally," but unconsciously I believe I did. We both came into the relationship with a dump truck load of unresolved emotional baggage, and our marriage ended with even more emotional baggage that we dumped on each other. With all the emotional baggage that I have dealt with in relationships, it is no wonder I am so cautious of being in another one!

The love that we shared was mostly in bed, making wild and crazy love. Today I believe some of our passion was partly anger. We would fight like crazy, then go make crazy love until we were so spent that we couldn't move. It seems all we did was fight and make up, and we called it love. It was crazy love all right; we were both crazy! We probably fought just so we could make up in bed, because that was how we worked out our emotions. I know today that there is much more to loving someone than having sex, sex, sex all the time like we did. I think we spent more time in bed than out of it!

Meeting my Long Lost Mom

I decided I wanted to meet my biological mom about six months later. I guess I figured since there was no hope for a d ecent relationship with my stepmom, I would give my real mom a try. I longed for a mother, and she was my real birth mother, the one I spent my first six years with, but a real mother would never abandon her children the way she did. Another reason I wanted to meet my biological mom was because I had a weird idea of impending death for myself for some reason; why, I do not know, but I did, and thought I should meet my long-lost mom before that happened. I also believe losing my dad made me long for a parental figure; after all, she was the other half of my parents, the woman who brought me into the world, and the one I spent the first six years of my life with. I am by nature a very curious person, and I was curious to meet her.

I suppose I could say we reunited since my mother was not a total stranger to me, but it felt like she was mostly a stranger to me. Maybe she wasn't a total stranger to me, but it is for sure the whole situation felt very strange. The fact that it had been so many years since we had seen each other also made it feel very strange. *I started praying about meeting her, and God answered my prayer, but you know the saying, be careful what you pray for; you might get it!*

Though it might have been natural for me to want to meet her, I do not think my expectations of it were. I think I had a fantasy about her, like she would somehow make everything ok for me, and make all the buried hurt in me go away. Wrong! Not only did she not make things better for me, but she made them worse. On talk shows they portray these beautiful, heartwarming reunions between children and long-lost parents hugging and crying, "Oh, my baby! I am so happy to meet you!" "My mom! Finally, I get to see you after all these years!" There should be a follow up show in a year, to see how warm and wonderful it is. Seriously!

I will never forget the day I met my mom. First, let me explain how we met. It was not through her searching for me; it was through my sister's boyfriend's aunt, who happened to know my mom. My sister told me about her whereabouts, and I called her. I do not believe my mom would have ever contacted me on her own; she just wouldn't, perhaps out of guilt and fear of rejection, and due to her lack of true caring. But curiosity got the best of me, and so there I was one day shortly after my 18th birthday, staring into the face of a woman I could barely even remember, saying, "hi mom," as if it had been twelve days instead of twelve years that we had been apart. It was very, very strange being around her. Really, how do you react to someone you know is your mom, but only have very vague memories of, a mother who abandoned you? Just like not remembering my young years with my dad, I do not remember much about my young years with my mom. I do have a few vague memories of her when I was young, but that is it.

On talk shows they always show these emotional, tearful reunions. What, no tears either? No, not from either one of us; in fact, it was very unemotional. We were both uncomfortable, not knowing what to say or how to act. What could I say? Oh, hi mom, how are you after all these years? What have you been up to all this time? What could she say? Oh, I have been working mostly. I haven't had much time for anything else, like visiting you and your siblings. She handled her nervousness by chain smoking, sitting on the edge of the chair like she wasn't sure if she should stay or leave, and I was thinking the same thing. I wasn't sure if I wanted her there or not, and I am sure she sensed it. How do we act? What should we say? I don't remember much of what was talked about, but it was not much about the past; it seemed more like idle chatter. Then after about an hour of this chit chat she left, giving me a family photo album. She had been hoping to see my brother, but he was working and didn't return home in time before she had to leave, so she returned the next day to see him, and we all three visited. I don't remember much about that visit, except that it was strange.

I am not sure how I felt afterward, or even if I felt much of anything. Was I happy to meet her? Relieved that my curiosity got met? I do not recall feeling much of anything consciously, but I am sure I was subconsciously. Bubbling underneath the surface of my nonchalant attitude were emotions I was unprepared for, especially anger and hurt. I was hospitalized with Hepatitis about a month after meeting her, something my ex-junkie man so generously gave me, and my mom came to see me at the hospital, bringing me some books to read. I will admit it was a comfort to have her there, especially since she was not there for me when I was sick in the children's home. I do have one memory of her cuddling me as a young child when I was ill, so I suppose she did care about me some. I can admit it was a comfort to have her back in my life, but I was uncomfortable with the comfort, because of other stronger feelings of anger and hurt, from a child who did not know how to handle this ever so emotional situation, and even though the anger and hurt had seemed to fade with the memory, the feelings were still there, only buried. *And it seemed like I was a little girl again on the sidewalks again...*

A Girl Interrupted

As my story unfolds it becomes clearer why, in retrospect, I had so much ambivalence toward my mom, and whether I did the right thing by pursuing her. The only thing I can say with certainty, is that knowing myself to be such a curious person, I probably would have always wondered about her had I not met her. What if? You know the saying about *curiosity killing the cat*. Maybe I should have just met her once out of curiosity and then let it go, and let her go, and more importantly, let the past go, but I opened the door and in she walked. If I had had better boundaries from the very beginning, I would have handled the situation differently, but I did not have a clue about boundaries then. Maybe I could have/should have closed the door, but I didn't. She wanted me back in her life and I wanted her back in my life, but it was a love/hate relationship that was not healthy for either one of us. I believe I thought that by having her back in my life she could heal my childhood wound, but she did not heal it at all; in fact, all she did was reopen the wound and make it hurt again. You know how it is when you have a scab you keep picking at? It just keeps bleeding, but if you let it alone, it will heal, and then all that is left is a scar. By meeting my mother, I kept picking at the scab of my childhood wound, but that would never have happened had I just left it alone. I always say, **I can live with a scar, but not an open wound.** Too bad I didn't know that then! I would have saved myself from more pain. It was bad enough she hurt me as a child, and here I was letting her hurt me again. For any former foster child who is attempting to reunite with parents, I say, "proceed with caution."

I wish I could go back in time and do things differently, but as a friend of mine said, "Carol, you made the best choice you could at that time." I'm not sorry I met her, but I do wish I would have let it go after one visit. It just was not a healthy relationship and we both suffered. What I really wanted was for her to fix my childhood abandonment and she couldn't. It was too late.

A Volcano Erupting

 What happened emotionally after I met her? My deep-seated feelings of anger, hurt, sadness, and deep pain, created depression and anxiety. And underneath it all was probably also a deep-seated love for my mom, which really created anxiety. I was a mess, but of course I did not know it at the time. I honestly did not know what I felt. All I knew was that I was uncomfortable. Would I have still had these feelings to deal with in therapy years later, where so many former foster children end up at? Probably, but the impact would not have been so volcanic. It was just too much for me emotionally then.

I felt like a volcano ready to erupt whenever I was in her presence. The volcano did finally erupt years later while she was visiting me, reducing our relationship to ashes.

I was only 18 when I met (reunited?) my mom, which can be a troubling time for anyone of that age but add to that the fact of having serious unresolved emotional baggage of abandonment, and it is not hard to see the problem I had. Young adults normally still want their parents in their lives as they are maturing into adults, but my situation was not normal at all! Instead of feeling like an 18-year-old girl ready to spread her wings and leave the nest, I felt like a bird going back to the nest, in need of refuge I never had. I was not aware of any of my thoughts or feelings about this; all I knew was that I was very insecure. I was trying to spread my wings and fly, without anyone showing me how.

A man who shared a story in the FACT book said, "I spent my whole life looking for a mother I never had, and never found." Wow, could I ever relate to that! That is how I feel now, like I never truly had a mother, which I have had to grieve. What I have learned from my experience though, is that I can and do mother myself today. My experience has also made me a more loving and nurturing person toward others. I am super sensitive to people's emotional needs, especially to the less fortunate children and animals who are in such need of love. I believe the fact that I did not have a mother has made me motherlike to people in general, because I am so sensitive to my own unmet mothering needs. It has certainly given me a motherly heart toward foster children. I think of myself as a mother to the motherless. There is always a positive to a negative situation if we look for it. *Out of the ashes I rise!*

I called myself *a girl interrupted* because that is what I was. I was going along with my life the best I knew how at the time, then my mom came along and interrupted it. I am not sure where I was heading without her in my life, but I sure found out where I was heading with her in it, and it was not a good place! I didn't realize how much I was affected by her coming back into my life because my painful stuff was stuffed real deep, but it was there and ready to come up whether I was ready for it or not. Why, I ask myself today, did you really want to meet her? Seriously, I would have been better off with an older woman as a mentor, someone who could help steer me in the right direction as a young adult. My mom steered me right off course into the wrong direction, and right back to my childhood. I was eighteen going on six when she came back into my life. When I needed to grow up, but instead I was regressing, which was not good. I ended up feeling more lost and alone than ever, like I was out in the ocean being tossed around in the waves, and the waves were my emotions! *Jesus, help me!*

Just Forget About the Past and Go on From Here

What I did not realize then, is that my mom and I were doomed from the very beginning of our new relationship. We were expecting things from each other that neither one of us could give to the other, which only served to hurt us both more than we already were. She wanted me to *just forget about the past and go on from here.* Those were her constant words to me. In other words, let's just pretend none of the past existed, that she had always been my mom, even though she wasn't present in my life. Let's just pretend that there is no hurt, and just hope for a good relationship now. Let's just pretend that she didn't walk out of my life when I was only six years old and leave lasting scars. Let's just pretend.

My mom obviously was not a very bright woman about psychological issues. I told her once that she should talk to a therapist about the lasting effects of abandonment. She was not only clueless about any long-term effects of my childhood abandonment; she was not concerned. Her narcissistic personality made it all about her, not her children. All she wanted was to play the victim and play the blame game, taking no responsibility for her own actions. It was everyone else's fault, including my dad's, who went way overboard to save our family shipwreck. With the attitude she had, there was no hope for any kind of true reconciliation. The loving thing for me to do would have been to recognize this early on and let her go, with love and respect. Sometimes true love is letting go, but it takes wisdom to do this, which I lacked then.

I was SO lost, like a child wandering around in the woods alone. Who am I? Where am I? Where am I going? Would someone please help me? *I never found anybody to help me then, except Almighty God, and He came to me in the most profound way, saying, "my child, I am here for you." Thank You Dear Heavenly Father and Jesus, for helping me find my way Home!*

A Spiritual Experience

My life became even more interrupted shortly after meeting my mom. In September of 1973, Dale decided we were moving out to Montana, so we packed up our few belongings in a 1955 Chevy and headed out to *Big Sky*

Country, otherwise known as *God's Country. I choose not to go into any great detail about what happened, only to say I had developed a strong urge to seek God at this time, and was blessed with a very personal, beautiful, and special spiritual experience with Jesus, in which I was taken up into the Heavens. Yes, I heard Angels sing three times for me, which was the most glorious music you can imagine, and Jesus filled me with His Holy Spirit. I wanted to stay in Heaven with Jesus, but was firmly told, "you cannot leave yet. It is not your time. You have things to do here." I know now that the thing I had to do here was this work for foster children. I wish I could convey the love of Our Heavenly Father and Jesus, but no words can even come close.* I would say more about my experience, but most people do not understand, and would think I am crazy. I do not want to convince others I am not, and it does not matter anymore to me what others think anyway. It was a personal experience meant for me. The only reason I chose to say anything about the spiritual experience in my story is because it is crucial part of my life story and has a lot to do with my work; otherwise, I would not say anything. Other spiritual people have confirmed what I experienced, but I don't need anyone to. I know 100% what I experienced. I wonder why people would even be so amazed that Jesus came to me the way He did. Jesus is All Powerful! He can come to whoever he chooses, and He chose to come to me!

When I say I love Jesus, I say it not just because I know He loves me and has done so much for me, but also from a deep and beautiful experience with Him. The love I have for Jesus cannot adequately be expressed in words, as it is beyond words; it is spiritual. And I am not capable of even understanding how Jesus did what He did for me, but I do know without a shadow of a doubt that He did. I am cautious about sharing this because of my fear of being thought of as strange, but we are living in a more spiritually open time today.

What I find amazing is that Bozeman Montana, which is where this spiritual experience took place, is in the Bridger Mountains. Jesus is the Bridge to God, and FACT is based on the Ten Stepping Stones and the Bridge to Healing. How amazing is that?! God is so amazing!

Getting Help in All the Wrong Places

One of the people who thought I was crazy was Dale, and he put me into a psych ward for a few days. I started getting depressed right after I got out, mostly because I did not want to be in this world anymore after being in Heaven. I felt so lost after what I had experienced. Jesus showed me my true home, and now I am stuck here? I felt displaced. What am I supposed to do now? Unless someone has had a spiritual experience like that, one cannot really understand what I am saying, but I have read stories of others who have gone to Heaven, and none of them wanted to return here either! There was a book called *Embraced by the Light*, in which the author expressed her own difficulty in readjusting to this life after experiencing Heaven, so I know I am not alone.

So where do I go from here? I experienced a vision of Heaven, only to be kicked out. I felt so lost and depressed. I wasn't really suicidal; I just didn't want to be here. God, can I please leave? Since I was depressed about not being in Heaven, I felt I should reach out for some help, but I reached out in the wrong direction! Where did Dale take me? To the state hospital in Montana, of all places! For crying out loud, I did not need to be locked up; I just needed some therapy! I remember so well talking with the woman at the intake office, and her asking me what my childhood was like, and me responding with, "what's that got to do with anything?" She did not say anything, but she was probably thinking, we got a keeper here! What did my childhood have to do with anything? How about everything! I think it is hilarious now! I remember banging on the doors the first night there, and yelling, "let me out of here!" I realized right away what a huge mistake I had made going there, but it was too late. I was stuck there for the time being. I was a girl interrupted all right! Just like the movie!

Never ever tell a psychiatrist you have seen Jesus! I was so incredibly naïve to think they would believe what I experienced. They wanted to know why I was there, and when I explained I was depressed after having such a beautiful spiritual experience, I was diagnosed large doses of medication for schizophrenia, along with Thorazine, which I did not need. I became a zombie quickly! I did not go in there crazy, but that place was about to make me so! When I first spoke of my spiritual experience, they asked me if I were hearing voices, and I would make them mad when I replied, "only yours." They were determined to make me schizophrenic. I found out years later, that if you take medication for a mental illness you don't have it, it can make you mentally off, which is what happened with me. I started getting paranoid from the medication they gave me, and then when they caught me not taking my medication, they locked me up, which was a nightmare beyond belief, all closed in this small room with no way out, crying to get out. That experience left me being extremely claustrophobic. I was in that awful place for about a month, and it was a month too long! The only good thing about the place was all the other people there, who thought I was loads of fun! I had some strange experiences while I was there. *There were older people who asked me to touch them, because they said I could heal them, and I loved caring for them. I do not know if I healed anyone, but I do believe they felt comforted by my presence because they sensed the Holy Spirit of Jesus.* They all loved me and were very protective of me. Truly, I never felt so loved in my whole life! There was something about the way I emotionally and mentally connected with the people there that was incredibly special. And I will never forget the way everyone crowded around me to say good-bye when I left. I will never forget them.

Halfway Home

I came back home to Illinois, not knowing what was before me, only that I was leaving the mental ward and all my fellow mentals to be in the real world with all the other mentals. People act as if the people in psych wards are the most mentally off. I disagree. I believe most people in psych wards are there because they are too sensitive for the world out here. They can't cope! I'm not saying there aren't real mental disorders, but in my opinion the whole world is mentally ill. As I sit here writing in 2020, our world is in total chaos. That is crazy! People being violent in our streets is a lot more insane than people who have emotional and/or mental disorders they are coping with. In my opinion, people often point fingers at people who are mentally ill as a cover for their own mental illness. It is so much easier to judge others than to judge yourself. And believe me, the people who run the psych wards do not have it all together. Nobody does.

That being said, although I was happy to be out of the mental ward, I wasn't much happier to be in a half-way house, which is where I stayed for about five months. I was forced to go to vocational rehab, which I hated. My mom reentered my life there, along with the depression and anxiety that had been lifting. Seeing her was like adding fuel to the fire, but I honestly did not know this at the time. All I knew was that I got very depressed after she visited me. I did not see the connection between my emotions and my mom reentering my life, but I am sure my therapist did!

Therapy

What does my childhood have to do with anything?

I was forced into therapy, where I persistently denied having any emotional problems from my childhood. *"I don't know what my childhood has to do with anything!"* I hurled at the therapist. I think it is funny now, but back then I really thought I knew what I was talking about. I remember one woman, God bless her, who had amazing patience and tolerance with me. She really cared about me and tried so hard to help me; she just would not give up on me, no matter how angry and defiant I was with her. I remember yelling at her, *"I don't want to talk about my childhood!"* Everything she said to me went right over my head. "You're angry about your childhood; let's talk about it," she said to me, to which I would reply, *"no, let's not talk about it! I'm not angry about anything, except having to be here!"* In my opinion, she was the most understanding one of all the people I dealt with during that time. She continued to reach out to me off and on for a few years, going the extra mile for me when I was suicidal. ***She was also an Angel God sent to help me, but I was not grateful for her like the teachers I had as child.*** I resented her at the time, because she was trying to help me deal with my crappy childhood, which I did not want to deal with! It would be years before I really dealt with it in therapy, but even if she didn't accomplish all she wanted to with me at the time, I believe she did plant a seed. ***God bless that woman for being the understanding and loving Angel that she was! Thank You God!***

A FACT Premonition

Another seed got planted during this time, but I do not remember it being planted. It was not until 1984 that my brother brought it to my attention. I called him because I was having a difficult time emotionally after my mom visited me here for the first time. I will never forget that day. I was in a very overwhelmed emotional state, so much so that I came home from work and broke a heavy antique chair against the floor. I guess I was a little angry? He told me while he was visiting me at the halfway house in 1973-1974 that God prophesied to him that I would form something new for foster children. I did not remember him telling me this at all. It came as a surprise to me when he told me in 1984. I wondered what it might be that God showed him, but I just let it go and didn't think anything more of it until a few years later.

Years later when I finally got serious about therapy, my therapist told me that being taken away from my mom was the worst thing that could have happened to me as a child. Why didn't I see it when I was younger? Why was I in so much denial as a young girl? It was all about surviving. Children do what they must to survive, and I just did the best I could to survive. I wasn't unique in my coping skills. I have talked with many former foster children who survived in their own ways. Since facing the truth that yes, it was traumatic, and yes, I have been deeply affected, I have also come to terms with the fact that my childhood abandonment will always haunt me some; I just know better how to deal with it today, but instead of dealing with it in therapy back then, I denied it and used whatever defense mechanisms available to avoid my past, as it was just way too painful for me. *I am not going there! No way!* I was screaming inside. Where I did go, was to the bottle.

Battle with the Bottle

I already mentioned that I drank as a teenager some, but only for a short time, and mostly due to peer pressure. I was really the wholesome *girl next door* type, a young girl who loved walking and riding my bike in the country, sitting outside on the porch doing my homework, being a cheerleader, visiting with an old neighbor lady, and going to church. When siblings tried getting me to smoke and drink, I told them I did not want to. I was, and still am, the sweet one in the family, and was made fun of for that. Deep down I wanted to live a clean and sober life, but with my dad gone, and reacquainted with my mom, I was full of emotional baggage that I was not equipped to deal with. I needed something to help me cope, to soothe the wound, and alcohol and drugs became the salve. I did not know why I decided to start drinking; all I knew was that I wanted/needed to. I did not consciously say, *"you are in a lot of emotional pain from your crappy childhood, so you should start drinking to cope with the emotional baggage,"* but it is exactly what I said unconsciously.

The bottle that I had only been acquainted with in the past, now became my best friend. Whereas I only dabbled with alcohol in the past, it now had a much stronger appeal for me, and the same could be said of cigarettes, which I had dabbled with and gave up when I was a young teenager. Everyone knows booze and cigarettes go together, and they sure did for me. The more I drank, the more I smoked. Just go into any bar and you will see that. Just like I wasn't looking for my first beer as a 15-year-old girl, I wasn't looking for it when I was 18 either; it just happened to come my way, and I seized the opportunity. I suppose it sounds funny to use the word opportunity, but that is how I perceived it then. I had an opportunity to have a new career, in drinking! I was not looking for this new career, but it came knocking on my door! How lucky could I get?! Remember me? My name is booze. So nice to see you again! I am offering you a new career! And the only resume I needed was my past drinking job!

I left the half-way house in May of 1974, and Dale took me home, which was to a trailer in Decatur, Illinois. I barely even got a chance to unpack my bags and settle in when he informed me that we were leaving for Florida; why, I didn't know, but back then I didn't need to know; I just went wherever he and the wind took me. We left without him paying our last month's rent, so some of our belongings, including the family album my mom had given me, now belonged to the landlord, which I was upset over, but my attitude was, oh well, that's life! Where Dale went, I went. Stand by your man. So off to Florida we went, staying with his sister for about a week before we wandered up to Alabama, where we stayed in a very rundown old motel for about a week until he found a house.

It was while residing in this old motel that booze made its entrance into my life again. I decided to go out in the lobby to watch some tv and have a smoke while Dale was sleeping, and an older man offered me a beer. Just like I took my first beer when I was 15, I never even thought about what I was doing, whether I should or should not drink it; I just took it and drank it. Then he offered me a few more beers, which I also drank with gusto. He was probably trying to get me drunk so he could have sex, just like when I was 15, but I was too naïve to know this, and too happy to have the beer to be concerned about it. What happened next is funny to me now, mostly because I was so serious about it. I walked into our room where Dale was half asleep, shook him gently and said, "I know what will help me--- booze!" I was so excited about this amazing revelation! I'm not sure what his response to me was, but knowing him, he probably just gave me funny look and went back to sleep. Crazy girl!

At the time I really did believe that booze was the answer; the answer to what I am not sure I even knew, but I just knew I needed something to help me with something, and booze seemed like the answer. It was my hope. It would be the friend I needed so badly. Little did I know at the time that my friend would stab me in the back, time and time again. I can relate so well when I hear people in AA talking about this. Here, I will be here for you. You can talk to me. I will make you feel better. Alcohol is the biggest liar, thief, and backstabber anyone could have, but I was so desperate for a friend of some kind at this time in my life, that I took its hand, and wandered into the darkness of alcoholism. I always say at AA that I drank for emotional reasons; it was my escape from the pain. It was my baby bottle!

A Gypsy Life

After a short time in the motel, we moved into a small house, and I took a job for a few weeks in an egg packing factory, which I hated. Dale decided that Alabama was not where he wanted to settle after all, so we took off. Well, ok...whatever you want was my attitude. I never questioned him about anything because I was depending on him to provide love and stability for me. I honestly did not see how unstable and lost he was, when we were really two lost souls trying to find refuge in each other, the blind leading the blind. We both came from unstable childhoods and had a lot of unresolved emotional baggage, which of course we were both clueless about. And so, it was with this shared emotional instability that our life together became an adventure, living like gypsies for about a year.

We left Alabama in the summer of 1974 and went to Santa Fe for about a month. For some reason he took off on me while we were there, then changed his mind and returned the same day. I'm not even sure I was aware of what was happening, but he informed me after he returned that he had planned on leaving me there. Abandon me? Why? Years later when we discussed our past together, he admitted to me that he had wanted me to grow up more. Really? Like he was so grown up and mature! How hilarious! He had me living like Bonnie and Clyde, and he wanted to point a finger at me and tell me to grow up? He was ten years older than me, and wasn't very mature for his age, so why would he expect an 18-year-old girl to be so mature? I ended up being the mature one when I made a sound decision to leave him!

Dale decided that Santa Fe was not where he wanted to settle after all, so we went back to Illinois to settle down there. He always had an intention of settling down, but we would be moving on down the road before we barely had a chance to unpack! It was my childhood all over again, but hey, it seemed normal to me, so I never thought much of it.

I believe that there is no such thing as normal; our perception of normal is whatever our experience has been, and unfortunately my childhood experience was chaotic. The only constant thing in my childhood was change, so moving around seemed very much like the normal way of life for me. I believe Dale and I were both restless souls, searching for a home we never had. I know I really wanted security like I had with my dad, but man oh man, Dale sure was not the right man to provide it! I always say I have daddy issues, and it is for sure I did back then!

We settled into a friend's old farmhouse out in the country when we returned to Illinois, which was more to my liking, as I was now home where I really wanted to be in the first place. I never wanted to leave my home; it was always him wanting to leave, and me following him. Dale got restless again after a few months and decided to go live with his sister in Delaware. He went there by himself to get things in order, then I followed him on a bus. I cannot remember if he had any well thought out plan for us, but it did not work out if he did, as we ended up living with his sister's family, which did not work out at all.

His family thought I was strange because I was so quiet. They kept pressuring me to talk, which I resented, so I told Dale I was moving out to take a job as a nanny for a man who had custody of his two young daughters, which I did from January-April of 1975. I wonder if fate sent me to this job, as the children's mom had abandoned her daughters, which

I could so relate to. I respected the father for not abandoning his children, just like I have respect for my dad for not abandoning his children.

I hated saying goodbye to the little girls, but Dale wanted to leave, this time to go back to Sweet Home Alabama again, which of course I agreed to. *Stand by Your Man* was my motto all throughout my first two relationships, but when I think about it now, I do not think of myself as being so loyal, as I do stupid and naïve!

Bonnie and Clyde on the Run

Dale expressed an urgency to leave immediately, so we hopped on a train, and settled around Montgomery, Alabama, where we lived in a small room next to a fruit stand we worked at. I never ate so many peaches in my life! And I loved talking with all the southerners! It was strange that I was so uncomfortable talking with Dale's family but was totally open and friendly with complete strangers. We were only there about a month when Dale informed me that we were moving again, this time to a trailer out in the country not far away, where I got acquainted with fire ants. I never will forget standing outside and feeling these fire ants crawling up my legs, and me taking my pants off and running around trying to get rid of them!

After living in this trailer not even a month, Dale informed me that the reason we had to leave Delaware was because of a bad drug deal. The criminal activity in Delaware was probably linked with Alabama, but I'm not sure. What I was sure of though was that I didn't want to live like Bonnie and Clyde! Oh Great! I had already moved twice in two months because of his criminal activity. I was living on the run with a criminal, who I was an accomplice to. Bonnie and Clyde were on the run! But Bonnie was about to be on the run from Clyde! It was not an easy decision to make, especially since I don't do alone well and really wanted to stand by my man, who I really believed I loved, but I think my fear about the situation made my decision for me. It was an impulsive decision that I made as soon as he told me about the criminal activity he was involved in, which now I was involved in. When I think about this crazy situation now, I wonder what my dad would have thought about it. He would crawl up out of his grave and shoot him!

Bonnie Leaving Clyde

That was it! Despite all my insecurity, and how in love I was with Dale, I somehow conjured up enough sense to tell him, "I am not going to live like Bonnie and Clyde," and Bonnie immediately left on a bus to Illinois. I am amazed that I was able to be strong enough at that time to leave him, but I had just enough sense and fear about the situation to realize I needed to leave. I did not want to end up dead or in prison. What I should have done was take one of his stolen guns and point it at him to make a point! I am leaving you!

I will never forget a man I sat next to on the bus, who told me how special I was, and that he really liked me and wished I would go with him. I told him I was going home to Illinois, and that I was going to get good and drunk as soon as I got to my sister's. He told me he did not understand. "Why would such a sweet and innocent girl like you want to get drunk?" he said. I am not sure what my reply was, but it was probably something like, "I just want to." It is amazing to me how outspoken I was about getting drunk, like it was the most natural thing in the world to me. Maybe he thought it was strange that I would want to drink because I seemed so sweet and innocent to him, but it was because of my innocence that I wanted to get drunk. I could not cope with the reality of my dysfunctional life! I may not have fully realized how dysfunctional my life was, but I was at least stable enough to know I needed to leave the dangerous situation I was in with Dale.

I remember getting off the bus and hitchhiking to my sister's house. Everyone was hitchhiking those days, but when I think about that now I wonder what I was doing. *God sure was watching over me!*

Party Time

I hitch hiked the rest of the way to my sister's home after I arrived at the bus station, which was so incredibly stupid and naïve of me, but I never though anything of it. It was so common back then in the hippie days. *God certainly was watching over me!* I was happy to be at my sister's place, and true to my word, I got good and drunk, along with my sister who was already a full-blown drunk. We partied that whole summer in bars, where my sister hustled drinks for us by flirting with the men. My sister wanted booze and men, but I just wanted the booze.

My 20th Birthday

I will never forget celebrating my 20th birthday. I took twenty of my sister's valiums while drinking large amounts of beer. Did I really do this? Yes, I really did do something that stupid. Was I suicidal? What the hell was I thinking? What was I trying to do, kill myself? It was a lethal combination, and yet I did it without any real concern of killing myself. I might have been suicidal, but I don't remember consciously feeling so; I just wanted to get good and high, which I most certainly did.

The alcohol and drugs weren't the only things that could have killed me that night! My sister drove off the side of the road and got us stuck in a ditch, but luckily some guys we knew from the bar happened to drive by and rescued us. I was so messed up I could hardly walk; my legs were like rubber, but we made it home alive, and I woke up the next morning. It is amazing that I did not die that night.

Thank You God, for saving me that night! Unfortunately, this was not the only time I was that foolish and self-destructive, and in need of God's strong and amazing Hand to help me. When I think back on all the times that I could/should have died in my young years, there is absolutely no doubt in my mind that God was protecting me. Spiritual people in my life have all told me that I have many Angels around me, which I wholeheartedly believe. I also believe that part of the reason God spared my life so many times was because He knew I would be doing this work for foster children, which is a testimony for them about His Love. It truly is amazing that I survived all the messes I got myself into when I was a young girl. I should be dead.

I will never forget the time a woman came up to me in church years ago and said, "I feel led by the Holy Spirit to tell you that you have many Angels around you." She also told me that I had a strong spiritual hunger, which is so true. God has not only sent me Angels, but messages when I needed them.

I jokingly say that when God was passing out angels, he looked at me and said, "I'm going to give that girl at least ten to twenty. She's going to need them!" I have a sense of humor, thank God.

Jesus the Shepherd

God was always watching over me, His wayward and lost child. I love the idea of Jesus as a Shepherd because I know I was lost. People talk of being saved at church, but I know what I am saved from! Me! I have been saved from myself! God has amazing love for his lost children. There is a song I love called The Reckless Love of God, which is about Jesus leaving the ninety-nine sheep to go in search for the one that is lost so He can bring him back home. That's what I feel Jesus did for me. When I look back on my past, I am truly humbled, as I see His Hand. He has been protecting me all my life. I got myself in so many messes out of sheer stupidity and naivety, messes that I could have died from, and yet here I am, a living testimony to the Grace of God and His love. Thank You Jesus, for being my Shepherd and guiding me back home to You!

Happily Ever After!

After about two months of constant partying with my sister, I received a letter from Dale, who declared his undying love for me and his desire to marry me, which of course I was thrilled to hear. He had not wanted to get married before, even after his divorce was over from his first wife. I don't remember all the reasons he gave me for not wanting to marry me, or if we ever even talked about it much, but I think he was simply scared to make the commitment to marry again. He had an ex-wife and three children, and he knew we would never have children because he had gotten a vasectomy, so it was not fear of more children. It was common for couples to just live together in the 1970's, so we weren't going again the social norm at that time. There must be some truth to the saying *absence makes the heart grow fonder.* Time apart had apparently made him realize how much he loved me, that he was ready to make the leap into marriage. There is song called **Let Her Go,** which best expresses this—**never know you love her till you let her go.** If he didn't know how much he loved me before, he thought he did now and was ready to make the commitment, or so it seemed anyway.

I wrote a letter back to him, also expressing my undying love for him, and said "yes" to his marriage proposal. On August 1, 1975, we were standing in a courthouse saying, "*I do.*" Our honeymoon was spent at a motel, making crazy love like we always had before. This was it, I thought! How incredibly dumb, naïve, and in love I was. I wish I could turn the clock back and give myself some sense I lacked then, but I can't. Life is a series of lessons, often painful ones, and this one would end up being a huge lesson for me, one that nearly destroyed me. I always say I know I have a heart because it can be broken, and it got broke big time by him. I forgive him and myself today, him for hurting me, and me for being so naïve and not walking away sooner. With my abandonment issues, I was simply too vulnerable and needy at the time to leave, until it got so toxic that I felt forced to.

A friend of mine told me years ago that it was a good thing our marriage ended, or at least one of us would probably have ended up dead. I tend to agree with her, as it was getting extremely toxic between us.

Nothing can destroy a relationship like infidelity, and according to an ex-police officer I knew years ago, it is one of the main reasons for murder. As senseless I seemed when I was a young adult, I finally ended up using my head when things got really bad with Dale, even though it broke my heart to do so. There are times when I should not let my heart rule my head, and this was definitely one of those times.

Unhappily Ever After

This is it! quickly turned into *this is shit!* Within a week of being newlyweds, my dream of *living happily ever* after turned into *unhappily ever after.* My new husband, the man who had expressed his undying love for me and vowed to forsake all others, decided to forsake his wedding vows and vowed instead to have other women. My pure and romantic girlhood dream of marriage was shattered one day when Dale walked into our apartment and expressed his desire to have an open marriage, that he wanted to swap with other couples. I don't remember exactly what I said in response to this, but I believe it was something like, "what do you mean, an open marriage?" I never thought in a million years that my husband would come home and tell me this! It was very shocking to me. I had always had a very pure and romantic idea of marriage, so this truly was a shock to me. Although I recall feeling shocked, I don't recall feeling angry, sad, or hurt about it. Knowing how I dealt with my emotions as a child, I believe I crawled into my shell and tried to numb out with alcohol. It was like I went along with a drive that I never wanted to go on, with Dale driving and me passively sitting in the passenger seat pretending like I was ok with the drive, when in fact I wasn't, but I didn't know to express that even to myself, let alone him, so I just passively went along with all his behavior. What I know today is that is abuse.

If a husband of mine said that to me today I would say, "no way!" And then I would say, "go away!" But I was so incredibly young and naïve, and so very dependent on him, that I was not strong enough to stand up to him or walk away. We just got married! Are you kidding me? I was aware that there were a lot of people having open marriages in the 1970's; I wasn't oblivious or ignorant to the fact of the times, it's just that I wasn't one of those people who was open to the idea of an open marriage. What I should have said to Dale was, "you want an open marriage? Then you can close the door on our marriage." Or how about, "you want to swap? How about you swap women for divorce papers!?"

What made his request for an open marriage even more disturbing, was his lack of concern about my feelings. It really was not even a request; it was a demand. There was no discussion about it. He did not say, "how do you feel about the idea of having an open marriage?" It was just him informing me that this is the way it was going to be, period. His whole attitude was, I want other women, whether you like it or not. He was very cold and selfish about it. I have concluded that Dale was possibly a sociopath, with no conscience, which is so scary!

This what I felt like doing but didn't!

Going Down the Toilet

This is the part of my story that I have anxiety over sharing, as this is when my life really started going down the toilet. This is when my drinking really escalated. This is when I lost myself, my real self. I have always said that my drinking was mostly due to emotional pain, that I wanted to numb out all my painful feelings. Not only was I drinking more heavily now, but I got scary skinny, not so much because I was anorectic but because I was more interested in drinking than eating. Who wants to eat and blow their high? Not me! My cigarette habit had also escalated. Smoke, drink... When I drank heavily, I also smoked heavily, going through at least two packs of cigarettes a day, which was just another addiction for me. All I wanted to do was stay high and numb out.

It really hurts my heart and soul to write about this part of my life with Dale, because the core of who I really am was nearly trashed completely. I am so repulsed over this behavior that I allowed with my ex that I cringe inside, and I feel so sad for the innocent and wholesome girl I was before I met him. I cried as I reflected on my dysfunctional life with him. I never realized how emotionally traumatizing it was for me to be treated with such disrespect by him at the time, but I realize it now. Just like when I was young girl, I accepted the trauma like it was normal, like it was a way of life for me, which I find incredibly sad now. It was so heartbreaking for my sweet and innocent girlhood dreams to come to this sick relationship. My marriage to Dale broke not only my heart, but my spirit. It is no wonder I felt the need to drink so much! It was my way of coping with all the emotional trauma and pain. It was soul murder.

What was particularly shameful for me about this situation was that not only was I allowing this immoral behavior in my marriage, but Dale's motive for wanting this open marriage was not just about wanting to have fun; it was about money. I do not believe I was even aware of this in the beginning. I thought it was just about him wanting to have fun with other women, but not long after this open marriage began, he informed me that his wealthy friend would be helping us buy a house, a new van, etc. Oh really? In other words, I felt used. While writing my story I felt angry and hurt about it, that a husband could do that. And he said he loved me. No loving and moral man would ever want his wife sleeping with other men. The swapping ended after a few months, but the hurt from it didn't. But today I forgive him.

My drinking increased during this time, as did my insecurities. I was not a very secure person to begin with at this time, and his behavior with other women only fed my insecurity more. I took it very personal that he wanted other women, that there must be something wrong with me. I thought I must not be pretty enough, sexy enough, etc. Why wasn't I enough for him? He was enough for me, so I could not understand why I wasn't enough for him. It never dawned on me then that there actually might be something wrong with him! I know that today, but back then it really hurt my sense of self-worth and made me feel like less of a woman. *God works in mysterious ways though, and something happened around this time that made me feel better about myself, something that also changed the course of my marriage. It may seem strange and immoral to say this, but I truly did see it as a blessing from God.*

A Sweet Affair

Something sweet and surprising happened one day while Dale and I were out and about, something that changed the course of our marriage. Dale left me alone with one of his friends while he went elsewhere to do some drug business, and a sweet affair began between me and his friend that day. His friend really liked me and told me so, but he never came on strong toward me; he was very tender and kind in his approach toward me. He sat in his chair looking at me for a few minutes, then said, "there is something so tender, soft and beautiful about you." I had been feeling very insecure and vulnerable around this time, which I guess he sensed. He came up behind me and started rubbing my neck and shoulders, then he tenderly took me by the hand and led me to his bedroom, where he tenderly held me and stroked me. There was a tenderness between us, a tenderness I was not getting from Dale, which felt like a blessing at the time. This man was like a breath of spring air for me. *I believe he was another human Angel God sent my way. Some may say I was being immoral, but I say God works in mysterious ways and knew I needed some tender loving care.*

I remember one night when he walked me home from his place (he just lived right down the street from me), and we were holding hands, then he took my face in his hands and kissed me very tenderly when we sat down on some church steps, which I thought was so sweet! He obviously did care for me, which I loved. I certainly wasn't getting that kind of tenderness from Dale! I so desperately needed the tender love he showered on me. I ended the affair after a few months, but he was special to me. I felt like I gave me back some innocence that I had lost with Dale. I felt precious and loved. Maybe in was being naïve in thinking that he cared about me, but I really thought he did. He was like a breath of spring air at the time.

Dale took off for Florida when he discovered I was having an affair and had his own affair. He was the one who started the open marriage, yet he could not handle it when I had an affair. You want an open marriage? Ok! You got one honey! What goes around comes around! Karma truly is a bitch, and it came back to him bigtime when he lost me.

I received a phone call from Dale, informing me of his affair, and his intention of not coming home until I grew up. ME grow up?! He had the audacity to tell me I needed to grow up, when he was the one who was so immature and selfish that he wanted an open marriage?! He is the one who needed to grow up! At least I was mature enough to know that a true marriage should be Godly and pure, not swapping with other people! He was blaming me for something he started and would not take responsibility for! What a jerk! It still amazes me how dumb and naïve I was. *God surely was watching over me when I was with him!*

While doing this autobiography I called Dale to get some information about our past together, and we talked about our past together. He apologized for the hurt he caused me and I forgave him. I realize today that we were just two dysfunctional people with childhood wounds who didn't know any better at the time. I really can't hate him anymore for things he did anymore than I hate myself for allowing it, and I don't hate myself for it. There is only peace and forgiveness between us today, but no contact. He has his regrets about me, but I don't about him. I am glad I had the sense to move one. I knew I wanted a more stable life. But I didn't leave with hatred. I just left and said goodbye. And I ended up with a much better life.

Haunted by Abandonment

I was only 21 at the time, and still very insecure and out of touch with my abandonment issues. I did not have a clue what or why I was feeling, only that I was in some pain I wanted out of, which I tried doing by drinking and drugging. I was drinking so heavily that I just took my beer to bed with me. All I wanted was to pass out into oblivion. Although I wasn't consciously in touch with my childhood abandonment issues, subconsciously I was and did not know how to handle them. My fears of abandonment came back to haunt me during this time, and the only way I knew how to get rid of my childhood ghosts was to stay drunk, which I did quite well for a week or so. Although it was not unusual for me to drink, I didn't usually want my booze as a bedfellow! I remember watching a movie of Marilyn Monroe's life story, in which she did the same thing. Interestingly, her childhood was remarkably like mine, and she could not handle the abandonment any better than I could. All I wanted was to chase these ghosts away. Please leave!

In retrospect, I wonder why I didn't have the sense to leave him after this traumatic experience. I think my fears of abandonment and being numb emotionally prevented me from fully realizing how traumatic it was. Numbing out is normal with trauma.

Am I an Alcoholic?

As this binge continued, I realized I could not keep drinking and decided to go ER for help, which I did not get. I told the doctor about my marital situation and that I could not stop drinking, and all he said was, "you need to go home and work out your marital problems," and I replied, "well, that would be nice if I could, but my husband is off having an affair!" I decided since I couldn't get the help I needed, that I would help myself! I went to the good old country doctor, the same man who had taken out my tonsils, and he gave me a prescription for sleeping pills, which I took the whole bottle of while at the bar drinking, then I told someone to call 911.

I ended up in ER getting my stomach pumped, then sent up to the psyche ward, where I woke up the next morning strapped down because I was on suicide watch. I really didn't want to commit suicide, but it took some convincing on my part to get the psychologist on the psyche ward to believe me. I only had to stay a few days, just long enough to get my bearings and convince the psychologist I wanted to live a sober life. I also had to make a commitment to go to group therapy, which I reluctantly agreed to.

My mom came to visit me in the psyche ward and said, "no man is worth taking your life over." I honestly don't even remember calling her, but apparently I did. I guess I felt like she would be a comfort for me, like I really wasn't abandoned after all. What I find ironic is that my original abandonment by her was what was triggering this abandonment by Dale, and here she was giving me advice. If she only knew how much her abandonment of me when I was a child triggered me to do this, she might have kept her mouth shut! If I knew then what I know now, I would have said, "you aren't worth taking my life over either!" If I understood at the time how the two situations were so closely related, I might have said to her, "I do not handle abandonment well, mom! And do you know why??? It's because you abandoned me as a child!" But I did not have a clue about any of my unresolved emotional baggage at the time, so I did my time there and left, resolving not to drink any more. I really did want to get sober and live a wholesome life, but I just wasn't ready to face my emotional baggage from my childhood.

Sober for a Change

I was let out of the psych ward on the condition of mandatory group therapy, but the same woman who had helped me in the past got irritated with me because I took the prescription medication without showing up regularly for therapy. She persisted in trying to get me to talk about my crappy childhood, which I still resisted. I did not want to talk about my childhood! She would say, "Carol, I know this isn't easy for you to talk about, but it will help you," and I would reply, "ok, I will try to go do therapy, but I'm sober now and doing all right." I felt like screaming, "would you please leave me and my past alone! The only issue I have is being here talking about issues I don't have, and the only thing I am angry about is being here!" Considering all the denial and defiance I had as a young adult about my childhood issues, people who read my story should find it amazing that I even founded FACT and wrote my story!

I thought my life would be smooth sailing now that I was sober, but I was wrong. *Something traumatic happened shortly afterward that almost wrecked my life for good, had it not been for the Grace of God.*

Again, I am left pondering and wondering how I could have ever even been involved with this man at all, let alone stay with him after being repeatedly traumatized. It took another serious trauma for me to be serious about leaving, and this one left a big wound in my heart and soul that took a long time to heal. But the scar does remain.

Bonnie Arrested for Clyde's Crime!

While Clyde was off in Florida playing around with his new woman, Bonnie got arrested for his criminal activities! One day when my friend was visiting me, a police officer walked up on the front porch and announced that he had a warrant to search the house for drugs and possible stolen guns! What?! I was considered an accomplice because I was his wife, even though I knew nothing about anything. I am innocent! Oh my God, how could this happen?! I'm not sure what I said to the cop who arrested me, but knowing me, I did not say much. I was probably frozen with fear, just like when I was a child. Scary! I was hauled off to jail, where I stayed for a week before my wealthy friend bailed me out, thank God! Dale ended up coming up to Illinois to face his charges after a week or so, and we went to court. Our wealthy friend kept us both out of prison, which I am so grateful for. This was a felony he got me involved in! Lord! *God was surely watching over me throughout this ordeal.*

When I think about how close I came to going to prison for Dale's criminal activity, I am not only frightened, but truly angry that he put me in such a dangerous situation. It was so scary going to jail for a week and wondering if I would go to prison. I didn't know what was going on. I ended up getting a year's probation and my record was cleared, but that was so scary. Why didn't I leave him then? That should have been enough for me to leave, but he wanted to work things out with me, so I agreed to give our marriage another try. How incredibly naïve I was back then. I was dumb and dumber!

This is another reason I am so easily intimidated by anything legal. I hate courtrooms!! I don't even remember being in the courtroom when the judge sentenced me. Last year I started having anxiety when I was legally threatened over a trivial issue and kept asking myself why I was so upset over something that logically was not going to happen, and then it hit me! Of course! I had a legal situation when I was put in foster care, and I had a legal issue when I got arrested, which I felt powerless and frightened by. I had not even realized until last year how deeply those situations affected me, especially the felony arrest. I recently watched a true movie called *Guilt by Association,* which was about a woman who was put in prison because she knew about her fiancé dealing drugs, and as I sat there watching this drama, I realized that could have been me. My whole life was put in jeopardy because of his criminal activity, which was so frightening. When we talked on the phone in 2021 he apologized for this, and I forgave him.

Thank You Lord, for being the Supreme Justice!

On my Own

I got my own apartment shortly after I got sober, which felt both strange and good. I guess since Dale thought I needed to grow up, I decided to spread my wings. I worked at an Elks Club, which was not the most wholesome job for a young girl trying to stay sober, but I managed to stay sober until Dale reentered my life. Why did he come back? Why did I take him back? I felt good on my own without him. He said he wanted me to grow up, but maybe he got scared and came back to me once he realized I might just be fine without him. When I reflect on my time with him now, I think I was just too young to understand what was happening, and he was too messed up from drugs to understand either. Today what is important to me is that I do understand things better and made my peace with him. It's in the past where it belongs. Peace.

Still the Same

We were back together, but our marriage was not working out, nor was my sobriety. I started drinking again as soon as we reunited and was fired on the spot from the Elks Club for being drunk. Not only were we both drinking and getting high again, but his promise of fidelity flew right out the window. He brought a strange man home one night, and I told myself, "this is it! I am not doing this anymore!" Something snapped in me that night, and I just knew I would never do that again, no way! I was done with his perverted ways, and I was almost done with him, but not quite yet.

Raped by a Friend

Dale decided he wanted to move to Florida again not long after we reunited, and while he was there getting things ready for me to join him, I was raped by a friend of his who came by to see him. I naively thought he called me into the back bedroom to discuss something private, but instead he forced himself on me. I was not strong enough to fight him off, but I told him to never come back to my house again. I told Dale about it later, but I do not think he thought much of it, which made me angry. I was raped! I told the guy's girlfriend what happened, and she accused me of seducing him! What?! It is no wonder women are afraid to speak up when they get raped. If I knew then what I know now about childhood sexual abuse and rape, I would have handled that situation much differently. I would have cussed that man off and then I would have given him a punch in the face!

A Last Ditch Effort for Love

The love I had for Dale was almost dead; there was just a spark left, and it was that spark that put me on another bus, this time to Sanibel Island, Florida. I cannot believe how stupid I was back then to keep on trying to make that marriage work. It should have been over the first week of our marriage, but I thought I was in love and stuck it out. Isn't that what women should do, stand by their man? I had a very old-fashioned idea about love and marriage, which was a difficult idea for me to let go of. One thing I know for sure today, there is just no way I would tolerate any of that abuse now! That was not love! At least not the kind of love I believed in. That was abuse and insanity! I would never tolerate a man cheating on me today, no way! I have jokingly told friends that if a man cheated on me again, they might be seeing me on the news for homicide! That's Carol! She done shot her husband!

It's good to keep a sense of humor about this stuff!

A Loveless Ending

I hate writing about this part of my life, as it ended up being the worst part of all. I decided to make a last-ditch effort to save my failing marriage. I was either tenacious or stupid, probably both, when I got on another bus and headed down to Florida. We were both happy to see each other and made love immediately. We were living in a small cottage right on the water, which was beautiful. I naively and hopefully thought that this time it would be ok, that he was past all the womanizing, but I was wrong.

I met his old lover while I was there, which did not help my insecurity at all. I didn't think I was pretty back then, and I felt even less pretty when I saw how beautiful she was. I was very intimidated by her, but I also liked her and was pleasant toward her. I remember her telling me, "Dale doesn't love me; he loves you." That eased some of my insecurity, but not all of it. The fact that I found poems written by him to her while they were having an affair, convinced me that he really cared for her.

It was December 1977 when I arrived in Florida, and by February 1978 I was sickly skinny (about 90 lbs.), addicted to Valiums and sleeping pills, eating them like candy, along with an increased alcohol consumption. I was addicted to everything I could get my hands on. I was a mess. A BIG HOT MESS! A wreck. I was ready to die but didn't know it, nor did I really care. The hurt and pain I was in was apparently bigger than any fear of death. I was looking for a way out of my mess but made a bigger of myself trying. I must have had a deep denial about the severity of my addiction, as I don't really think I was completely suicidal; I just couldn't cope with the painful marital situation. Deep down I knew I had to leave Dale, but my fears of being alone and abandoned left me without the strength to do it. I was in severe emotional turmoil, and I felt like the only way I could deal with it was to numb out, which I did very well during this time.

I went to a whole new level of dissociation, from not just daydreaming about being somewhere over the rainbow, but to being somewhere over the rainbow. Even my older brother told me that I was altered while I was there, and he is right. I can't quite put it in words what happened there, but my spirit knows it. I didn't just leave my body; I left the planet! I was wanting to just leave all my pain behind like I did as a child looking at the stars when I was thrown outside.

Somewhere Over the Rainbow...

The promise of fidelity Dale gave me upon my arrival there was short lived, again. He told me about a month later that he was having threesomes with a married couple and wanted me to be involved. I can't remember how I responded to this, or if I did at all. I don't recall saying or feeling much of anything when he told me this. I was just numb, body and soul. This is when it got really dark for me, and my alcohol and drug abuse skyrocketed to a lethal level. At this point I believe I was at least somewhat suicidal. *I believe only God could help me at this point, but I was not praying for His help, not yet.*

Raped in a Blackout?

My drinking and drugging got out of control during this time, to the point where I was living on the edge of life or death. A strange man in a bar gave me some pills that I thought were valiums, and when I started feeling disoriented, I asked him if he would take me home, which he did, but I also believe he raped me. I wonder now if he gave me a date rape drug of some sort. I blacked out, and all I remember is waking up a day later. Dale told me he thought I was raped because I came home screaming. How stupid and naïve it was of me to take a ride home with a strange man! I could have been raped and killed that night! *Oh God, help me out of this mess! God did help me out of this mess, and there would be more messes I would need His help with.* In AA there is saying, *some are sicker than others,* and I believe I was back then, but most of my sickness was due to my childhood trauma, which made me a lost soul. *I love thinking of Jesus as the Shepherd, because I so identify myself as a lost sheep that He brought back home. I believe Jesus may have had to use the staff on me a few times, but He made sure I got home!*

Happy Valentine's Day!

Everything came to a head in my marriage on Valentine's Day 1978. Dale took me over to his swapping couple and had sex with the woman while I was in the room. The husband wanted to have sex with me, but I told him, "swapping is not my thing; it's his," and he left me alone. I wonder now why I even agreed to go with him. I think I knew deep down it would be the end of us if I witnessed it, that I would finally leave him. It was the straw that broke the camel's back. When I heard some noise and looked over briefly at them, I felt a knife go right through my heart, and something in me died. It was the worst hurt imaginable to me. Happy Valentine's Day, sweetheart! We met around that day, which made it especially hurtful. Any love I had for Dale died completely that day. My pure heart and spirit was shattered that day. A picture can describe a broken heart, but a picture can't really describe a broken spirit. There was a deep wound to my spirit that I can't really put into words, which took the love of God to heal.

When I decided to make my peace with Dale years later, he asked me if I ever had any loving feelings left for him after what happened, and I said, "no," which I know hurt him, but it was the truth. He told me he never forgave himself for hurting me the way he did, and I told him I forgave him. I was finally at peace with him. I feel bad that he feels bad, but the truth is the truth. One thing I know for certain today is that love is fragile and precious. Love can be killed, and he killed it. I learned so much about real love with my late husband, Larry. And Larry healed my broken heart. **What a gift from God he was to me!**

It Is Over!

We left immediately after he was finished having his sleazy fun, and I told him I was leaving him upon our arrival home. The way I reacted seems abnormal to me now, but I think I was so shell shocked at the time that I did not know what to feel or do. I never even got angry or cried. Nothing. I was just numb. I didn't love him, but I didn't hate him either; I felt nothing. I casually but firmly told him, "it is over with us." Although I did not understand myself well enough back then to know what I was doing, I now realize that I was being passive aggressive. When I end relationships,

I do it quietly and firmly, and I never look back. When it is over, it is over for for good. Dale mistakenly thought I was so forgiving that I would take him back, but he was so wrong. I closed that door for good! No amount of pleading to get me back would ever work. No love.

The next day when I reaffirmed that our marriage was over, he became enraged and left the restaurant and left me alone to care for all the customers in the restaurant, which I was not prepared to do. True to his self-centered nature, he didn't care about the mess he had put me in, nor did I at that point. I had just ended my marriage, and the only thing I cared about at the time was numbing out by getting drunk and high.

Meeting Husband Number Two

I put the closed sign on the front door, then got good and drunk at the waitress table. Not long after I sat down, in wandered a guy named Jim, a wandering hitch hiker who happened to wander into the restaurant a couple weeks earlier asking for a blood riser, and who I found to be rather cute. We had only been casual acquaintances, but as we sat getting drunk together that day, we talked about our lives. I explained my life with Dale, and he talked about his wanderings. He invited me to come stay with him since I had nowhere to go. I had to leave the restaurant, as my relationship with Dale was definitely over, and I was afraid of his anger, so I took Jim up on his offer to stay with him until I was ready to go back home to Illinois.

What I thought was just a friendship with Jim quickly turned into something more. How the heck did this happen? Oh, but of course, why wouldn't it happen? It just happened with Dale, so why should I be surprised? And why should I be surprised that I would be attracted to another man like Dale? I discovered years later that not only was Jim like Dale, but even worse in many ways! I should have listened to Dale when he told me, "Carol, he isn't who you think he is." It takes one to know one! I thought it was jealousy talking, but it was also a warning. Lord, I was so stupid and naïve. Here I go again! Anyone reading my story can clearly understand why I stated, *"I went through the school of hard knocks!"*

Drug Withdrawal

As my new relationship with Jim blossomed, we decided to get an apartment in Fort Myers, but we were only there a short time. The doctor refused to fill my drug prescriptions again because I was taking too many. You don't say, doc? I thought I wasn't taking enough! I was upset at the time, but I thank God now that the doctor knew best. Jim was also concerned about my drug consumption and encouraged me to stop. I really did not realize how addicted I had gotten to the drugs, but I sure found out when I was forced to stop. This time is rather fuzzy because of the withdrawal, but I do recall throwing up a lot, shaking, and not sleeping for about a week. It was scary for me, and I never wanted to get addicted to drugs again after that experience!

A Plea to Thee

I went back to Sanibel Island to get some belongings I left at the apartment I shared with Dale, but I started getting real bad withdrawal symptoms again and decided to sleep.

I desperately prayed to Jesus as I was lying on the bed, and I suddenly felt His presence and immediately fell asleep and did not wake up for hours. Again, God was faithful and helped me in one of my darkest moments.

I do not know how to describe what I felt when I say I felt the presence of Jesus, only that I knew it was Him. When I woke up, I not only felt refreshed and rested but euphoric, as if I were walking on a cloud. I had been lifted into a Heavenly place. Jesus healed me that day and His Spirit was all around me. I truly do love Jesus, for who He is and what He has done for me. This happened on the eve of Easter, which I thought was amazing.

When I speak out about my love for Jesus, I am truly doing it from the heart. I have a strong Love connection with Jesus. He has always been faithful in rescuing me in my darkest hours.

I love You, Jesus!
Jesus, the most loving and beautiful being ever!

On the Run

As I was walking down the road to get the rest of my things I left at Jim's, Dale tried to run me over with the car! He wanted to kill me because he was so enraged about me leaving him. After all the hurt he caused me, I am the one who should have been trying to kill him, and here he was trying to kill me! It was totally insane! The fight or flight adrenaline helped me outrun him, but barely. I believe he seriously could have hurt me, even killed me. When I mentioned this incident to Dale years later, he told me he did not remember doing it, but I do remember it, and it was scary! I get a silly vision of this now, Bonnie running away from Clyde!

I know Dale missed me when I left, but I did not miss him at all. I was glad to have him OUT of my life! I never wanted to reopen that door. He kept trying to get me back, and even threatened suicide once, but it was as over as over could be. Once he was out of my life for a few years, I began to wonder…who was this man I was with for five years of my life? Like all the other traumas in my life, I could not fully comprehend how bad it was with him until I was away from him. We usually don't see how bad something is until we are away from it, at least it's that way with me. After having spent so many years with my late husband, who was the sanest man I ever knew, I fully realize now how insane Dale was.

A Final Goodbye to Dale

I decided to say my final goodbye to Dale right before I left Florida. He had calmed down some and asked me if we could take a walk on the beach together at sunset, which I agreed to. Sad to say, it was the best time we ever had together. Our relationship was over, and for the first time I felt like we were friends. He asked me if could spend one more night with him, and I said, "yes," but not because I wanted to be with him, but to show him it was over. This happened before our divorce was final and while Jim was off somewhere wandering, and he definitely knew after that night that it was over. Our love was dead. I know he cried a river over me, which I had compassion for, but it was over. Despite all the hurt and pain he caused me; I still couldn't hate the man. It is almost impossible for me to hate anyone, even those who have hurt me. I remember him telling me about a year after we parted, "Carol, you really are a caring woman." One of my prayers today is, ***"Lord, keep me tender hearted, but not so tender hearted that I am stupid and naive!"*** I have been learning since my husband passed that I need to toughen up more, and not let my heart rule my head!

Moving On with Jim

I moved on with Jim, but my life was still unsettled. I went back home to Illinois on a bus and visited with some family, while Jim hitchhiked to his home state of Michigan. I decided to join Jim in Michigan for about a month, then went back home to Illinois and got settled in an apartment. My plan was to live on welfare until my divorce was over (welfare paid for the divorce). Jim joined me in Illinois, but it felt rather strange at first to be with him.

The expectations I had of Jim getting his good job back at Chrysler fell through and he ended up working in a restaurant instead, which was a disappointment to me, as I really did want to settle down and have a normal life. I was tired of living like a gypsy. I wanted a home and stability. I had always wanted that. It was never my idea for Dale and me to travel all over creation; it was his. I was just being loyal and standing by my man. The instability with Dale was another reason why I wanted out of that relationship.

My divorce was final in the summer of 1978, and I started working, but we had to move from our apartment to an efficiency apartment because it was cheaper. I had a few different jobs around this time, mostly in restaurants, and I didn't have the initiative to do any better. I did go to the DAV and was told I could get some college tuition if I attended before the age of twenty-five, but I was already twenty-three at the time and couldn't see myself doing this, so I just dropped the whole idea. I didn't feel disappointed; I just brushed it off because it was not important for me. Considering that I was emotionally immature for my age, it makes sense that I felt like that. I have heard that foster children are usually behind ten years emotionally, which makes perfect sense when you think of all we have gone through. Some people might be offended by this, but I'm not. There are worse things I could be than an emotional retard! It keeps me younger! One thing I have learned as I grow older is not to take myself too seriously. I'm sure God doesn't!

A Ninny

Isn't love all that matters? If two people love each other enough, isn't that enough? I lacked the good sense as a young adult to know that it takes more than love to feed you and keep a roof over your head! I was so young, naïve, and romantic when I was in my early twenties. I was a foolish ninny! Somebody should have tried knocking some sense into me then, but I probably would have just taken the blow and kept on going! It took years for me to start using my head instead of my heart, but thank God I finally did, or I would have never married Larry!

With Larry I used my head and let the heart follow, which ended up being the best decision and the best relationship ever! I got stability and love with Larry, which is what I always wanted. **God is so good!** When I first met Larry, my ex-sister-in-law made a comment to Larry about me marrying him for money, and I told Larry, "well, what am I supposed to do, go find the worst bum on the street and marry him?" We laughed about that! Of course I took into consideration that Larry had a good job, that he could provide a home and stability for me! I would be an absolute fool not to consider that, especially after everything I had gone through with my ex's. I already tried the streets! No thanks! I will take a home any day! And a husband who is not a cheater or a beater!

Dale's Back

It was around the time that Jim and I moved to another apartment that Dale reentered my life. He came over one day and struck up a friendship with Jim, which seems odd to me now, but I was still very naïve then and my boundaries were not good. I should have told him to leave but did not. Why would Jim want him there? Since they were both potheads, I assume it was for free pot, but I am sure it was also a way of Dale getting a foot in the door to get me back.

One day Dale came over and offered to hit me up with heroin, which I foolishly let him do. Then he came by the next day and did it again. Wow! How incredibly stupid and naïve could I be?? This crazy man tried to run me over with a car! Didn't it ever occur to me that he could kill me with an overdose, or that perhaps he was trying to get me addicted to heroin so I would go back to him for free heroin? If that was his plan, it didn't work. I told him, "never ever bring heroin over to me again because I could easily become a junkie." He never attempted that again, and I never did heroin again, but he still wouldn't get out of my life! If this happened today, I would not only have a boundary but a wall! I remember him telling me when he first met me, that he would never let anyone give me heroin, yet here he was doing just that. I am just glad I had the sense never to do that again! And I am glad I had the good sense to move on. I am sincerely sorry for the hurt he had over us, but life is a journey and I had to move on. The truth is, I never would not be who I am today had I stayed with him.

What I find so disturbing about this time in my life was my lack of boundaries. I had none, but I do now!

On the Move Again

Jim decided he wanted to go to Florida shortly after the heroin incident, and I thought, Oh Lord, here we go again. Didn't I go through the same thing with Dale? Jim was no more settled than Dale; in fact, in some ways he was worse, wanting to hitch hike all over the country. There were times early on in our relationship when he went off hitchhiking for a few weeks, but I did not mind as long he came back to me. Knowing what I know today about him, he was probably unfaithful to me while he was gone.

It was March 1979 when we went to Florida, but we didn't go alone. Dale decided he wanted to go to Florida too, and would we mind giving him a ride? Of course not. What's the big deal? He just wants a ride there. We'll drop him off and that would be the end of him, right? Wrong! This part of my story sounds so outlandish to me now that I must laugh! I was with my ex-husband and my current boyfriend, traveling to the same place I left the first and met the second!

But it gets even more ridiculous, believe it or not. Once we arrived in Florida Jim and I decided to get a motel for a few weeks until we could get more settled in our own apartment, and guess who wants to stay with us? Dale, of course. He needed a place to stay for a day or two, but a day or two ended up being a few weeks. I couldn't stand him being with us, but what could I do? I could have told him to get the heck out, but I didn't know the meaning of a boundary back then, let alone a wall, so I was stuck with an ex-husband living with us.

I started drinking more again, though I did not know why. I just needed to. I didn't even want to go to Florida, and I was with two unstable men who I foolishly allowed in my life. How did this happen? What was wrong with me? I was not conscious of how I was feeling because I was numbing out with alcohol, but subconsciously I was beginning to have serious doubts about Jim. The fact that he was so easygoing about Dale being in our lives was troubling to me; it showed a lack of respect for me and for us as a couple. When Dale and Jim approached me with the idea of a threesome, it was a hug red flag for me. Didn't Dale encourage the same thing when we were married? That is when I told Jim I wanted Dale out! The damage had already been done though, and I no longer felt the same way about Jim for disrespecting me like that. I found out years later that Jim was a worse pervert than Dale. He not only wanted other women but men too! I went from bad to really bad but didn't know it until I was on the verge of divorcing Jim. You know the saying about *jumping from the frying pan into the fire*. I have a sense of humor about this now, but back then it was hurtful, and of course the only way for me to deal with the hurt was to drink more, which I did the whole six months I was living in Florida.

Jim and I found an apartment in Fort Myers that was above the landlord's flower shop where I worked part time and drank full time. I believe the landlord wanted to give us free rent in exchange for sex, but I said, "no." This was a strange time in my life. I truly was living on the fringes of life, unsure and unsettled. I had a few other jobs there—one at a party store, one at K-Mart, and one at a sub shop, but my main career was drinking. I went to church for a short time, but I was not comfortable with it. I believe deep down I was trying to find myself back to the wholesome girl I had once been, but I was too lost to find her. **But God knew my heart and was searching for me in the dark.**

My Introduction to Alcoholics Anonymous

I was introduced to Alcoholics Anonymous in September 1979, right before I left Florida. I so vividly remember sitting in a room full of older people who told me how lucky I was to be there at such a young age (I was 24), as they were much older than me when they got sober. How fortunate

I was! What they did not know, was I was only there for Jim. He had the drinking problem, not me! That is funny to me now, considering I could drink him under the table. I was a lush! It must be the German and Irish in me! I knew deep down I was an alcoholic, but I also knew I did not want to give up my drinking. I remember sitting in the apartment, telling God, "I know I have a drinking problem, but I don't care," but apparently He did, as he found a way for me to be introduced to AA. My mind was in such a fog I can't even remember how I ended up there. Jim and I neither one wanted to get sober, so how I got there is a mystery to me. I did not see any good reason to get sober. Getting sober was the furthest thing from my mind. Give me another beer, thank you so much! I was about to reach a bottom that should have been enough for me to give up drinking forever, but I guess I still was not ready yet to surrender to sobriety, and I was not ready to surrender to God.

As I always say, "it gets darkest before the dawn," and this time in my life is a testimony to that. Jim came home one day and informed me he wanted to go to New Orleans with a couple he met, because there were better jobs there. Sure, why not? I should have asked him, "who is this couple?" I found out once we were on the road that he was a severe alcoholic, and she was a prostitute. Wow, just my kind of people! I was not crazy about Florida anyway, so going somewhere new seemed like a good idea. My life was already unstable and I was drinking heavily, so I thought nothing about packing up and moving again. Moving was a normal way of life for me. Someone from a stable background might think it was strange the way I was living like a gypsy, but I did not. Doesn't everyone live like this? No, they do not, but it took some time in AA to finally figure out that my life was unmanageable, and I was insane! The first step in AA is *admitted we are alcoholic and our lives are unmanageable* and the second step is *came to believe a power greater than ourselves could restore us to sanity*, which I couldn't relate to. I did not see my life as unmanageable or insane because that is all I ever knew from the time I was a young child. It seemed quite normal to me. It was not until I got sober and got to know people who had more normal lives than me, that I was able to see just how unmanageable and insane my life was.

A Trip to Hell

The unmanageability and insanity in my life was skyrocket to such a level during the next month or so of my life that even I could begin to see it. It was so crazy that I don't even have all the details because my mind was in such a fog from all the alcohol I was consuming. What I do remember is that what should have taken us a day to get to New Orleans, took us at least ten days. We partied all the way, stopping at motels, how many I do not remember. I remember Jim having sex with the prostitute, and I remember her wanting to have sex with me, which I declined. Theresa really liked me, so much so that she wrote me a poem about her thinking I was beautiful, which I thought was both nice and odd since she was a female. It wasn't easy for us to leave a motel once we were settled in, but we were on the road and that is what people on the road do. T. provided for us by prostituting at truck stops, which she thought nothing of. It was as natural as breathing to her. She seemed to have no conscience about it, which seemed rather odd to me, but she was providing the alcohol, whatever food we ate, and the motels, so who was I to question her morals? When I think about this trip to New Orleans now, I can't believe how crazy it all was, but the time in New Orleans was even crazier. Scary crazy. This is when my life spiraled out of control, and I hit the bottom of hell. *I needed God's help like never before!*
What I find so sad about this experience is that I was so lost I forgot to reach out to God, but thankfully he didn't forget about me. How humbling.

Homeless in New Orleans

We went in search of jobs when we finally arrived in New Orleans but couldn't get any because local job references were required, which of course we didn't have. One would think we would have investigated the situation beforehand, but we didn't. I assumed this couple knew what they were doing, which obviously they did not. We were able to get help from the Salvation Army for about a week or two, then we got temporary jobs for about a week, but that wasn't enough for us to get an apartment, so we were stranded out in the streets with our car as the roof over our heads. Vagrancy is a crime in New Orleans, which had us concerned. I may have been drunk, but I was not so drunk that I did not care about being homeless and possibly ending up in jail! What are we going to do now? I was stuck in New Orleans with a prostitute, her alcoholic boyfriend, and a boyfriend who was not worth two dead flies, with no way out! *Lord, help me please!*

We were in New Orleans about a month when T. suggested I prostitute, which of course I did not want to do. We were out one night bar hopping when she made this suggestion, and Jim was so drunk and upset about the situation that he hit three parked cars, which was another thing we could have gone to jail for! I went into a blackout while drinking whiskey and don't remember the rest of the night, but I do remember the next morning very well. I woke up in a junk yard of all places, hungover and very sore from Jim beating me. My God, how and the hell did this happen? I guess if I needed to reach a bottom I found the perfect place to do it. What better place to learn a lesson about drinking than to wake up in junkyard in New Orleans? I don't remember much of that day, but I do recall feeling desperate for some help. Desperate people will do desperate things. What am I going to do to get myself out of this mess? "Lord, help me out of this mess and I swear it won't happen again!"

The only answer I had to this question was to take T.'s suggestion to prostitute. What else could I do? I was desperate, and desperate people will do desperate things. By the time I decided to prostitute, we didn't even have money for food, or for the booze we wanted. I was in New Orleans, where prostitution is prevalent, so I let T. help me. Most of my time there is fuzzy in my memory because I was so drunk, but I believe I was only with a few men that T. set me up with, then I decided to call my wealthy friend in Illinois for help. Help!

Whenever I speak of this bottom at AA, I always say, "I think I would have shot myself that day in the junk yard had there been a gun in the car." People who know me have a hard time believing I could ever have been in such a horrible situation, but I was. It seems surreal to now because it was such a long time ago, and I am so not that person anymore. The sad part is, I never was that kind of person. I like to think some bottoms are necessary, and maybe that one was necessary for me, but it was hell. *I have had a hard time forgiving myself, but I know God seen my heart and forgave me, so who am I not to forgive myself? I mentioned to a therapist about me prostituting, and all she said was, "Carol, a lot of people do that when they are desperate. Don't beat yourself up over it. God doesn't."*

I am so thankful that God is so loving and forgiving. He realized that I wasn't bad, just lost and in need of a Shepherd.

I called my mom for help, but she wouldn't send me any money because she thought I would use it for alcohol. I understand her rationale, but I needed her help to get out of New Orleans, and she let me down. I was truly angry at her about this for a long time. How could my own mom deny me help when I needed it so much? For crying out loud, I was stuck in the streets in New Orleans, which is one of the worst cities in the US, and she would not even lift a finger to help me. But hey, she wasn't there for me as a child when I was in foster care either, so why should I be surprised now? Maybe she thought she was helping me by not sending me money for booze, but she wasn't. She left me stranded and abandoned, again. Maybe she did help me to reach a bottom I needed, but it still hurt me that she wasn't there to help me when I needed it the most.

I got so desperate for help that I finally made a phone call to my wealthy friend, and Dale just happened to be there visiting, and we talked. I told him, "I am in New Orleans, and I need help," and he said, "Carol, that is no place for a girl like you to be." I agreed; it was no place for a girl like me to be, but I was stuck there whether I should be or not, and I needed help!

Dale helped by having his friend wire me money, but our car broke down in St. Louis and we had to stay in a motel until he could pick us up. Maybe Dale did this as a ploy to get me back, but I do believe he was genuinely concerned about my safety also. He let Jim know he was angry about getting me into this horrible situation.

I was never so happy to be back home in Illinois! Dale took me over to a friend's apartment, the man I had an affair with, and when I told him that I had to prostitute to make money for an apartment, he discouraged it. He said, "Carol, you aren't the kind of girl to do this; please don't do it." And I told him, "I don't know what else to do." He had always been so sweet with me when I had an affair with him, that I slept with him then because I was so desperate for some love and understanding. A friend. I didn't regret it. I needed his love and tenderness. I felt like he was the only one who really cared about me at that time.

I wish I could say that I took my lover's advice, but I didn't. I was back home, but I had no home. I needed money for an apartment, food, etc., so I continued to prostitute for a short time, until I had enough to take care of my basic needs. This whole time period was so traumatic, and I was drinking so much, that my memory is fuzzy again, but I believe I was only with two men, but it was two men too many.

The one man was all right, but the other man was dangerous. He refused to pay me, then put a gun to me when I said something to him about wanting my money. I said, "ok," and got out of his van. *Lord, have mercy! I could have been killed that night! God surely was watching over me! Thank You, Jesus!*

Though I did not make the connection about my childhood abuse and the prostitution then, I do now. I gravitated to two older men, one in New Orleans and one in Illinois. Why? Because it was familiar, not just with the man who sexually abused me but with a god father I had who gave our family food and clothing. I was looking for love wherever I could get it. *My innocence was stolen during this time, and only God could give it back.*

Once again God was watching over me, and I survived what could have been a much worse situation. It left an emotional scar, but that scar has made me more understanding and compassionate toward others who are homeless. And I love and appreciate my home like no other!

As painful as this homeless experience was though, this bottom was not the end of my drinking, but it was a turning point for me that I needed. A seed was planted for sobriety, sanity, and stability, though I did not realize it at the time. *The seed was planted deep and would need more time to break through the hard ground, but with enough nurturing it would sprout and grow by the Grace of God. When I reflect on my past,*

I feel as though God was always planting seeds for me. He has always done for me whatever I could not do for myself. His love was relentless, and still is.

Living on the Fringes of Life

Although I was happy to be back home in Illinois, things were not good between Jim and me at all. Our disastrous homeless experience had destroyed our relationship almost beyond repair. We were both bitter and blamed each other for what happened. The trust between us had died, but we didn't know how to end the relationship. Our love had nearly been destroyed, yet we pretended otherwise because we weren't strong enough to say goodbye. I was very much aware that love can be killed, as I had already seen that happen in my first marriage, but what should I do? Leave? We both had abandonment issues from our childhood that made it nearly impossible to part.

When Jim and I first met, there seemed to be an innocence and sweetness about our relationship. I remember us holding hands while walking in the park. I remember him loving the song *Sweet Caroline* because it reminded him of me. Our relationship was pure and untarnished in the beginning, but only for about a year. Our love went downhill as soon as Dale reentered our life. I believe Dale purposely set out to destroy Jim and mine's relationship, in hopes that I would come back to him, but that would never have happened. Never. Jim told me years later that he always knew I had never really gotten over Dale, but he was wrong; I got over HIM, I just never got over the deep hurt. My heart was not truly with Jim because it had been broken by Dale, and Jim knew this. I didn't realize how deep my hurt went at the time, but I do now. *Jim could not mend my broken heart and spirit, but God did send a man who could, and did. My dearly beloved late husband Larry was the man who healed me from my past hurts, and I have even more love for him because of this.*

Jim and I managed to get settled in an apartment and lived on unemployment and welfare for about a year and a half, and although we didn't have much money even for food, we always found a way to find the money for alcohol. Alcoholics will always find a way to drink, and we were no exception to the rule! We stayed in this apartment for about a year and four months, which was a long time for me to be in one place, but I loved being settled in one spot. We were still living on the fringes of life, but at least I was not homeless, which I was grateful for.

It was during this time that a light bulb went off in my brain and I really wanted to be settled. Having a home and security took on a whole new meaning for me after the homeless experience in New Orleans. Like all the other bad things that have happened in my life, I am not happy it happened, but I am grateful I learned from it and gained a lot of wisdom, humility, and gratitude. *There is a lot of wisdom in the saying, 'the devil meant for harm, God used for good.'*

Jim and were both drinking heavily and having nasty spats, which would result in him packing his bags and leaving, only to return within a short time. It got to be a joke... "here, let me pack your bags; see you in about an hour." One time he took off for Florida for about a week, and when he returned, he told me he had sex with a man while he was gone, which I was so disgusted with! Now I am thinking, who IS this man? Even Dale didn't do that! It would have been bad enough for him to cheat on me with a woman, but it was even worse with a man! I was so shocked by it, I don't think I even knew how to handle it. I believe this perverted behavior went on a lot behind my back while we were together, but I didn't find out the full extent of it until we were divorced. Lord, how did I ever pick this guy? What was I thinking? And the answer is, I was not thinking. One thing I know about myself today is that I do think. I grew up.

Although our relationship was not in tip top shape, we did have our sweet moments. I remember him coming home with a gift for me, a watch I believe, and I told him he should not have bought it. As poor as we were, he did something special for me. He may have done it out of guilt over being unfaithful to me, but I wasn't on to him yet about his infidelities; I was still stupid and naïve. There was also a time when he left little love notes all over our apartment for me to find, which I thought was so sweet and romantic. We were really trying in our own way to mend the relationship, and one of the ways we thought we could mend it was by getting married. Here I go again…

Married Again

Despite our volatile relationship, or maybe because of it, we decided to get married, which is insane when I think about it now. We thought we could fix our relationship by getting married? Really? Our relationship was a mess before we tied the knot and became a bigger mess afterward. I honestly can't remember who approached the idea of marriage, but knowing me, it was probably more my idea than Jim's, though he was in favor of it also. We were both insecure about our relationship at this point but didn't know how to handle it. We didn't know how to be together, but we didn't want to be apart either. It is never easy saying goodbye to someone, but it is nearly impossible for former foster children, who have such deeply rooted fears of abandonment. I wish I knew then what I know now, but I wasn't quite ready yet to graduate from the school of hard knocks.

When I reflect on my first two relationships, I am amazed at my own stupidity, and I am also amazed at my own lack of self-worth. That I would allow these two men to abuse me is incomprehensible to me today.

Jim had already physically abused me in New Orleans, and he also beat once when he returned home drunk one morning after being gone all night. And I married this man after he did this to me? What was wrong with me? I know women who have allowed much worse abuse than this, but I was not raised with physical abuse, not did I ever believe I deserved Jim's abuse. I allowed it because of my fears of abandonment. Jim was so abusive that he encouraged a drunken neighbor to beat me! I can't remember if he beat me or not, but just the fact that he encouraged it was abusive. Today I would never ever tolerate abuse like I did then.

A Psycho Move

Everything came to a head at this apartment in February 1981, when the abusive neighbor threatened to kill Jim and me. I can't remember why he wanted us dead; maybe he was just a psycho drunk, but we took his threat seriously and told the landlord that we had to leave immediately! This was a scary situation for both of us, especially since this man killed his own dog shortly before he threatened us.

We actually moved into the same apartment I had on my own when Dale and I were separated. What is the chance of that happening? Maybe God was giving me a message? If He was, I wasn't listening. I find it rather humorous now when I think about living in the same apartment twice! Wow, talk about moving around a lot! *But I believe God knew what He was doing even though I didn't. He put me in the right place at the right time.*

Despite the bleakness of my life at this time, in spite low I felt about myself, there was still a spark of hope somewhere deep inside of me. *God will come to us in our darkest moments when we need Him the most, and He came to give me a message of hope through my older brother, who sent me a long letter expressing that God prophesied to him about me doing great things.* I remember reading the letter and thinking it was crazy! I preferred being drunk over being sober at this time in my life, was living on welfare, and married to a man who could have made a living on a street corner, and my brother was telling me I would do great things. I did not know what to think of this message from God, nor did I care to think of it. All I cared about was surviving and getting drunk! I wish I had kept that letter, but I lost it somehow in the shuffle of moving around. But I never forgot what it said. Hope? *I may not have thought there was hope at that time, but Almighty God did! Thank You God, for sending me this beautiful message of hope!*

My Second Try at AA

I tried AA again in Illinois in early 1981, but I was still not ready for sobriety. I had quit smoking a few months earlier, which I was happy about, but I traded in food for cigarettes and was overweight, which I was not happy about! I knew I would eventually lose the unwanted pounds, which I did. I also knew my dad would be happy about me quitting smoking, which helped motivate me. He did not want me to die like him, nor did I. I made the decision to quit smoking when I started waking up with a bad smoker's cough. I quit, and never had a desire to smoke again. *I prayed for God to take the desire away, and He did.*

Unfortunately, I did not have the same will to stop drinking, though I was beginning to want something better for myself. Something in me did want sobriety, or I would not have gone back to AA. I have heard many people in AA say, "AA messed up my drinking for good," which was true for me. The old timers in Florida messed up my drinking for good! There had been a seed planted in Florida that was trying to come through the hard ground; it just needed more time. As of September 3rd, 2021, I have been sober for thirty-five years, and am now one of those people who messes up other newcomers drinking! Though the darkness at this time left me in doubt as to what I wanted, the veil was slowly lifting. It truly does get darkest before the dawn, and the light was about to come. Hope was on the horizon. *God was working again!*

Hope is Here

God did bring me hope, but I did not know it then. Hope came with a neighbor, an old woman who lived next door to us. She was near death from brain cancer, and I was caring for her because I cared about her, and she really liked me and trusted me. I guess she thought of us as her children in a way because she didn't have children. We ran her errands, cleaned her apartment, and cooked for her, etc. Nora and I had a special bond, and I will never forget her. She gave me a few of her things because she knew she didn't have long to live and preferred giving them to us instead of her family, who were like vultures. She also bought us a used car so we could run her errands. *God really does provide in ways we do not expect.* If it had not been for Nora's love and kindness, Jim and I would not have had the means to come to Michigan, where my whole life turned around. *When I speak of Angels God put in my path, Nora was definitely one of them. My Heavenly Father, I thank You from the bottom of my heart for thinking of me during my darkest times. I am so humbled by Your Graciousness. In spite of all my stupidity, in spite of all my waywardness, You have never turned Your back on me. You loved me when I could not love myself.*

There is a Christian song I love a lot, called Waymaker, which speaks of God always making a way. Even when we don't see it or feel it, He is always working and finding a way. I am blown away when I look at my life and see the way God has worked things out for me. When I thought there was no way, somehow He found a way. But what I am really blown away by is that even when I wasn't even looking for a way, He knew I needed one. At this time in my life I wasn't even interested in finding a way, let alone asking for one, but He knew me better than I knew myself and knew exactly what I needed. He truly is a Waymaker, miracle worker, promise keeper, light in the darkness, my God, that is Who You Are!

The Hand of God

It always amazes me when I look back over my shoulder and see the hand of God, and how he used my darkest times to move me forward toward the Light of His goodness, and ultimately to give Him glory. What an awesome Father we have! Despite all my failures, shortcomings, self-destruction, and backslidden ways, he managed to make this mess called my life, and make it into something beautiful. He took all the loose threads of my life and weaved it into a beautiful tapestry.

I enjoy taking things that look like junk, such as an old antique table, and turning it into something beautiful, and I believe part of the reason I enjoy doing this is because I feel that is what God did with me. God found a way for me to come to Michigan, because He knew in His infinite wisdom that it was what I needed. He had plans for my life all along, but I never knew it because I was not paying attention, but I am *sure glad He was! I was too busy surviving to be thriving, but He found a way for me to really become alive and thrive, in Him.*

I love to worship God, which I do by listening to Christian music all the time in my home and in my car. *When I look over my shoulder, I see the Hand of God and it gives me great reason to worship Him! I often dance to my Christian music!*

Lord, how do I ever thank You enough for all You have done for me?

A Short Separation with Jim

Jim took off and left for Michigan about three months after we moved. It came about because I had been drinking and cooking, which is not usually a good combination for me! I can burn a pan being sober, so you can imagine what I can do drunk! One night I had the apartment so smoked up that we could hardly breathe, and Jim got so fed up that he left. I thought he would be back like before, but when morning came and he still had not returned, I got upset and decided to go on a drinking binge, which lasted about two weeks. I decided to go on a beer diet to help me lose weight. It is astonishing how alcoholics will justify their drinking. I need to lose weight; beer should help!

Jim called me from Michigan to let me know he would come pick me if I wanted to move there. I did not hesitate to say yes. I had to stand by my man, right? One thing is for sure, and that is nobody could accuse me of being disloyal; I was loyal to a fault, even when I shouldn't have been! My brother happened to be in Illinois at the time and helped me move my things out of the apartment, then took me to my sister's, where Jim picked me up from a few days later. And off we went to Michigan! I had mixed feelings about moving this time—part of me was scared, and part of me was looking forward to the change. I already knew I liked Michigan because I had been here once before when we first met in 1978. Another reason I didn't mind moving to Michigan, was because it is only a state away from Illinois, so I didn't feel so far removed from my family and my home state. The longer I was here in beautiful Michigan, the more I fell in love with it, especially once I got married to Larry and traveled around the state. *I am so thankful for God blessing me!*

A Fresh Start in Michigan!

What surprises me now about moving to Michigan, was my initial resistance to it. I was leaving Illinois where my roots were, where I had always felt the most at home, and where most of my family lived, which left me feeling rather uneasy about leaving. Change has never been easy for me because of my childhood, but I was rather looking forward to a new life in Michigan.

What is so ironic to me now, is that the very reasons I hesitated to leave Illinois, eventually became the reasons I was glad I left. Yes, Illinois was where my roots were, but they were not particularly good roots. And yes, Illinois was where I felt at home, but only because it was familiar, not because it was a healthy home. And yes, Illinois was where most of my family lived, but my family is very dysfunctional, which was not healthy for me to be around. I get along with everyone in my family, but the past and all the dynamics involved is emotionally unhealthy for me. In time I learned boundaries with my family, but it took years. I am a firm believer that had I stayed in Illinois, I would not have gotten sober and moved forward in my life. *Leaving Illinois and coming to Michigan was the best thing I could have ever done for myself, and even if I did not see this right away, God did! As I write my autobiography, I look over my shoulder and see the Hand of God throughout my whole life.*

Miracles!

I could never have foreseen my future here, that this fresh start would evolve into what my life is today—that I would find a home, get sober, finish high school, go on to get a college degree in Psychology, graduating with high honors, form FACT, write the FACT book, and now my autobiography, and last but certainly not least, was my marriage to Larry, who changed my whole life and helped me heal from the past! I am so humbled by the love of God and how He brought me here, and how He continues to bless me and use me for His higher purposes. I am a Christian, and Jesus is the love of my life; everything else follows from that. When people ask me why I did this work for foster children, my honest reply is, "Jesus." I did it out of love for Him. I did it for foster children also, but my love for Jesus motivated and inspired me the most. Jesus said, "be there for my children," and I was faithful to his request. Jesus gave me a heart for Him, and for foster children. What I say is "Jesus called me and I listened." What a joy it will be when I see Him in Heaven someday and He tells me He is pleased with what I did!

A Burden Lifted

I remember having a sense of hope while we were traveling to Michigan. It was May 1981, Spring was in the air, and I was looking forward to the change. I felt like a burden was being lifted from me; I felt freer and lighter as I was leaving Illinois. Hope was in the air.

We settled into an apartment in River Rouge, a town around Detroit. I wasn't drinking as much, as I was quickly losing weight and did not want to overconsume my calories. My goal was to be slender again. Fat was not me! Not only was it unhealthy, but I felt horrible about the way I looked. I am way too proud to let myself go. I started feeling good about myself and having a better outlook once I was my slender self. I was also feeling healthier from not smoking. I hadn't realized how smoking had affected my health until I quit! *I asked God to take the desire away for cigarettes, and He did, and replaced it was better health.* I could breathe again! And I had more energy! Feeling healthier from quitting smoking gave me a desire to feel even healthier; that is why drinking was beginning to lose some of its appeal, but not enough yet to get sober.

Jim and I were getting along better. Moving to Michigan was positive move for us as a couple. The fights we had in Illinois ended. Money was tight because he was the only one working when we first arrived, but it was not so tight that we didn't have enough to drink!

Around July 1981 I believe I had a miscarriage. I wasn't upset about it because I knew we were not stable enough to have a child, but I did take it as a sign of hope that maybe I could in the future if we were more stable. I think seeing my sisters struggling on their own to raise children turned me off. I always knew that if I ever had a child it would have to be under very stable circumstances, not living in poverty. I never ever wanted a child to have to go through what I went through as a child, and I knew there was no way I wanted to raise a child on my own. I may have not had a lot of good sense about men at that age, but I did have good sense about having children, which I am grateful for.

A New Home!

We were in this apartment about three months when Jim lost his job, and once again we were looking at seriously living on the fringes of life and facing the awful prospect of being homeless again, which of course petrified me. I remember walking along the street one day and saying out loud, *"God, please, no! I can't go through THAT again! I will never lower myself to the streets again! Never again! Please God, help us!" God heard my prayer and answered it faithfully and quickly.*

Jim paid his dad a visit that day and he told Jim to bring me over for his approval, so the next day we went over there, and his dad liked me instantly. He even told me I reminded him of a girl he loved years ago. On August 29, 1981, we moved in with his dad, who let us stay there rent free, under the condition that we keep the house clean, take care of the yard, the snow removal, and cooked for him, etc. I was thrilled to be there! I finally had a stable home, some security, and a father-in-law who loved me like a daughter!

Hallelujah! It was a Godsend from Heaven, and I have thanked God so many times for providing what He knew I so desperately needed at that time. My Heavenly Father gave me the foundation I needed to build my new life on. God is so good, and I am so amazed how he has worked in my life. God also has a sense of humor!

A Drinker's Paradise

Not only did my new father-in-law love me like a daughter, but he was also a heavy drinker, who loved taking his new kids to the bar with him and buying us all the free beer we wanted. I was in Heaven! A drinker's paradise! Great! I have a home and all the beer I want! It was party time! And party I did! I normally didn't do the bar scene, preferring to do my drinking alone at home, but since I was with Jim and his dad, I felt safe and had a good time. As you can well surmise, my drinking increased. I started going on weekend binges, drinking from Friday night well into Sunday morning or evening. I was working at a small hamburger joint right around the corner from home, so I wasn't drinking much during the week, but I sure did look forward to the weekends! I was a binge drinker.

I find it ironic that I was now in a drinker's paradise and was beginning to get tired of it. People in AA say all the time, "I got sick and tired of being sick and tired." I can so relate to that. I was getting sick and tired of the hangovers, and I was also tired of feeling bad about myself. The light was beginning to dawn on me that perhaps I might like to give up alcohol. I was having pains around my liver, and having had Hepatitis, I knew that was a warning that the alcohol was taking its toll on my body, which scared me. I decided I genuinely wanted to stop drinking, but despite repeated promises to never drink again, I would be at it again, often the same day. It was beginning to dawn on me that I could be an alcoholic, which frightened me. I was beginning to feel out of control. Whatever made me think I ever had control over my drinking? I never did have control; I just thought I did. I thought I controlled my drinking quite well, by staying drunk!

This binge drinking lasted for about six months, then something happened that changed my outlook on everything and frightened me into seriously wanting to give up alcohol. Our old neighbors in River Rouge invited us over for a weekend of partying. Sure! Let's party! We had partied with them before, so I thought nothing of it. It sounded like fun! But the fun ended up making me run! It ended up being another bottom, and the one that made me seriously want to get sober. I am not happy that it took a bottom like this to get me sober, but at least it got me sober. I am shocked when I look back at how incredibly naïve I was in my younger years.

God sure has been watching over me! I am utterly amazed at my own stupidity and naiveness when I was younger. I always say, "when God passed out Angels, He looked at me and said 'I am going to give her at least ten, because she's going to need them!"

Raped Again

We had been partying all weekend, and I was drunkenly and innocently dancing around like I enjoy doing, when a friend of our neighbors got turned on by my dancing and decided to rape me. I knew he had a reputation for being a bad biker type, which really scared me. Oh God, not again! He forced me into a back bedroom and tried for about a half hour to penetrate me, but he was too drunk. I was crying and praying the famous prayer, *God, if you get me out of this mess, I promise I will not ever drink again!* God heard my prayer, and an amazing thing happened. He finally looked at me and said, "you know, you seem like such a sweet girl. I'm going to let you go. I'm sorry I did this to you." He let me go and I ran out of that place so fast!

What made this incident even more traumatizing was the fact that my friends encouraged him to rape me, and even held Jim back from trying to help me. This was a terrifying experience, and a real wake up call for me. A lot of people say in AA, "I didn't always get into trouble when I drank, but alcohol was always involved when I did get in trouble." That is the way it was for me. Alcohol was trouble for me. It was like a two-faced person pretending to by friend while stabbing me in the back. My friend called me the next day to apologize, and I told her, "you are not a friend; don't ever contact me again. I do not want anything to do with you." I cannot believe how trusting and naive I was then. I could not believe a friend would do something so horrible as to encourage a man to rape me. Lord, the messes I got myself into. ***God has worked overtime for me!***

Although I do not believe God caused this, as I know God would never want me to experience something so frightening, it certainly did work out for my good, as this is when I finally decided to quit drinking, and I truly from the bottom of my heart meant it this time. I realized that drinking was always involved whenever I got myself in messes, and I was tired of the messes. And God was probably getting tired of cleaning up the messes! This was a dangerous mess that could have left me dead. I decided that day that I wanted to be clean, sober, happy, joyous, and free. I decided I wanted a better life. Some people must hit harder bottoms than others, and I guess I was one of them. I just knew I did NOT want any more bottoms like this. This was the critical turning point for me.

There is a saying I heard in therapy, *the harder the ball bounces, the higher it goes*, which perfectly describes me and my life. I am amazed when I look at everything I have gone through and then look at where I am now. On September 3rd, 2021, I celebrated thirty-five years of sobriety. There is a saying in AA, *don't quit before the miracle*, and the miracle is that only can you get sober, but you will want to stay sober. That miracle happened in my life! I only attend AA about a once a month or so now, and when I do attend, I refer to myself as a recovered alcoholic, not a recovering alcoholic. *God relieved me of not only the bondage of alcohol, but also the bondage of self. I love the AA Third Step Prayer— 'God, I offer myself to Thee—to build with me and to do with me as Thou wilt. Relieve me of the bondage of self, that I may better do Thy will. Take away my difficulties, that victory over them may bear witness to those I would help of Thy Power, Thy Love, and Thy Way of life. May I do Thy will always! Amen.' This prayer is on my refrigerator and mirror as a constant reminder that the only one standing in the way between me and God, is me! Today I do not want to be in bondage; I want less of me and more of God. I want to be free!*

Getting Sober

The miracle of sobriety happened, but not overnight. Although I was quite serious about quitting drinking, I did not realize how serious the disease of alcoholism was until I tried to stop drinking on my own; in fact, I had not even thought of alcoholism as a disease that could kill me. I had not thought of going back to AA at this point because I thought I could quit on my own. I stopped the weekend binges but was still trying some controlled drinking. What a joke that was! I kept track of the days I drank on a calendar. Who does that? Would a normal drinker do that? I tried so hard not to drink, then would get disgusted with myself for not being able to. I would even pour the last beer down the kitchen sink and vow never to drink again, only to be at it again, often the same day. I was beginning to see that I had lost control, which scared me. I hated the feeling of being out of control. There should have been no question that I was an alcoholic. I always say, "if someone thinks they are alcoholic or if they think they aren't, they probably are, because people who don't drink don't sit around wondering about it at all!" I was beginning to realize that I needed help quitting, which led me to reconsider AA.

I think it's funny now when I think about the way I thought about controlling my drinking. Anybody who is trying to control their drinking is obviously out of control with their drinking! Alcoholics are so hilarious! And I was no exception!

My Third Try at AA

This roller coaster ride lasted from March to September 1982, until one night as I was standing at my kitchen sink, I spoke out loud, "God, I need a sign. Send an airplane overhead right now if you want me to go back to AA." I got my sign immediately. An airplane flew right over my house! God often answers prayers right away, and He most certainly did this time! He got my attention! I was hesitant to go back to AA, as I had tried it two other times and it hadn't worked, but I found the third time around that you have to work it! I also found out that you must want to be sober more than you want to drink, which I honestly did now. Now I had real hope for sobriety.

I walked into the doors of AA for the third time on October 1, 1982, never to seriously drink again, though I did have seven (the magic number for me!) minor relapses from this time until September 3, 1986, when I had my last drunk.

I started having marital problems with Jim once I got sober, largely because he didn't want me sober. Our lives were going in two different directions. The codependent relationship we had while drinking was ending and he was threatened by it, which led me to go to Al-Anon for a short time. I believe it was around this time that he began seriously cheating on me, though I didn't find out the full extent of his behavior until we were divorced. He put on a good front and was very sneaky about his behavior. If I had known about the infidelity I probably would have left him sooner, but I was mostly in the dark, and I was so codependent with him when I first got sober that I couldn't leave anyway.

I am just glad I finally had the sense to leave him. I felt bad about huri

I'll Show YOU!

After a brief relapse with alcohol in April 1983, my AA sponsor at the time encouraged me to go to Sacred Heart Treatment Center in Detroit, which I agreed to. I never will forget what happened there. I had a defiant attitude toward the therapist about my marriage and got angry when she tried helping me see how dysfunctional and codependent my relationship with Jim was, so she let me have it. She said to me, "you'll never get sober." I don't remember how I replied to that statement, but I am pretty sure she was using reverse psychology on me. She knew with my defiant attitude, that if she told me that, I would want to prove her wrong, which is exactly what happened! I might as well have said, "I'll show you! I WILL get sober!" If that is what she was trying to do, it worked!

It was while I was there that I got educated on the disease of alcoholism, which put some healthy fear of alcohol into me. I found out that I was at the tail end of the spectrum of the disease, which truly frightened me. I also found out that the disease progresses much quicker in women than it does in men, which might explain part of the reason why I was more eager to get sober than Jim was. I was only there for about two weeks, but it was an educating and enlightening time for me.

The night this happened with my counselor, I was in bed praying about what I should do—should I stay there for the whole time, or should I leave? I did not want to be there for a long time, nor did I really think I needed to be. I really thought AA was enough for me. *As I was praying with my eyes closed, I heard a voice speak to me, "GO WITH THE FLOW... THE FLOW IS LOVE...." Wow! How amazing!* And what is amazing, is that those words of wisdom are continually blessing me. I am always reminding myself of these words of wisdom. If I ever find myself going against the flow, I remind myself of these words of wisdom. *God's Love truly is the flow in my life today.*

I ended up leaving there the next day because I got kicked out for telling someone off, but I was perfectly ok with it. *I felt like God had answered my prayers and I was moving in the right direction. I WAS*

GOING WITH THE FLOW AND I COULD TRUIST THAT THE
FLOW IS LOVE. I had a spiritual experience that enlightened me and
gave me hope. Thank You Lord, for speaking to me in my time of need!
When I think of this spiritual experience now, I am truly amazed at how
God works. There I was just being quietly disturbed, and the Holy Spirit
spoke to my spirit!

Finishing High School

About a year after I got sober, I decided I wanted to finish high school, so I took evening classes at a high school nearby, which I rather enjoyed. I got all A's in my classes, and was encouraged by a teacher to go to college, which I began contemplating. I was only about three classes away from getting the actual high school diploma when I decided to take the GED course so I could pursue college quicker, but then didn't pursue college because of my personal life, and finances. In God's time this would happen, but this was not the right time. I will never forget getting my GED and how proud I was to have finally finished high school. I did quite well on the GED and was even told that I was in the 97% of people who did very well on the English part, which made me feel good. English did seem to come rather easy for me throughout school.

When I did finally pursue college and took English Composition, I did so well on a paper for a documentary of a high school in New York that the professor sent my paper to the high school. I was not super confident when I first entered college, so this was a boost to my ego that I needed then.

My life was flowing alone nicely now. I had a few different jobs from the years 1982-1987. I had a waitress job, a telephone soliciting job, a pizza making job, a childcare job (I love that one!), a motel maid job, and a cashier job. I changed jobs like I did homes when I was younger!

Around the fall of 1987 I decided to quit my cashier job and start my own cleaning business. A friend of mine in AA had her own business and encouraged me to do the same. I was tired of working for minimum wage and putting up with bosses, and I figured since I knew how to clean so well from working in a motel, I might as well make some better money doing it. *I prayed about it and God worked it all out.* I started getting cleaning jobs, and by the time I left my second husband in 1989, I was well enough established that I could afford to support myself.

A Visit with My Mom

My mom came to visit me for a week in July 1984, which I both loved and hated. We had a good visit together, but my ambivalent feelings toward her started surfacing after she left, which I had a hard time handling. All the feelings I stuffed in the bottle were beginning to surface, which made me uncomfortable and anxious. I think part of my anxiety was due to feeling separation anxiety like when I was six years old and separated from her, though I was no more aware of it in 1984 as I was when I was a little girl in 1961.

Anger Surfacing

Anger was beginning to surface, which I did not know how to handle. I will never forget the day I came home shortly after my mom's visit and smashed a heavy antique wooden chair, if you can imagine that! I was SO angry! I was told in therapy a few years later that old, suppressed emotions are magnified if/when they surface. The anger I felt as a child now surfaced as rage. I didn't understand the rage, but it sure was surfacing in a very big way!! That I would be able to smash a chair like is a bit scary to me now, but I had so much anger toward my mom then that it came up like a volcano eruption, and of course behind the rage was hurt. Deep hurt.

When I speak of my regret about reconnecting with my mom, this is a good example of that. This was the first time I had been around my mom for this amount of time. I had only gone out with her for dinner or short visits at her place, but never had I spent a whole ten days with her. It was way too much for me. If I knew what I know today about boundaries, it wouldn't have happened, but I didn't have a clue about boundaries back then.

I was getting alcoholic therapy then but was only briefly addressing my deeper, underlying childhood issues. This was a very crucial time for me. In the past I had always gotten drunk and/or high to numb out my feelings, which I did not want to do any more, but I did not want these feelings either! What do I do now? I felt like running away from it all, but I did not want to run back to the bottle. This was not an easy time for me, to say the least.

God, please help me! He did help me, by bringing another human Angel into my life, but this human Angel was so special and spiritual that she seemed more like a real Angel sent from Heaven. Thank You God!

CAROL LUCAS

An Angel Appears!

God also knew this was not an easy time for me and sent an Angel to help me. Her name was Lisa, and she crossed my path in October 1984 at a pizza place I was working at. She was a very spiritually gifted girl, who took a special interest in me. She told me, "God told me to come see you." I had noticed her staring at me intently when she was there before ordering pizza, then one day she seemed to appear out of nowhere and began talking with me while I was sitting outside taking a break. She told me she made a special trip back there to see me, which was unusual for her. She said that normally people sought her out, but that God told her to come to me. She never wanted any money; she only wanted to help me. When I asked her why she wanted to help me, she said, "if you saw a child drowning, wouldn't you want to save the child?" I replied, "yes, of course," and she said, "that's how I feel about you; you need help from drowning." She knew I had been through a lot of tragedy in my life and wanted to help me heal. She always called me sweetheart when we talked. *She emphasized that God would heal me.* I only knew her for a short time, but she changed my life. The last time we spoke she told me she would always pray for me. I believe her prayers for me were answered, as I began to see positive changes in my life after I met her. She was a true Angel, whose kindness I will never forget. *She was a gift from God!*

She next time I saw her she told me that three children put a curse on me twenty years ago, that they were involved in a Ouija Board and buried a lock of my hair while putting a curse on me (my aunt always cut my hair). I remember playing with a Ouija Board one night while I was living with my aunt, and I remember them being secretive while going outside, and not wanting me with them. *She told me the reason I had so many bad things happen to me was because of this curse, but she knew I loved God, and He was watching over me. The curse was removed by her prayers and burning special candles for me, and ultimately by God.*

She also told me that I was exceptionally good hearted, but had little peace, which was so true then. She also told me that many people saw goodness in me and were jealous of that quality. I did not see that then, but I do now. She told me I was the kind of person who was always doing good for others and would help open doors for them, but doors were never opened for me. That was also true, but that changed after she did her special prayers for me.

I remember so vividly the last time I saw her. I had to walk about six blocks through a bad neighborhood to get to her house (I did not have my own car yet), and I told Lisa and her mom I was afraid to walk home because some guys had been gawking at me on my way there. *They reassured me and said, "don't worry; you will be safe. You are very special to God; you have many Angels around you."* That must be true, because on the way home it seemed like there was an invisible shield around me, as if the guys could not even see me. Right before I left their house, Lisa's mom said, "in the future many people are going to admire you." I didn't think much of it at the time, but of course I know now it has to do with my work for foster children. I didn't know what to think of that at all; I just shrugged it off, like I did when my brother told me he seen me doing great things. *This was not the first time God sent an Angel to Me, and it wouldn't be the last. Whenever I have really needed guidance or protection, He has always sent me the right person at the right time. I call them human Angels. Thank You, Lord!*

A Geographical Cure

In January 1985 I decided to move to Albuquerque where my brother lived. He encouraged the move because of all the crime in Detroit. Although it was true I didn't like Detroit, it was also true that subconsciously I wanted a cure for my crumbling marriage. With me moving forward in sobriety, and Jim still flip flopping around, we were going our separate ways, and I thought a move would help, but geographical cures don't work; I took my dysfunctional marriage with me! My brother jokingly said that every state should have a sign that says, '*this state won't work either!*'

I decided to leave Albuquerque after being there about a month. It was a beautiful place to visit, but it didn't feel like my home, so I told Jim I was leaving and took a train back home. I also didn't feel ready to make any big change in my life, and I missed my AA friends. I should have thought about this before I moved, but I wasn't sober enough or sane enough to know what I was doing then. My subconscious mind was making my decisions back then, not my conscious mind. And my subconscious mind was full of unresolved emotional baggage.

Jim and I Going Our Separate Ways

Jim came back to Detroit shortly after I did, and we were settled again, but we were not settled *with* each other. I was staying sober and pursuing school, and he was still flip flopping between sobriety and drunkenness, preferring being high. Jim also smoked pot and cigarettes, and I often found him out in the garage sneaking a joint, but I didn't say much about it. I was getting more content with doing my own thing, and just let him be. We didn't argue a lot; we just didn't have much of a relationship at all, except sexually, and even that seemed more lustful than loving. He wanted to watch porno films and do perverted things, which I was not interested in. I know now that he was a sex addict, but I didn't know it then; I just thought it was strange.

What is even stranger though, is that he could have been a rapist. Not long before we moved to Michigan, around the same time he beat me with his boots, he told me he had to stand in a line-up for a rape. Once I realized he was a sex addict, and sex addicts often rape, I couldn't help but wonder if he really did rape a woman. Boy, can I pick 'em! I managed to pick two womanizing sex addicts, one who was a sociopath, and one who might have possibly been a rapist! I can have a sense of humor now and laugh about it, but it sure wasn't funny then. How and the heck did I manage to pick two men like that?! *I know now that God surely was watching over me!*

I was doing my own thing with sobriety and school from January-August of 1986, but then something happened that changed our marriage drastically. He decided he wanted to meet his long-lost mom, the one who had abandoned him to foster care when he was just two years old, so I helped him in the search. The search ended up being easy, as his mother was living close by in Detroit.

He seemed happy at first to meet her, but apparently the same thing that happened to me when I met my mom, happened to him. His suppressed feelings came out, and he couldn't handle the situation. He didn't come right out and say it, but I could tell he was uncomfortable, as his drinking, pot smoking, and sex addiction increased after he met his mom

Be careful what you pray for; you might get it.

A Family Visit with My Mom

Right around the same time he met his mom, my mom came to visit again, and Jim and I decided to visit with his mom while my mom was visiting. What perfect timing! What a warm and fuzzy family gathering that was, right? Wrong! The vibes were so bad in the room. I remember that day so well. We were all three sitting around chit chatting, when I suddenly started talking to my mom about my childhood sexual abuse, and blurted out, "how could you let that happen to me?!" She seemed a bit surprised about my outburst, then said, "that never happened to you." I told her that it DID happen to me, then she said, "well, that happens to a lot of people." In other words, she was telling me it was no big deal that I was sexually abused. I lost my temper and got very angry. My feelings that had been bottled up from childhood finally erupted like a volcano, and they erupted all over the room that day. It seems so bizarre now when I think about it, these two women who abandoned their children sitting there, neither one of them knowing what to say. They were both put on the spot. I don't remember how Jim responded to my outburst, but I believe it triggered his own anger, as he got very quiet and uncomfortable.

I can tell you the trip home was not pleasant, and it became even more unpleasant when we arrived home. I remember sitting in the living room looking at my mom, and I suddenly had another emotional volcanic eruption, one that had me flying out my front door to get away from her. I could not control my anger; I was seriously angry to the point of wanting to drink, so I went to visit an AA friend in the neighborhood, who suggested I go home and politely tell my mom that she needed to leave, which is exactly what I did. I told her I wasn't comfortable with her being in my home anymore, and I thought it would be best if she left. I wasn't nasty with her; I just told her that she needed to leave for the sake of my own sanity and sobriety.

I wrote her a letter expressing all my feelings shortly after she left, which she responded to with a bad attitude. She was always on the defensive, never taking any responsibility for the hurt she caused me, which I had a real issue with. I did not want anything to do with her after this. I just wanted to scream at her, "are you EVER going to apologize for abandoning me?" But she never did. I will never really understand how a mother could abandon her own children. And I will never really understand how a mother could never even apologize for doing so. It is this behavior of my mom's that led me to make the conclusion that she was a narcissist, who only really cared about herself.

Another Geographical Cure

Only a month after this volcanic visit with my mom, I decided to leave Detroit again, this time to go back to Illinois, which was a worse geographical cure than the last one. Jim and I moved again, this time with more emotional baggage than we had when we went to Albuquerque. We got an apartment near my sister in a small town, but Jim took off within only a few days. I woke up one morning to find a $100 and his wedding band on the kitchen table. There was no note, but I did not need one; the message was loud and clear. I'm leaving you!

My Last Drunk

Interestingly, he left the day before his mom's birthday, which was September 3rd. Jim was not just running from me; he was running from his own pain, but emotionally I felt abandoned. I was beside myself with emotion, and decided to get drunk, so my sister and I went to Hammond where we lived as young teenagers, and sitting there on a bar stool was none other than the man who had given me my first drink and raped me. I ended up going to his apartment across the street and drinking all night, but I blacked out quickly and can't remember what happened, but what I do remember so well is waking up the next morning wanting to die. I felt as horrible as I did in New Orleans, if not worse. I had almost two years of sobriety when this happened, so I was not only upset over Jim leaving; I was also upset over the loss of my sobriety. They say that alcoholism progresses in your body whether you drink or not, and I found this to be true, as I had awfully bad withdrawal symptoms this time—shaking a lot, etc. They say in AA, that if you don't remember your last drunk, you probably haven't had it. Well, I do remember my last drunk, and I don't ever want to feel that way again!

What to do I do now? I was emotionally overwhelmed and felt somewhat suicidal, so I went over to a woman's house I had visited when I first came to Illinois to inquire about AA meetings in the area. She was in AA herself and understood what I was going through, which was a huge comfort. She never judged me. She welcomed me into her home and said, "if my husband left me, I might get drunk too!" *She was a Godsend that day, another Angel God gave me in one of my darkest hours.* She comforted and reassured me it was only a relapse, and not to beat myself up over it, that I could get sober and stay sober. She also told me something I never forgot. She said, "honey, you just don't love yourself enough, but you will as you stay sober longer." How right she was! I do love myself in a healthy way today, but it took time and a lot of healing from my past to do so.

One thing I realized today is that the reason I felt suicidal was because the man I drank with triggered me emotionally. All those years ago and I am only now realizing this. Another layer of onion.

I Surrender to God!

I took a train back to Detroit and got very involved in AA and church. I needed a lot of support during this time, which I got from my AA and church friends. Although it was initially rough, this time alone without Jim ended up being a time of growth for me. *My AA sponsor at the time encouraged me to go to her church, and I went up to the altar and surrendered my life to Jesus during a Sunday morning service.* I thought I had surrendered before, but after this last relapse I realized I had not totally surrendered. I worked the 12 steps of AA diligently after this last drunk, and I was already fully aware that the third step says, *"surrendering your life and your will to God, as you understand Him,"* so going up to the altar wasn't necessary, but I chose to do it as an act of humility. *It was my way of saying, "I am surrendering all to You." And I meant it with all my heart. This was a huge turning point for me. This is when my whole life began to change, both inwardly and outwardly. I SURRENDER!*

This was a time of great uncertainty for me, as I didn't even know where Jim was or if he would ever come back, yet my faith grew by leaps and bounds. I was going to AA and church regularly, and feeling much closer to God, depending on Him for everything. I was involved in intercessory prayer for Jim but *be careful what you pray for; you might get it!*

I received a phone call from Jim in February 1987, telling me that he was coming home, that he had a DUI in Florida and wanted to leave; in other words, he only wanted to come home because he was in trouble and wanted to skip state, which is what he did. We tried to work things out when we got home, but we were on two totally different paths at this point. I had grown up a lot in the six months he was gone. I was not the same person, and he did not like the person I had become. I tried to get him to go to church with me, but he wasn't interested in that. He came right out and told me he missed me drinking with him. We did decide to renew our wedding vows that spring on our anniversary, but any happy reunion we had was short lived. I believe it was around this time that his sexual addiction got worse, and when he was having an affair with a woman he worked with, but I was not aware of all his infidelities until after my divorce from him. He managed to fool me for a long time because he was so sneaky, and I was still rather naïve about men and love. But not for long. I grew up real fast after my second divorce.

Therapy?

It was around this time that I decided to get some therapy for my deep-seated issues that were quickly surfacing, but I did not get good therapists for that. One therapist told me all I needed to do was move forward with doing positive things, which I was already doing, so I left that therapist and went to another one, who told me I just needed to forget about the past and grow up. I was becoming consciously aware that I had these deeper-seated issues from my childhood that I needed and wanted to heal from but did not feel emotionally supported by these therapists.

What seems ironic to me now, is that as a young adult I had a therapist encouraging me to work through my childhood baggage when I didn't want to, and now that I was willing and ready to, I was being told I didn't need to! The past must be dealt with, and you do it by working through your pain and gaining insights, not by burying it. I tried that for years and look where it got me! Drunk, high on drugs, depressed, anxious, suicidal, in dysfunctional relationships, and in psych wards! Obviously, just letting go of the past did not work for me!

What I find rather humorous is that years ago I didn't even think I had any issues from my childhood, and now here I was with all this baggage. Where can I unload my baggage? Help!

A FACT Seed Planted

I was beginning to realize that my drinking and drugging was largely due to my unresolved emotional baggage from my childhood, and that my sobriety could be in danger if I didn't resolve it. One thing I knew for sure was that I wanted to stay sober more than anything, so I was serious about wanting help with this emotional baggage. I was at a turning point but didn't know where to turn.

This is what led me to pursue FACT. I searched for a support group for former foster children but found none, which surprised me. I thought for sure with all the support groups out there that there must be one for former foster children, but there weren't any. This is what planted the seed in my mind for a support group of my own. I have always had the attitude that if I want something done, I should do it myself. Maybe it comes from learning early on in my childhood that I couldn't depend on anyone, like when I wanted to be fed and figured if I can't get anyone to make me oatmeal, then I will make my own! It is ingrained in me to be independent.

As I began seriously pursuing the idea of a support group for former foster children, I began thinking of a name for it, which was given to me one day while I was watching tv. A commercial came on for *ACT* mouthwash, and it instantly hit me! *Fostered Abandoned Children Together!* (the *FACT* name was later changed to *Fostered Adult Children Together. God is so amazing in the way He works! FACT* was only a seed in the ground then, though I did start coming up with some ideas for it. In the fall of 1988, I met a man in AA who was also a former foster child, and he was supportive of the idea, but my life was about to change in a big way, and *FACT* would have to wait. *God's timing is always perfect, and this just was not the right time for FACT.* But it was the perfect timing for me to get out of my dysfunctional marriage and move forward in my life.

Divorced Again

I made the decision to leave Jim in January 1989. I started a cleaning business in 1987 and had enough jobs to support myself, and I also had my own new car, so I was well on my way to independence, which felt good. I could finally get out of my dysfunctional marriage and move forward in my life. I knew I had to leave, and apparently so did Jim, as he agreed to the divorce. I'm sure he was hurt that I left him, but he also knew it was the right thing to do. There were no harsh words spoken or any attempts at changing my mind. He probably seen this coming for a long time and wasn't surprised. We both knew it was inevitable, that we couldn't go on living the façade of a happy marriage, and I knew for sure that I couldn't live in the same house with two alcoholics. Jim and his dad both drank a lot, and I did not want to live in that environment anymore; it was not good for my sobriety. I wasn't afraid of drinking anymore, but it still wasn't comfortable or healthy for me to be in that oppressive environment. Leaving was one of the hardest decisions I ever made, yet also one of the best decisions I ever made. No pain, no gain. I felt like a bird leaving the nest—somewhat afraid, but ready to spread its wings. I was free!

Though I was a bit surprised that I finally left Jim, my friends weren't. Many of them said, "Carol, I wondered when you would finally come to your senses and leave him. You should have done that a long time ago." Well, maybe I should have left him sooner, but I was not ready until I was ready. There is a time and season for everything, and the time was now right. I had to have myself financially situated to do this, which I wasn't before now. I suppose I could have gotten welfare, but I wanted to take pride in supporting myself, which I could now do. I also wanted to make sure I had done everything I could to make the marriage work, which I now felt I had. I grew up believing I would only be married once, and here

I was getting divorced for the second time, which did not make me feel good at all. I did not want to feel like a failure for the second time. Lord, what was wrong with me, that I couldn't get it together with men?

On My Own

Freedom was both scary and exhilarating. It was scary because I had never been on my own before, and except for the two brief times I left Detroit, this home with Jim and his dad had been my home. I had been there over seven years, which was the longest I had ever lived in one place my whole life, so this was not an easy move for me. What I did have though, was the comfort of knowing I was welcome to go back home to my ex-father-in-law's, even though I wasn't comfortable being around Jim. His dad was still genuinely nice to me; in fact, when I asked him what I should call him now that his son and I were divorced, he said, "what have you always called me?" I replied, "dad." That settled that issue. Just because I was divorcing Jim did not mean that I was divorcing his dad, so I continued having a good relationship with his dad, until Jim got so hateful toward me that his dad and I thought it best that I discontinue visiting. Jim's dad hated the way Jim treated me, but he felt caught in the middle because Jim was his son, which understandably made him uncomfortable. Jim got his way by ending the relationship physically, but he could never change what was in my heart toward his dad. I will always be thankful for the love he showed me.

Thank You, Heavenly Father, for giving me an earthly father figure when I needed one!

Even though it was scary, and I was uncertain of my future, it felt good to be free from my dysfunctional marriage. I always say I would rather be alone by myself than be alone in a marriage, which is how I felt with

Jim toward the end. At least I could be free to do what I wanted when I was alone.

A good friend of mine let me live with her until I was able to save the money I needed for an apartment, and in May 1989 I moved into a lower flat close to my old home. It felt good to have my own place, the first ever really. I had only briefly lived on my own once before when Dale and were separated in 1977, and it was through public assistance, not from me supporting myself. But now I was truly on my own and supporting myself! I did not have much materially, but I managed to furnish my flat cheaply, and was thrilled to be independent! Even though at times it felt overwhelming to have to be responsible for all my bills, it still felt good to know I could be on my own and support myself. *I trusted God to give me what I needed, and He always provided.* I was busy working and still going to a lot of AA meetings, but I went dancing at an Alano club on the weekends. I rarely danced with men when I went out dancing; I was happy to dance all by myself, which I still am! I dance a lot at home to Christian music, and sometimes to rock and roll. I love it!

Alone Without a Man

The most difficult part of being alone was being without a man. I had always had one in my life until now. I was only seventeen when I met Dale, and I immediately met Jim after I left Dale when I was twenty-two. I knew I wasn't ready for a serious relationship, yet I didn't want to be alone, and struggled emotionally because of this. I have never been promiscuous; I am way too much of a moral lady for that, but there was still the temptation to be involved with a man, which briefly led me astray a few times. I don't do alone well, but I don't do immorality well either, so I was stuck between a rock and a hard place.

There was a man I liked a lot, but he was emotionally messed up more than me. He was also a former foster child, who was as emotionally unavailable as any man could be, but I was attracted to him! Of course! Why would I not be? With all my issues of abandonment, and two failed marriages with two abusive men, why would I be attracted to anyone but someone like this man? It makes perfect sense to me now. I was attracted to him because he WAS emotionally unavailable! I did not know that then, but God did! *Thank God that relationship did not work out! God took him away to Jamaica for a few months, to make sure I did not get involved with him!*

In April 1989 I crossed paths with a man I had been acquainted with years ago, who expressed his love for me, but I kept wanting this other man who was emotionally unavailable. Back then if there were ten men lined up, I guarantee you I would pick the sickest one of all! I can laugh about this now, but it wasn't funny then. I find it sad that I was running away from the very love I craved. A man who would love me and not abandon me scared the hell out of me! I would eventually want a loving man, but I was far from ready yet.

The guy who loved me kept expressing a desire to see me, and I finally gave in since I had been celibate for almost a year. The song *Fooled Around and Fell in Love* perfectly describes what happened with us. What was supposed to be a fun night got more serious, but it didn't work out because we were both freshly divorced and scared of a serious relationship. I remember going up to him once and asking him if he would like to go out for coffee, and he said, "that would be nice sometime," but sometime never happened. I'm not sure who was more terrified of commitment, me, or him! I am grateful now that our relationship never went further, as I found out years later that he was a full-blown sex addict! Lord, if I had gotten married to him, it would have been complete disaster! He would have made Dale and Jim look good compared to him!

Moving

In May 1990 I had to move from my apartment due to finances and not feeling safe there. The old man who lived in the upper flat was harassing me, which frightened me. The land lady told me he supposedly killed his own mom by throwing her down the stairs, so I had good cause to be concerned. Oh great! Here I go again! Running from another psycho killer! Why does this stuff always happen to me?! I can laugh about it now, but it was not funny then; it was downright frightening! I also believe I got triggered back into my childhood when I was sexually abused by the old man. I did not feel safe. I couldn't get out of that place fast enough!

God always takes care of me, and He made sure I got out of that dangerous situation fast! I moved into an apartment a few miles away, which I wasn't happy about, but at least I was free from the psycho man. What I was not free from though, was my past, and it followed me to my new residence. The change scared me because I was so far away from my familiar neighborhood. I didn't like this change any more than I liked the change in my childhood. For someone who hates change, I sure have had a lot of it in my life! I counted all the different places I lived when I was younger, and it was around sixty. No wonder I love my home so much!

I will never forget this move, as it was the beginning of some serious emotional trauma. I wasn't completely in touch with my feelings yet. I was somewhere between being numb and feeling. My frozen feelings were thawing out, and it was painful. Like when a frostbitten hand hurts when it is thawing out, I was thawing out emotionally, and it hurt. I didn't understand then what was happening, but I do now. The feelings that I stuffed as a child were now surfacing, and it was scary! What is going on?! Can I refreeze my emotions? I must have been scared to death as a young girl being moved around! As painful as it was for my emotions to thaw, I know now that it was the only way for me to heal from my past. Like I said in the beginning of my story, though it was scary and overwhelming, I had to *be real and feel to heal.* But believe me, the last thing I wanted to do was *be real and feel to heal!*

For anyone reading my story who might think it was easy for me to revisit my traumatic past and all the feelings associated with it, think again. This was tough stuff! I get irritated with people who think this is easy, like you can just fix it with a few therapy sessions or a weekend retreat. That is nonsense; it is not real.

The fact that I am now doing EMDR therapy is proof that this isn't easy stuff to deal with. And it takes a strong person to face this stuff. What I would say to anyone dealing with these issues is, "be patient and gentle with yourself. It is painful, but you will get through it and heal."

Be real and feel to heal for me meant *getting down and dirty in the mud.* I have gone places emotionally while working through this painful stuff that I wouldn't wish on anyone, and it is for sure I don't ever want to go there again! *And thank God I don't have to!*

A Family Tragedy

I was barely settled into my new apartment when I received a phone call from my brother, who told me that our older brother had been killed in Kentucky on his way home to Indiana. How or why this happened has never been fully resolved, and out of respect for everyone concerned, that is all I choose to say about it. The only thing I need to express is how I was affected by it. I was extremely upset over his death, so much so that I had to run to my therapist when I was informed about it. I had a few issues with this brother from my early childhood, of not feeling safe around him. As was stated in my state file, I was picked on some by my siblings when I was left alone with them, especially the older ones who were jealous of me just because of the attention my mom gave me, and this brother was one of them. I was stuck right in the middle of a sibling war!

It is only natural for there to be sibling rivalry in a family, especially one of that size; we were not unique. With ten children trying to survive on their own with and an absent father and a part time mom, it is only natural that there would be discord, but I was a young and sensitive child; the only thing I understood was that I did not feel safe. Ten children in one house can be wreak chaos, and me being such an extremely sensitive soul, all the noise and chaos overwhelmed me. I still hate noise and chaos!

Real Therapy

I made the decision to get into some serious therapy shortly I was divorced in May 1989. I was read to get real and deal with my past. I was finally ready to take an honest look at myself. I was told by a therapist that most people seek therapy in their 30's and 40's, so I was in the norm. I was now thirty-three, divorced for the second time, and was old enough and fed up to get help, as I did not want another divorce!

I entered therapy believing it was going to be a wonderful, healing journey, which it ultimately was, but I sure was not prepared for all the pain involved. No wonder I ran from therapy in the past! Not only was I dealing with my divorce and all the change involved, but now my brother's death, which was so painful. I was emotionally overwhelmed to the point of having anxiety. This was not a fun time for me. I'm not sure what I thought real therapy was going to be like, but I sure did not think it would be like this. Maybe I thought after a few sessions I would have it all figured out and go on my merry way; I don't know. Maybe I thought I would cry a few tears and be done. I'm ok now. If that is what I thought, I sure had it wrong.

All the anger I had stuffed in the bottle was surfacing, and as much as I wanted to stuff it back down, I simply couldn't anymore. Like it or not, my feelings were surfacing. Emotionally I felt like a jack in the box. I know now that purging my feelings was healthy, but at the time it was just awful. At times I thought I would not make it through therapy. I remember telling my therapist I was afraid I might go crazy from all the overwhelming feelings, that I wouldn't stop crying if I started, but he reassured me by saying, "Carol, you are more likely to go crazy by not feeling your emotions and crying. You won't cry forever." Maybe I did not cry forever, but I sure cried a river of tears during this time.

When I speak of human Angels God brought my way to help me, Frank was one of them. He helped me more than he probably ever realized. We remained friends even after I ended therapy, and one day on the phone he said, "Carol, I have been around many people throughout the years, and very rarely have I ever met someone who is so unconditionally loving as you. It's a rare quality." That was the highest compliment anyone has ever given me. I never thought much of it at the time, but I have come to realize the truth in his words as I have grown older and wiser. Jesus said, "and the greatest of these is love." *People who know me well tell me I am loving, and I say it is because God's loving, Holy Spirit lives in me. God is Love.*

Frank suggested I go to ACOA (Adult Children of Alcoholics) not long after I began therapy, so I attended a few meetings. I figured since Jean was an alcoholic and I had a dysfunctional childhood, it couldn't hurt to give it a try, but I didn't feel completely supported there, which I expressed to Frank. I told him that the people at ACOA didn't understand my abandonment, which he agreed with. He said, "I wanted you to go there so you could see the difference in your childhood. The abandonment you went through was worse. Being taken away from a parent is the worst thing that could happen to a child, and it happened to you."

I walked around for years not realizing how devastating the abandonment was, so it was nice to finally have someone tell me the truth, that being abandoned as a child was traumatic, and that I was deeply affected by it. He validated my childhood hurt and pain, which I needed. *Thank God for Frank!*

Frank already knew my desire to form FACT, and highly encouraged me to pursue it. He also encouraged me to pursue college. He told me the same thing my dad did, that he thought I was bright and ambitious. They say all it takes is one person who believes in you to make a difference in your life, and I have been blessed with more than one, which I am grateful for. *God knew I needed the encouragement and made sure I got it from the right people, including Frank!* Frank was somewhat of a father figure for me, so I respectfully listened to him most of the time. But I didn't listen to him when it concerned personal relationships, at least not in the beginning.

I was comfortable talking with Frank about relationships with men. One thing he said that I eventually took to heart was this: "Carol, before you get into any sexual relationship, be friends with the man first." He knew I had gotten sexually involved with both of my ex-husbands right away and wanted to spare me further pain, but I didn't listen well enough. I must have had selective listening! Instead of taking his sound advice, I got hijacked by my heart and my hormones! Although I didn't take his advice to heart right away, I did learn a valuable lesson about relationships, and I grew up big-time! It was through this bum relationship that I truly came into my own and grew up. Growing up can be painful, but as the saying goes, *no pain no gain.*

Friends with Benefits

I eventually took to heart Frank's advice about not getting sexually involved with men right away, but not before I got hijacked by my hormones and made a mess of my life again. Was I ever going to learn?

In July 1990 I met a man who grabbed my attention, and I lost what good sense I had. I was in my 30's, my hormones were raging, and I wanted a man in my life. It was supposed to be *friends with benefits*, but he quickly fell in love with me and messed the whole thing up! How did this happen? I knew I wasn't ready to get serious with anyone, and certainly not with a man who was living more on the fringes of life than I was, but I do have my issues of abandonment and do not do alone well, so I went along with this relationship off and on for a few years, and even let him live with me some. I knew in my heart this was not what I really wanted, and I also knew it was not morally right, but I also confess that I just didn't care then. I was alone, vulnerable, and still very needy. Being alone has always been the biggest challenge for me. I always say, "I don't do alone well."

In January 2022 I was still winding down after a shaky time during Christmas time 2021 and had a young man pray over me at church, and he prophesied that I would soon have a peace that I had never had before, which is now coming true.

As of March 2022, I have been without my husband for almost three years, and I confess that it has been hard for me, but I am doing alone better than I did when I was younger. That I can even say that is a miracle! I am so comfortable in my own skin today that I am perfectly ok with being alone if that is what God wants for me. I have more peace. *Thank You Jesus!*

Another Move

I moved out of my sardine can apartment in October 1990. I was happy to be moving out of the claustrophobic apartment into a spacious flat where I could breathe and not have to put up with noisy neighbors. I was also relieved to be away from a neighbor at the apartment complex who had backstabbed me. Why did I always have issues with negative neighbors who wanted to harm me? I have learned the hard way that I need to keep good boundaries with neighbors, to be friendly but not overly friendly. I need boundaries, and walls if they are necessary!

Although I was quite happy to be moving into this new place, the six-year-old little girl in me was not! I was scared to death! I had terrible panic attacks while moving, which I tried to control by laying down, resting, and praying after I got most of my things moved in, but it seemed the harder I tried controlling the anxiety, the worse it got, so I finally got up and just started yelling, at who or what I don't know, but I got my feelings out. Frank told me I was in more danger of going crazy by not having my feelings than stuffing them, and he was right. I felt crazier trying to hold down my feelings than I did when I got them out. I felt calmer after my screaming rant and was able to get it together enough to go out to the Alano Club to hopefully get help for getting some heavy things moved into my flat. Luckily, a woman I knew helped find two men who helped me move my things in, which also eased my anxiety. They both happened to like me and took me out to eat afterward, which made me feel cared for.

A friend of mine years ago said to me, "Carol, there is something childlike and vulnerable about you that makes men want to take care of you." It does seem to be true that I have always drawn men to me who are caring and protective toward me. I can live with that! *I am grateful God has brought men into my life like that.* I am not so independent that I don't need a man, nor do I want to be. One of the things that drew my husband to me was the fact that I needed him. He was always protective of me, and I loved that about him; in fact, it is one of things I miss about him the most!

I remember going to my next therapy session and telling Frank about my panic attacks while moving, and that I didn't understand why I would be so afraid of moving since it was only a few blocks away, and him saying, "Carol, it doesn't matter how far away you're moving; you're getting in touch with your feelings from your childhood." Oh, is that all? Holy crap! No wonder I ran away from therapy so many times in the past! I wanted to run again after he said this to me, but it was too late; the feelings were already erupting like a hot volcano! No wonder I drank and drugged! But I did not want to drink and drug anymore, nor did I really want to run away from therapy anymore, so I was stuck with my painful feelings whether I liked it or not. At least I was feeling, which made me feel alive. No matter how painful a feeling is, I would much rather feel it than be an emotional zombie!

It is now 2023 and I am doing EMDR therapy, which is helping me a lot. *God led me to the right therapist for this. It's a perfect fit and he is very dedicated to helping me heal from my past trauma.* I am very blessed and grateful for his help.

Being Strong and Vulnerable

When I say *be real and feel to heal,* that is what I am talking about. I had to go way back there in my painful childhood and feel all those painful feelings I stuffed as a young child, the feelings I couldn't feel then because I felt like I had to be so strong to survive the trauma. Feeling my emotional pain as a child was a luxury I couldn't afford. It was too much in survival mode. But strong for me today is not about being strong by stuffing my pain; strong for me today is about being vulnerable and letting myself cry when I need to, which I did a lot of during this time. I may seem like an overly emotional person to some people, but I don't care. I want to be human and feel my feelings. Even Jesus felt sad and cried, so why shouldn't I? Jesus understands our humanity because he lived as a human being here. He had his own pain to deal with and cried. If our Creator had a need to cry, then He certainly understands our need to cry. I always say, *"God gave us tear ducts for a reason, to use when we need to." God knows I had a lot to cry about!* I will never forget what Frank said early on in therapy when I started apologizing for crying in his office one day. He said, "Carol, if I had gone through everything you've gone through in your life, I would be crying too!" He also told me that he did not agree with the lack of emotional support in AA, which I agree with. AA is a great place to go for sobriety support, but not such a great place to get emotional support. Many people get uncomfortable with others sharing feelings, because they don't want to be in touch with their own. I was told that there are more three- and four-year AA tokens available than any other year, which makes sense, since it is around three or four years of sobriety that feelings start to surface. I know this to be true for myself. I received a few tokens in my early sobriety. I know now that once my feelings started to surface, I wanted to escape from them. Instead of allowing myself to drown in my tears, I wanted to drown myself in alcohol.

There were many tears shed during the seven years on my own, and I earned every one of them. Those years spent alone were extremely hard and painful for me, but they were also the years that I grew the most, emotionally, spiritually, and even physically. I have a picture of me at age thirty-nine that portrays the transformation that took place within me. I blossomed into a beautiful and mature woman. The saying, *'beauty comes from within'* best describes this picture, as there is a radiance about me that shines from within. I was still struggling emotionally, and I sense the hurt and sadness in my eyes, but sadness is better than anger, which I had huge amounts of six years earlier! Anger came first, then hurt, then sadness. ***I believe healing is like a metamorphosis that happens so gradually we hardly notice, at least that is the way it has been for me. I woke up one day and realized I had turned into a beautiful butterfly! But only by the Grace of God!***

College

My aspirations and dreams were beginning to change as I was maturing. The only thing I knew when I was first divorced was that I was happy to be free and independent, but I began to realize about two years later that I wanted more out of life. Although I had dabbled with the idea of pursuing college after I finished high school, I never moved forward with it because of my insecurity about outgrowing Jim, but now that I was on my own and emotionally free from him, I was also free to pursue my dreams, and one of them was going to college. I grew up feeling like I was dumb because I flunked first grade, so I think subconsciously that was part of the reason I wanted to pursue college, but I also wanted to do it for my dad because he had wanted that for me. I also had a goal of perhaps wanting to work in a children's home, which required a degree. I had encouragement from my dad, teachers I met when I was taking adult ed classes, an older woman who was a mentor, a spiritual guide, and Frank. I felt confident enough that I could do it, so I made necessary arrangements for financial assistance and took the SAT test, and I was on my way. I entered college in August 1991.

I was both happy and scared about attending college, but mostly happy. I felt a boost in self-esteem immediately, and a sense of freedom. It felt like an adventure, as if a whole new world opened for me. College broadened my horizons. I found out from taking an IQ test that it was higher than I imagined (130). I was shocked and thrilled to find out I was that smart! Wow! As I stated on the back cover of the **FACT** book, *I got my education in the school of hard knocks and later graduated from the University of Michigan with high honors*, but the first school is where I gained my wisdom, not college, but I am still proud of my college education.

I never forget things that make an impression on me, and since I majored in psychology, what the professor said in my first psychology class stuck with me. I had barely settled in my chair on the first day, when he said, "if you're majoring in psychology, you are here because you have psychological issues." I couldn't debate that! I knew I had issues! Big issues! Psychology was for me! The professor also said something simple, yet profound about relationship that really stuck with me. He said, "it's better to BE the right person than to FIND the right person." Wow, did I ever need to hear that! How true, how true. I did not fully appreciate those words until I had some education in the school of hard knocks and met Larry, but I live by those words today.

I will never forget the day I went into my Abnormal Psychology class and told the professor I thought I had every mental disorder in the book. He just smiled and reassured me that we are all a little mentally ill. I breathed a sigh of relief as I walked away, knowing I wasn't so uniquely mental after all!

Although I learned a lot in my psychology classes, I learned even more outside the classroom by reading books through the years. I tell people I could teach a course on the NPD (narcissistic personality disorder) because I have read seven books on it, trying to understand and deal with those who have it. These days my way of dealing with narcissistic people is not to deal with them! I run from them! When it comes to them, I don't have boundaries; I have walls!

My life changed a lot once I was in college. It became more mature and grounded. I stopped socializing so much and spent more time alone, which was good for me. There had been too many people around me before, and many of them were negative people who were draining my energy. I was now spending quality time alone, not only doing homework but also praying and meditating. I was quieting down and maturing. I met a Christian woman in April 1991, who I turned to for guidance and prayers. She was another Angel that God sent me! She helped me SO much! They say in AA to find a sponsor you want to be like, but I never found anyone, so I turned to her. She was very spiritual and wise, and I gained much wisdom through her. She prayed with me a lot, and I know she prayed for my schooling. *People talk about God being kicked out of school, but I always say that as long as there are tests, God is still in school, because I suffered from test anxiety and always prayed a lot before tests! I know He heard my prayers, or I would not have made it through college. Thank You, God!*

Friends with Benefits and More

Shortly after I started college, I let my friends with benefits guy move in with me, but the benefits for him was not just physical; it was also a roof over his head! I decided to give him a try, which was a big mistake. I was getting more accustomed to being alone emotionally, but I was getting tired of carrying the financial load all by myself. My old roommate was supposed to have moved in with me but was not financially able to, which left me alone trying to support myself in this new and more expensive place. I let this guy move in believing he would do his part financially, but he didn't. I kept hoping he would get it together, but he wasn't even stable enough to keep a job.

I was cleaning the landlord's house during this time, and I remember how he looked at me once when I told him about my financial situation, like, what a loser; what are you doing with a bum like him? The question I should have been asking myself at that time should have been, "Carol, why aren't you asking yourself the same question?!" This seems ridiculous to me now, but that just goes to show you how insecure and needy I was at that time. This situation is laughable today. I must have been desperate!

What I have come to realize today is that having my basic security needs is very important. Without the basic survival needs met I couldn't strive for the higher things in life because I was too much in survival mode. In other words, I don't just survive today; I thrive! *Thank you God! Thank you God!*

Another Move

In March 1992 I had to move out of this flat because I couldn't afford it, and we separated for a short while, which should have been a good long while if I had any sense! You would think I would learn the first time with him, but I didn't. I had more lessons in the school of hard knocks where he was concerned. Lord, was I ever going to get wise about men?

I was not prepared financially to move out of this place into another flat, so I took a small room in a boarding house, which I hated! It was so small it made the apartment I had seem like a palace. I was only there a couple weeks, then a good friend offered to let me stay with her, which I did for about two months before finding another apartment. This was a very chaotic and stressful time for me. I was trying to take summer classes amid all this turmoil, which was extremely difficult.

Before the year was over, I moved four times, lost my mom, and almost got murdered. I was so happy to see 1992 end! What a year!

I know that God was with me through it all. He was faithful! And although I didn't see it then, I was growing emotionally and spiritually, largely due to a very good spiritual mentor named Jeannie.

Evicted

The next apartment I got was not in a good area of Detroit, but I was grateful to at least have my own place again. I moved in during June, with a promise from the landlord that he would have a refrigerator for me soon, which never happened, so I refused to make the next month's rent. I came home one day and discovered the landlord had broken into my apartment, then he evicted me. I did not want to fight with him over this, so I left after only a month of being there, but I was afraid of him during the short time I had left there. Oh no, not another psycho! After reading about all the threats from people living around me, it should be clear why I am so grateful to have my own home in a safe neighborhood that is far away from Detroit and the metro area. *The only time I even go into the city is to visit the Little Rose Chapel in Taylor, Michigan, and I always pray for God's protection while I am there, which I know God gives me.*

Settled Again

I moved into another flat in August 1992, which was not in a much better neighborhood than the previous one, but at least I was free of the nasty landlord and out of the demon infested apartment (the neighbors told me there were demons in the house), which was a relief. I was also close to my spiritual mentor, who helped me tremendously. I was so stressed out during this time. The anxiety was high, and my nerves were shot! I decided to give my boyfriend another chance right after I moved in this new place, but this time I had better boundaries and didn't allow him to live in my flat. I was getting wiser and making better decisions. I had been praying for us to reunite and my prayer was answered. You know the saying, *be careful what you pray for; you might get it?* I would end up being sorry I prayed for, but not just yet. I was glad to have him back in my life, even if he was unstable. I was so afraid of being alone that I felt like he was better than nobody at all, which I find rather pathetic now. It's obvious from reading my story that I did not do alone well at all back then.

My perception of this situation now, is that I could have had the whole cake with another man, but instead was accepting crumbs from this guy. I guess I thought that was all I deserved; after all, I had accepted crumbs all my life. Wow, have I ever grown from that time! Today I know I deserve the whole cake and would never consider having only crumbs! I not only had the whole cake with my husband; I had all the decorations on top, with lighted candles! *I find it sad that I felt so underserving back then, but that is just where I was then, which is not where I am now, thank God! Today I know I am just as deserving as anyone else, because I know I am just as much God's child as anyone else! Everything changed within me when I truly began to perceive myself in God's light. Thank You Lord, for revealing this truth to me!*

My Mom's Death

I found out in June 1992 that my mom was dying from COPD. I was trying to prepare myself emotionally for her death, while struggling to keep a roof over my head. I was strong during this time, doing my best to control my emotions so I could survive and function, just like I did as a child. Crying felt like a luxury I could not afford then. I was in survival mode and felt like I had no other choice than to tough it out. I told myself, "you must be strong." I didn't feel strong, but I kept forging ahead. This was no doubt the most stressful time on my own.

I called my mom on her birthday, October 22, to say goodbye, which was very emotional for me. We had decided a few years prior that we would make the best of the time we had left, and we had even exchanged letters, so superficially everything was ok between us. I wished her a happy birthday, she told me she was close to death, then she told me she would always love me, and I told her I loved her. I realized during the brief conversation we had that day, that all the hurt I had was largely due to the bond we shared as mother and child. Although I did not have a strong conscious memory of this bond, I believe subconsciously I felt it. I was overcome with emotion not only about this but also the fact that she was leaving me forever this time. There was no more hope of anything more between us.

I was not emotionally prepared when I got the news of her death on October 29th. Nobody is really prepared for the death of a loved one, and losing a parent is never easy under any circumstance. I was so overwhelmed with emotion that I was unsure if I should even go to the funeral. I knew I was too upset to travel to Illinois alone, so I took up a friend's offer to take me. She encouraged me to go, telling me that I needed to make closure. I did not make complete closure at this time, but at least I did the respectful thing and said goodbye. *Thank God for good friends! She was another human Angel!*

Our Last Family Gathering— My Mom's Funeral–Me on Left

It felt strange being at the funeral and observing her in the casket. There was a family gathering at my sister's house, which also felt strange. It had been years since our family had gathered for anything, and here we were on this solemn day, gathering for a final goodbye to a mom who had abandoned all of as children. After all those years of no family, it felt really strange to be with them. I did not stay long at my sister's because me and my friend both needed to return home, and I also wasn't comfortable and felt out of place with all the drinking and carrying on. Illinois had long since felt like my home, and I wanted to get back home to Michigan. We went through my mom's meager belongings before I departed, and I chose to take a crucifix and a ring of hers. My sister found a roll of film and had it developed a few years later, which were old family photos. I did not get these pictures until 1999, but what a huge blessing they were when I did! I got to see family photos, and photos of me as a baby, a toddler, and up to five years old. I discovered that I was an extremely sweet and adorable looking little girl! I was so innocent looking, like a cherub angel, with a

CAROL LUCAS

round face, big eyes, and small lips. My mom put a sticker of a little girl holding a duck on a letter she sent me years ago and told me the little girl reminded her of me. She was right; the little girl looked like me. At least she remembered what I looked like as a child.

A Double Whammy of Grief

I was deeply affected by my mom's death, so much so that I had a heavy heart. Not only did I have deep grief over the final loss of her at death, but I also had deep-seated grief from the loss of her in my childhood, which felt unbearable. The facilitator at a grief support group I attended explained to me that I had a double whammy, that my grief was more severe because I was losing her twice. I had so many mixed up and ambivalent emotions about her. It felt like I was back on the sidewalks again, except this time I had no choice whether I should step on a crack. She was gone forever. This was a final goodbye. There could be no more reconciliation between us, whether I desired it or not.

I struggled a lot with guilt over not getting close to her like she wanted, but after talking with my spiritual mentor and her reminding me that it would have only caused me more pain than she had already caused me, I was able to let the guilt go. She was never there for me as a child when I was in foster care, and yet she wanted me to be there for her. Why was it so hard for me to put my own emotional and mental health first? Why should I even believe I was responsible for her? I did not owe her anything; in fact, she really owed me. I was told by a therapist years ago that I probably mothered my mother because I was such a loving child. I came to realize that it would have caused us both too much pain had we gotten any closer. The bottom line is, I gave her the best I had, and I accept that today. It took more time and therapy to fully realize this and let her go with love, but I am happy to say today that I have. I no longer have a love/hate relationship with her. I have peace in my heart today about her.

I had already gone through a lot of turmoil in 1992 but was soon experience more, which would rock my world to the core and change my whole world. I would forever be changed by a just a brief few moments of time.

In September 1992 I had an encounter with a gifted woman in a store parking lot, who gave me a warning that I needed to be careful, because a man wanted me dead. I have had encounters with psychics before, so I took this warning seriously. *I also pay attention to things that happen randomly, as I believe they come from God.* I asked my spiritual mentor about it, and she agreed that I was in danger, and specified that I should be careful about shopping in safe neighborhoods.

I already had a lot of faith in God's protection of me, but I would soon have a whole lot more! Today I remind myself of the Power of Jesus when I called out to him. Only by the Grace of God am I alive to tell my story of His Amazing Grace!

A Close Call with Death

For He shall give his angel charge over thee,
to keep thee in all thy ways

The warnings I received became a horrible reality a few months later. I don't even like thinking about it, let alone writing about this close call with death. It's difficult for me to write about because it is traumatic revisiting it, but it's necessary for me to do so to be real and share my whole story. ***Most importantly, it is ultimately a testimony to the power of Almighty God.*** This experience profoundly affected me in both good and bad ways. If I could rewind my life and undo this trauma I would, but that isn't possible. It happened, and I need to deal with the reality of it. I could go on and on with the ifs and whys, but that isn't going to change the reality. The only thing I can change is me, which is ultimately what happened through this experience.

It was December 3rd, 1992. My boyfriend had asked me to come over and visit him at his new apartment a few miles away, which I agreed to. I put on a long flowy skirt he liked seeing me in and was on my way out the door, when something told me to put on some jeans instead, so I did. ***And thank God I did!*** I had a vague sense of something feeling off, but I couldn't quite put my finger on what. I have strong intuitive and psychic ability, but back then it wasn't quite as strong as it is today, and I didn't always trust it like I do today.

I stopped by a party store on the way to get a money order, which I thought nothing of since I had shopped there in the past when I was married. I had always felt safe before, but I was unaware that the area had degenerated badly into a crime and drug infested neighborhood. My spiritual mentor had warned me to be careful about only shopping in safe places, but I had no idea how unsafe it was. Unfortunately, I was about to find out.

As I was walking out of the party store, a black man grabbed me, put a gun to my left side as he put his right hand over my mouth and said, "if you scream, I'll kill you." He then forced me over to the side of the last building in a mini strip mall where a parked semi was, and brutally attacked me. What was particularly scary, was that he had me in between the parked semi and the building where it was pitch black. I told him, "you can have my money, but please don't hurt me," and he yelled, "shut up bitch!" He then proceeded to brutally attack me as he ripped my clothes off.

I knew as soon as he was forcing me over to the side of the building that my life was in danger, and of course I prayed right away, *"God help me, or I am dead!"* I knew in my gut that he didn't just want my money, but you do what you must do when your life is in danger. I tried fighting him off, but there was no way I could. He was like a vicious animal. He ripped my thick sweater in half with one hand, had my jeans down to my ankles, and whipped me around like a wet noodle while he pistol whipped me in the face. I cannot truly convey the terror I felt, or the brutality involved because it was so intense. There are no words for it. One would have to experience it to fully comprehend. The only thing that kept me going was adrenaline, but even with the adrenaline rush, he was beating me so severely that I was right on the verge of losing consciousness. I was so close, that whenever I recall this, I always say, *"I was only a breath away from death."*

I completely understand the saying, *my whole life flashed before me.* My whole life flashed before me in a split second, and the most prevalent thought I had was, *I cannot die now; I have this work for foster children to do.* I also had the thought that the attacker needed some help, that he had to have come from a traumatic childhood to be so messed up as to violently attack an innocent woman.

I am not exaggerating when I say this was a close call with death. It was so close that only Divine Intervention could help me, which is what happened. As I was nearing my last breath and about to lose consciousness, I screamed out, "Oh God, Dear Jesus, help me!" And as Jesus was coming out of my mouth, the man fled like a bat out of hell. I was too disoriented to clearly see the Angel, but I did see some light off to the left of me and perceived a Divine Presence. My spiritual mentor and other spiritual people have told me that it was a mighty Angel that appeared. Believe me, nothing short of a miraculous mighty Angel could have freed me from this evil. By the Grace of God, Jesus, and a Mighty Angel, my life was spared that night. Praise be to God Almighty!

My life was spared that night, but not my humanity or sanity! To avoid the possibility of my attacker coming back I walked up to the front of the building half naked, my jeans still down by my ankles and clutching on to my sweater, which was so humiliating for me. There were people gawking at me because they were so shocked, which made me angry, and I yelled out, "would somebody please go get me a robe from Value Village (a goodwill store in the mini mall)!?" Somebody got me robe to wear, which was a comfort, and right as I was putting it on a cop car pulled up. The police officer took a report and told me that a man driving by called on his cell phone to report a woman was being forced over by a building there. This was amazing, since this was 1992, not 2021. *Cell phones were rare then, but God made sure there was one around that night! God sent me another human Angel!* Another amazing thing about that night is the fact that I decided to wear jeans instead of a skirt. I would have easily and completely been raped had I worn a skirt, which would have been even more traumatic, but the jeans saved me. It was classified as an attempted rape and murder. The police officer wanted me to go to the hospital to checked for a concussion, but I refused. I told him I just wanted to go home where I felt safe, but I honestly would never truly feel safe after this horrible trauma.

After the police officer took the report, I called my boyfriend to inform him of what happened and asked him to please come pick me up. He was so upset that he told me he was going to go find the first ******* ****** he could find and kill him. I had to calm him down as I was trying to calm myself down. I asked him to take me over to a friend's house, but she wasn't home. A cop stopped us for some reason (probably speeding because he was upset), and thought my boyfriend was beating me because there was a baseball bat in the car. He assumed the worst because I looked upset. Lord, could this night possibly get any worse? I explained to the cop that he hadn't beat me, but I had been beaten by someone else. He just wanted to make sure I was all right, but it was embarrassing.

I don't recall this night well because I was in so much shock, but I do remember calling my older woman friend and telling her what happened, then she got my boyfriend on the phone and told him to stay with me for the night because I was in shock. I use the word shock because it is the only word that comes close to describing how I felt. There honestly are not words to describe the whole horrible experience and how I felt. It is beyond describing in words, nor do I really care to. I just want to forget about it! *And I will ask God to let it go when I am done writing about it. It was a very traumatic experience that I survived by the Grace of God.*

My boyfriend took me home early the next morning, which I believe he wanted to do. I remember feeling like he didn't care, but he did; he just didn't know how to handle it. Having read about trauma since this happened, I now understand that it was also traumatic for him, and he felt bad that he was not there to protect me. I remember coming home and curling up in a fetal position in my bed and saying, *"God, why don't you just take me? I am tired of this life." But God did not take me. I slept some, then I called my spiritual mentor and informed her of what happened. She told me she knew it was not my time to go, that God protected me.* She also told me I handled it better than most people would have because I was spiritual. I know I did handle it better than most, but believe you me, I did not go through this horrible trauma emotionally unscathed. Like I have said before though, *"I can't live with an open wound, but I can live with a scar."*

> *"A SCAR IS A WOUND THAT HAS HEALED. WE NEED TO BRING OUR WOUNDS TO JESUS, LET HIM HEAL THEM, AND USE OUR SCARS FOR JESUS. OUR SCARS MAY BE OUR GREATEST MINISTRY. ADRIAN ROGERS*

How I Handled the Trauma

How I handled the trauma in the aftermath is sad to me now. I refused hospital care because I hate hospitals so much, and yet the very next day I went to a scheduled gynecology appointment. Really? What was I thinking? To the average person this may seem strange that I would do this, but having since read about trauma, it makes perfect sense to me. I was just trying to survive a very traumatic experience by acting normal. Isn't that what I did as a child? Don't feel, don't be vulnerable; just be strong! It was ingrained in me as a child to numb out and be strong, and it was exactly what I did after I was attacked. When the gynecologist seen my beaten face and asked me what happened, I replied casually, "I got attacked last night." I was not emotional at all. He called a doctor over from the hospital to look at me to make sure I didn't have a concussion. It felt nice to have people concerned about my welfare, yet I was also uneasy because they were validating the trauma, which I just wanted to minimize. I was not oblivious to the fact of the trauma, but I didn't want to acknowledge the severity of it. I was used to trauma. I got attacked. It was no big deal. Just be numb and strong and go on with your life, which is exactly what I did.

Nineteen years later in 2011, when I finally did deal with the trauma, my therapist told me the fact that I had already had so much trauma in my life made me more resilient to this trauma. She told me many people would be locked up for good over such a severe trauma. I guess that is the upside to trauma, that what doesn't kill you makes you stronger. Seriously though, I feel sad now that I went through that horrible trauma, and only recently started crying about it, but at least I can cry about it now, which has been healing. The fact that I am sad about it now tells me I have worked through the trauma, as sadness is the last thing to be felt when grieving.

I left the gynecologist office with no concussion, but I do have a slight bump on my hairline that never went away, so there was some permanent damage that is a constant reminder of the trauma. I got another reminder of the trauma when I was in my Child Psychology class and the professor called me up after class to ask me what happened because my face was black and blue. I am surprised I even went to my class looking like that, but like I said, I just wanted to go on with my normal life. He encouraged me to get therapy, which I didn't do at the time. I told him I was talking with a woman on the phone from rape counseling, but I honestly just wanted to forget the whole thing! I am the one who went through this trauma, yet everyone else seemed more concerned than me. I thought it was no big deal. So what, I got attacked and almost murdered! I survived! I have survived other things and I will survive this! That was my attitude.

I now find it sad now that I could so easily accept this horrible trauma as normal, but all I knew at the time was that I had to act normal and keep on trucking. I did not have the luxury back then of falling apart in therapy. I saw Frank once after this happened, and he didn't seem to make such a big deal of it, so why should I? It makes me angry now when I think of his attitude, because he could have been the one to help me deal with this trauma. Maybe he couldn't handle the trauma; I don't know. I think the fact that he didn't validate the trauma supported my own denial about it. I remember when I left his office that day. He said, "so you got a little beat up, huh?" That is all he said! He should have been more validating and supportive than he was. Maybe if my own therapist had supported me, I would have dealt with it when it happened. Sadly, that did not happen. Instead, I buried it way down deep. I always say, *"it was buried in my subconscious mind, and when it finally surfaced to my conscious mind, it nearly drove me out of my mind!"*

Since being in EMDR therapy, I can now understand the trauma better. I handled it the best I could at that time.

What I Learned from the Trauma

What have I learned from the trauma? One thing I know for sure, is that there is no way God caused this. It was not in God's plan to have this happen. There was no lesson He was trying to teach me, though I did learn some valuable lessons from it. A lot of people try to make sense of everything by saying that everything is by God's design, that God causes things for our own good, which I do not believe at all! *God is love and would never ever wish such a horrible and evil trauma on one of His children!*

The sad reality is that we live in a world where evil exists, and I happened to encounter it. It was horrible, but I survived. *In the Bible it says, "what the devil meant for harm, God uses for good." I am not sure about any devil, but whatever evil that wanted to harm me, I believe God did use it for my own good.* The good that ended up coming out of this outweighed the bad, but it took time for me to see this.

One thing I know with certainty is that this close call with death increased my faith in God, big time! And even more importantly was that it increased my trust in my Heavenly Father, Who will never ever abandon me! What a huge revelation that was for me! Up until December 3rd, 1992, when I was saved from the most horrific death, I struggled with the belief that God loved me like he did everyone else, that I could trust Him. I found out that night that God does most definitely love me, that I could trust Him, and that He would never ever abandon me. If he can help me out of the most dangerous situation imaginable, then he most certainly cares for me in the normal, everyday things like shelter, food, etc. God meant it when he said, "I will never leave you, nor forsake you."

And what do I have that many people do not have? Faith in Angels! I know that God has Angels around me to protect me! What an awesome thing to know, that God in His Almighty Power can protect me from evil. I have faith today that is unshakable. I know many people who do not have faith that God can move mountains, but He can, and He does. He moved a big mountain for me on December 3, 1992, and I am forever grateful for that. I am not only grateful that my life was spared; I am also grateful God proved His Love for me. I experienced the Power of God that night, and I feel that God is leading me to speak out about it more, including in this book. It is the least I can do after what He did for me. What better good could come from that experience than to let it be a living testimony about Him and His Love?

The Dark Tunnel

I wish I could fast forward a few years to 1995 when I met my husband Larry, but unfortunately, I still had some dark and painful times before that. The three years (1992-1995) before meeting him were emotionally painful years for me. It felt very dark and lonely at times, but I also know they were years of great growth.

I remember reading a passage in some ACOA literature during this time that said recovery from adult children's issues is like going through a dark tunnel that you feel stuck in forever, but then the light finally dawns at the end of the tunnel and you emerge into the bright sunlight. I know this was true for me. I felt like I would always be in this dark tunnel all alone, lost, and hopeless. Where am I? Will I ever get out of here? Where am I going? Will I be ok when I leave this dark tunnel? What will be at the end of this journey through this dark tunnel? It was a scary and uncertain time for me. I didn't realize I was growing because I was so focused on the dark tunnel, but then the light finally emerged at the end. Wow!

What was at the end of this journey through the dark tunnel? Me! That was the beauty of it, though the tunnel was anything but beautiful while traveling through it. I certainly did not embrace this concept then, but I know today that I needed every dark moment and every painful emotion I experienced back then to bring me where I am today. As I say, *"be real and feel to heal."* I suppose it would be nice if I could just intellectualize this journey, but I would not be fully human if I did. Human beings are feeling, emotional beings, and thank God we are! We do need our intellect, especially when we get overwhelmed with our emotions like I am prone to, but that isn't where the true healing takes place; it takes place in our heart and spirit. Ideally there should be a balance between the heart and head, which I still help with according to my husband, who always told me that my heart was too big for my head! This has gotten me in more trouble than I care to admit to, and it continued to be a problem during these three years of darkness.

I have had some dark moments since losing my husband, and now doing my autobiography, and have been reminded of the dark tunnel I went through so many years ago. On May 7, 2021, I was feeling extremely emotional about some traumatic issues that recently came up that concerned my mom and the sexual abuse, and was praying while driving, when I noticed a beautiful sky that perfectly described how I felt at that moment.

God gave me beautiful sign of hope, the sun shining through the rain. I was so awed, not only by the view, but by the fact that God gave me this beautiful picture! Even through the dark tunnel, He was there. I was told by a gifted friend of mine that I was now going through a metamorphosis, which I believe was part of the reason showed me this beautiful light at the end of the tunnel. I am now in therapy healing from my past and doing EMDR. I am beginning to see the light at the end of the tunnel and look forward to being a beautiful butterfly. I feel as though I am emerging now. I feel a lot more whole, a lot freer, and a lot more peaceful. Thank YOU, GOD!

He is the Light in the darkness!

CAROL LUCAS

A Bad Move

My heart and my fears of being alone got me in trouble again with my boyfriend. Why didn't I learn the first time that it couldn't work with us? Why couldn't I use my head instead of my heart? I let my boyfriend move in with me again in December 1993, which was a huge mistake! I knew deep down this was not the right thing to do, not rationally or morally, but my fears of being alone clouded my judgment again and I was once again living with this bum who couldn't keep a job, and once again I was left wondering how I could be so stupid! You know the saying, "shame on you the first time; shame on me the second time?" Shame on me this time! Since the definition of insanity is repeatedly doing something and expecting different results, I had to wonder if I was insane. Why should I think it would be any different this time? It is good to have hope, but not like this! I went from hoping it could work out this time, to hoping he would get out of my house as soon as possible! ASAP!

He only lived with me this time for about a month when I told him he had to leave, but since he was so down and out with nowhere to go and I was too big hearted to just throw him out in the street, I let him stay with me until he found his own apartment, which was not for another year and three months! I was tender hearted and gentle when I told him it was over with us, but I was also firm. I told him he couldn't give me what I needed, that I wanted and needed stability. I was finally growing up and using some good sense, which was about time! It wasn't easy sharing a small house with a man you're no longer in a relationship with, but I managed.

What made the situation even more complicated and even laughable, was that we had five dogs in this small house for a short time. He brought his golden Lab, and I had my own dog Belle, who had three puppies in August 1994. I had a house full of dogs, but the dogs were easier to deal with than him and his sloppy ways! I wish I was more like a male friend of mine who had a similar situation with a man, and told him, "you have a place to go; you just don't know where it is yet!"

I Surrender All!

Once I made the decision to break it off with my ex-boyfriend, I was truly surrendering my life to God and trusting Him with all, believing He would bless me with a good man someday if that were His will for me. I got honest with myself and realized that I had been trying to control my own life, which had to stop. I wanted a better life with a better man, and I knew I deserved it. *I decided to wait on the Lord to bless me in His time, which I knew He would, if I was living a Godly and moral life. But it was up to God, not me, and if he wanted me alone for the rest of my life, I was willing to be ok with that. Father knows best.*

In April 1995 I was blessed with a message about my life, through a gifted woman I was working for. While cleaning her house the first day, she told me that when I walked in her home, she had a vision of me standing next to a man and holding a child. I wasn't skeptical about the man, but I was the child, as I really wasn't thinking of having a baby (I have since come to realize the child was probably symbolic of my work for foster children). She also told me about a special place called *The Little Rose Chapel*, where miracles happen.

I can testify that miracles do indeed happen there, as they happened for me more than once. *While visiting the chapel the first time, I got on my knees and told God that I wanted to surrender all to Him, that I just wanted peace and to draw closer to Him, that if he wanted me to be alone for the rest of my life, I was ok with that.* All I wanted was peace. About two weeks later I met my husband!

CAROL LUCAS

The gifted woman also told me that she mentioned me to a gifted woman she knew, and that the woman said, "that poor woman has had nothing but crap all her life, but God is going to put a man in her life very soon who will be like her knight in shining armor. He will take all her hurts away if she will let him." Wow! It was within a month of her telling me this that I met Larry. And Larry was my knight in shining armor, who did take all my hurts away. My husband healed me.

There was only one temptation I had during this time, and it was with the man I had a brief fling with years before. He lived down the street from me and didn't waste any time coming to see me after my ex-boyfriend left. I heard a knock on my door about three days later and there stood this man, who invited himself in and said, "I always wanted to sleep with you again." I thought, how about asking me how I am doing? Talk about blunt! I told him the next man I married would be putting a ring on my finger, and he said he couldn't commit to anyone because he didn't know how long he had to live. I knew he was telling me the truth because he had Hepatitis C, but I also knew he was a womanizer. I let him go and that was the end of that temptation! I was proud of myself for walking away, as I know he would have hurt me. I didn't get away from two cheaters to get involved with another one! I was finally using my head, which felt nice! I felt like I was finally growing up and maturing. I was able to make a sound decision based on good sense, instead of getting hi-jacked by my hormones and/or my fears of abandonment.

I went about my daily life, which mostly involved working and going to school, with some occasional dancing on the weekends at a singles club. *I lost some cleaning jobs in August 1995, which left a dent in my income, but I trusted God to provide, which of course He did.* I found an ad for a cleaning position while shopping at a Kroger grocery store, which I wasn't going to take because I knew it wouldn't pay as much, but I was desperate; I needed more money, so I took the ad and started working for a woman named Marilyn.

God Worked in a Mysterious and Miraculous Way!

Little did I know when I first met Marilyn, that God was working out my life in His mysterious and miraculous way, that only He can do. One day Marilyn and I were chatting after work about personal things, and she happened to mention that she had a brother who she thought would like me and wondered if I would like to meet him. I decided it was time for me to date, so I said, "yes." Why not? As I was driving home this feeling came over me that this was the man I had a premonition of about a year earlier when I was on my knees praying one night, of an older Christian man who would want to marry me. I just knew in my spirit that he was that man. Larry called me right away to make a date for the following weekend, and there was no doubt when I met him that he was indeed that man.

God is so good! After all the tragedy in my life, it may seem odd to say, but I see the goodness of God in the midst of it.

My Knight in Shining Armor!

Our first date was on September 22, 1995. Wow! What a memory! His sister sure was not lying when she said he was a gentleman. I had never been around a man like him before. He drove up in a beautiful, white Yukon, which were popular at the time, and my first thought was that he had a good job to be able to afford it. He knocked on my door and we took off, in search of a restaurant. He asked me where I wanted to go, and I honestly didn't know, as I rarely ate out, so he picked an expensive restaurant called Mountain Jack's. I remember him looking at me while we were at the restaurant like he thought I was real pretty, which made me feel a bit shy. We had a nice dinner, then he took me to the movie theatre.

I will never forget what happened on the way into the theatre. He asked me if he could hold my hand! I hadn't had a man do that since I was in middle school! I thought it was incredibly sweet, and I knew then he was a true gentleman. I think he had my heart then, though I didn't know it yet. It was SO refreshing to be in the company of a man so gentlemanly and sincere. After the movie he took me home and I invited him in for tea, which he accepted. We talked a few minutes, then I walked him out to his vehicle to say goodbye and he asked me if I would see him again, and I said, "yes. I like you. You're a nice guy."

I was so impressed with Larry's respectfulness toward me. Not once did he even try to kiss me, let alone make a sexual advance toward me, which I thought was so sweet and respectful. He impressed me as a man who was very moral, a true Christian man who truly respected women. I loved his realness. I felt like he seen me as a whole person, not just a sex object like other men in my past had. He respected me and I respected him for that. I truly had grown into a mature woman with some good sense, which was amazing considering my past choices in men. I found my soul mate, but I didn't fully realize it until we were together for a few years.

Although I knew he was a gentleman, I still had my fears, and one of them was infidelity, which we talked about on our first date. Larry reassured me over and over that he only wanted one woman. He always told me throughout our marriage, "I only want one woman who will love me." Well, I only wanted one man who would love me! I remember telling him that he scared me some, and he said, "why? I'm not going to hurt you," and I replied, "that's why I'm scared; I'm not used to being with such a nice man." But my fears subsided not long after we were married, and I was completely comfortable with him being such a nice man. I fully embraced his love because I knew I was emotionally safe with him.

Larry and I began developing a good friendship, talking on the phone a lot, and dating regularly, but our friendship soon blossomed into a beautiful romance that turned serious. Larry knew right away I was the one for him and proposed to me only two weeks later, with a stunning ring. Talk about fast! He made me feel like he was my knight in shining armor and I was his princess! He made me feel so special. When he gave me the ring and I asked him why he got such an expensive ring for me, he said, "because you're special." Wow! What a thing to hear from a man you have only known a short time! Although I was thrilled with the proposal and the ring, I did not immediately say "yes." I told him I had to think about it and pray about it, which I did. *I went to the Little Rose Chapel and sat quietly praying about my decision, asking God to guide me. I also had a vision of some land while I was there, which I know now is the land we bought years later. I left with a sense of peace that marrying Larry was the right thing to do.*

Part of the reason I was hesitant to say "yes" to his proposal was because my attraction to him was different than with my two exes'. I doubted my attraction to him at first because I didn't have a crazy in love feeling like I had in the past with other men. I am glad now I didn't! I think my two exes were fatal attractions! Whenever I speak of Larry I always say, *"I used my head and let the heart follow,"* which was SO true, and thank God it was! My attraction to Larry was very much grounded in reality, not fantasy. In other words, is he stable? Yes. Can he provide well? Yes. Will he offer me security and stability? Yes. Are our morals and values the same? Yes. Do we have similar interests? Yes. When I looked at Larry, I seen all these attributes and said "yes." "Yes, I will marry you, Larry!"

CAROL LUCAS

Larry was a very perceptive man who seen into my heart and soul. He knew he loved me, and he knew I was a woman who would love him. I remember asking him after he proposed, "why do you want me and not any of those women at Ford who make good money?" His reply was, "I don't like them women. I like you." He wanted a woman who loved her home and wanted to be a good wife. He also wanted a woman who loved the country like he did. He wanted a woman who would share his life and bed with him. He didn't want another career driven woman like he had in the past, who would be competing with him and trying to control him. I was the kind of woman he had always dreamed of. Larry wanted love.

We both knew in our hearts that it was a blessed union. There was no question in our minds that God had brought us together. It was a match made in Heaven! That God put this exceptionally good man into my life still amazes me. I will forever thank God for Larry! I will always love Larry! Always!

Since we were now engaged to be married, we both decided we were ready for deeper romance, which happened on Sweetest Day. He brought me out to his home, and we spent our first night together on October 14, 1995. He gave me a beautiful gold heart necklace, bought me some Sunflower cologne, and had a beautiful black negligee for me. Wow! Was I ever impressed! How romantic! What a memorable night!

The next day he took me down to meet his family, which was nice but uncomfortable. I wanted to feel accepted but sensed his sister was jealous of me and didn't want me with him. I have an extraordinarily strong gift of discernment. I know when people are sincere and when they aren't. Larry didn't believe me at first when I told him his sister didn't like me, but he did in time. I can see right through phoniness, and knew she was phony. I always see past the façade when it comes to people. When you grow up in a dysfunctional environment where you don't feel safe, you learn early on to be on guard. It is deeply ingrained in me.

Larry and I continued talking with each other and spending the weekends at his home. He treated me like royalty when we first met, taking me out to eat a lot. I will never forget the time he took me to Frankenmuth for the first time. I had never been there before and thought it was beautiful. It was during the Christmas season when all the decorations were out, and he let me pick out as many ornaments I wanted for our Christmas tree, and let us eat in a nice restaurant there, but the most memorable part was the carriage ride we went on. It was so romantic! We spent the night there and went shopping the next day. I remember him buying a nice leather hat, which he wore a lot. I will always keep that hat! I will never forget how impressed Larry was when I saw a dress in the window and intuitively knew it was the perfect dress for his daughter's upcoming wedding. He made me feel so special that weekend. Larry always said throughout our marriage, "we *are making memories.*" I feel the full impact of those words now that he is gone, as memories are all I have left now, and I treasure every one of them!

We could have gotten married right after his daughter's wedding but figured it would be best to wait until spring. This also gave us more time to get acquainted. He picked me up on the weekends and brought me to his home, which allowed us to get settled in with each. I discovered Larry was an exceptionally good cook! We got to enjoy some domestic bliss before marrying, which was nice. There was a natural harmony between us from the very beginning, which remained throughout our marriage. We just naturally got along very well. We never argued about things that a lot of couples do, like housework, money, lack of communication, sex, etc. We were soul mates, and that is why there was a natural harmony between us. I always say we were spiritual soul mates. I believe the main reason we were soul mates was because we were spiritually connected. **The Holy Spirit was truly what united us.**

Married for Real This Time!

I moved in with Larry in early March 1996, which was quite a memorable move. I decided to come out alone in my car with my two dogs, Belle and Trucker, but got lost and had to call Larry to get directions. Believe me, nobody can get lost like me! It was quite a comfort to know he was there to help me find the way to my new home. Larry always made me feel so safe and cared for, and it is what I miss the most about him now that he is gone.

We had planned on getting married on March 21 but postponed it a few days because of bad weather. By April 1st, the weather was pleasant, and we decided to take a drive to Ohio to get married. We had planned on getting married at a courthouse, but it was a group marriage, which turned us both off, so we decided to take a drive to Findlay, Ohio, where the mayor married us. I will never forget when the mayor almost said, "kill the bride" instead of "kiss the bride." Larry and I both thought that was so funny!

The next six months were quite memorable for me. I grew up with traditional values, believing a woman should be a good wife and take care of her husband, so it was very much ingrained in me to be a good wife. I took pride in my role as a wife, as he took pride in his role as a husband. I will never forget the time I tried to make waffles in the waffle iron and made a mess, but I sure did try, and we both laughed about it! I also remember the time I made some homemade bread that was more like brick than bread, but I made some more. I was determined to make the bread right!

We had a lot of good times in the beginning of our marriage. He came home every day to dinner on the table, then we spent time together in the evening, often going for Harley rides and getting ice cream.

My First Harley Ride!

I will never forget the day he took me out for my first Harley ride in April 1996. He was going out on his Harley and invited me along, but I was uneasy about it. I told him, "I am not a biker mama, all tattooed up," which he thought was so funny. He said, "Carol, just get on the bike once with me and see if you like it." I said, "well, ok," and so off we went, going a good distance in the country before coming back home. He asked me how I liked it, and I was surprised to tell him that not only did I like it, but I loved it! I might have been surprised at how much I loved it, but I don't think he was. I was hooked after the very first ride and went all over the place with him on the Harley!

The first fifteen years of our marriage were spent mostly on the Harley during the nice weather. We had so many happy times on the Harley! I have so many happy memories of us riding together! It was SO romantic being on the back of the bike with him, riding through the beautiful countryside. I especially loved riding later in the day when the sun was setting. I always said it felt like we were riding off into the sunset together. You can't get any more romantic than that!

The day before Larry passed on I told him the years went by too fast, but I know the reason they did was because they were such happy years filled with so much love and joy! I treasure all my memories with him and will always love him. I always tell people, "Larry didn't just change my life; he gave me a life I never had before." **He truly was a Gift from God.**

Our Beautiful and Romantic Wedding!

September 21st, 1996

We agreed to have a marriage ceremony later that year around the anniversary of our first date, so on September 21st, 1996, we were married in a beautiful Victorian Wedding Chapel that wasn't far from the Little Rose Chapel. I must say, we were quite the beautiful couple. I looked radiant in a beautiful Victorian wedding gown that I made myself, and Larry looked happy and handsome in his suit. It was a private ceremony with only a few friends and family. A friend of Larry's took some beautiful pictures of us that I put in a photo album, which I treasure. Even the pastor said he thought we were a blessed couple. We WERE a blessed couple and we both knew it.

What God has joined together, let no man put asunder were not just words to us; they were very real. ***God brought us together and God would keep us together.***

Our Life Together

Our lives together started out harmoniously, without any serious upsets or arguments. We sometimes got triggered by emotional baggage from our past relationships, but we were aware of it and were able to resolve it quickly. We would both sometimes have to remind each other that we were not the ex-spouses. Larry told me he loathed his first wife, so no way did I ever want to be compared to her! And God forbid he ever be compared to either one of my exes! Our life together was mellow and joyful once we became settled. We had both been in such unhappy marriages before that we both knew what we didn't want, and we didn't want to make the same mistakes again. I believe we appreciated each other even more because of this. Third time around was definitely a charm for both of us!

There is so much to say about our marriage and all the years we spent together that I hardly know where to begin, but I will begin by summing up my years with Larry as the happiest and most joyful years of my life. They started out joyful and they ended joyful. I was incredibly happy to be married to him and devoted myself to being a good wife. I always made him lunches to take to work and had dinner ready for him when he came home. He worked days when we first got married, so we spent our evenings together, which we totally enjoyed.

The only unhappy memory I have of him is when he passed. I keep waiting for the grief to end, but the reality is that it never completely will. But it has gotten easier.

Larry and I both loved our home a lot and were content in it together. My love for my husband and my home always came first. I was still working and finishing up with college, but I always made sure Larry came first. I never wanted him to feel like anything or anyone was more important to me than him, and I can honestly say that he always knew that. I never ever took him for granted. I always told him how much I loved and appreciated him. I truly did, and he knew it. Larry was so very precious to me.

We did a lot of home renovation, fixing the house the way we wanted. He talked of building a new home for us when we first met, but we were content with the one we had. Larry told me that his first wife never liked the home he built, that he built it for someone else, and he agreed. He told me, "sweetheart, I built this house for you; I just didn't know it at the time." I agreed with him, and said, "yes, and I am perfectly ok with it!" We had a lot of laughs about that! Larry built this house all by himself, even doing the electrical, plumbing, and heating, etc. He was a very smart man. I know what it is like to be homeless and/or living on the fringes of life, so I truly and deeply appreciated this home, and still do. I always voiced my appreciation for Larry and everything he did for me when we said our prayers together, which I know warmed his heart. Larry always knew I felt very blessed to have him providing security and stability for me. *I do not take my home for granted and always thank God for it!*

A Family Dream

With my new marriage came a hope and dream of my own family. I wanted a child, a chance to be a mother, and I thought I would at least try since the gifted woman had seen me with a child. That was my heart's desire at that time. I was already forty years old when we married, so I was aware my chances weren't great, but with fertility in my genes and God on my side, maybe I would get my miracle. I thought God would answer my prayer and my miracle would happen, but it never did. I tried for seven years; I had an operation to have my fallopian tubes opened, and even took fertility drugs, but I miscarried right away both times I got pregnant. The only other option was invitro fertilization, which we couldn't afford, nor did I believe in, so I finally gave up. Although I didn't get the child I wanted, I did gain a lot of wisdom.

I admit I did not give up gracefully at first. I was truly angry at God for not giving me my miracle, and had to grieve the child I couldn't have, but I also came to realize that although I had a strong desire for motherhood, I was also terrified of the prospect. I was on such a roller coaster ride for the seven years I was trying, that I was more relieved than anything to have it end. The ups and downs wore me out emotionally, and it wasn't good for my marriage either. It was a relief to finally let go and be ok with it. Also, Larry already had three children, and although he would have welcomed one of our own, it was not high on his list of things to do, which I understood and respected. Larry wanted a life with his wife, which is something he didn't have when he was married with children. When this dream was over and I honestly asked myself what was more important, a husband or a child, the answer was a husband. And my free time! I am perfectly content with no children today. My baby is my dog! Larry used to say, "he was ok with one child, and happy with none." Ditto. My perspective has changed as I've grown older. I've mellowed.

Forming FACT!

Although my dream of having a physical child didn't come true, my other dream of forming **FACT** for former foster children was about to. On September 9, 1999, which was national prayer day that year, I received a phone call from a woman in Detroit who was searching for a support group for former foster children. She had gotten my number from a self-help support group place where I had something listed. We both agreed to collaborate on **FACT** when I told her of my desire to form **FACT** meetings. I already had many ideas for **FACT**, but I thought two heads were better than one. It made more sense to me than doing everything alone, especially since the last word of **FACT** is **TOGETHER.** Pam and I met to discuss forming **FACT**.

What was also amazing about meeting Pam, was that she lived right down the street from where I was attacked. I couldn't help but feel that this was no accident. As my life flashed before me that night, my most prevalent thought was that I could not die because I had this work to do for foster children, and now I was working with a woman who was living so close to that scene. I took it as another sign about the destiny of *FACT.* **It was a God thing!**

My brother came to visit right after I met Pam, and the three of us got together at her home on October 7, 1999, and formed the *Ten Statement of Beliefs,* which is one of the documents of **FACT**. What took place that evening was so amazing that I cannot express it in words; it was a profound spiritual experience. I feel so blessed to have experienced that evening. *All I can say is that we all three felt the strong presence of the Holy Spirit in the room as we prayed for God's guidance in doing this, and all the ideas and words we needed seemed to flow from His Divine Presence. We were all amazed at what was put on paper. When I speak of God's Hand guiding mine, this is what happened that night in a* phenomenal way. It was a very memorable night that I will never forget. When I completed the Ten Stepping Stones, I was also amazed that there were ten of them, and I also thought it was amazing that there were ten children in our family, as if God ordained this, which of course I believe He did! God is so utterly amazing!

Statement of Beliefs

WE BELIEVE there is hope, through God as we understand Him.

WE BELIEVE and accept that we are powerless over the circumstances of our past.

WE BELIEVE in healing from our childhood injuries.

WE BELIEVE we begin to heal by facing our anger toward people who injured us.

WE BELIEVE releasing those who injured us leads to healing.

WE BELIEVE we have a rightful place in the family of man.

WE BELIEVE we are neither slaves of the past nor master of the future.

WE BELIEVE our isolation ends when we share our pain.

WE BELIEVE that in finding others who are lost we find ourselves.

WE BELIEVE there is purpose with God.

I Believe God Believes in the Ten Statement of Beliefs!

The Beginning of FACT Meetings

FACT was formed in the Spring of 2000, and I even had a website with all the documents available for others to download for FACT meetings. Pam found a room at a church for us to have FACT meetings, and for a short time (about two months) there were four of us who had meetings, until there was a dispute about how the meetings should be run. I wanted things to be more organized than they did, with some leadership on my part, which they resented. We all wanted unity but had a different idea of what that should involve. They wanted everyone to be able to cross talk at the meeting, which I knew from being in AA and other support groups, would never work. Each person should be given a chance to speak, then at the end of the meeting there can be crosstalk if anyone wants it. There was another issue with Pam wanting to more involved with the website than I wanted. The third issue was monetary. I decided to make *FACT* a non-profit organization, which Pam and the others also wanted to control, and I said, "no way!" I felt like I couldn't win with them, which I believe stemmed from their jealousy of me. I already knew from experience that things can get ugly once jealousy is involved, so I decided to bow out gracefully before it reached an ugly point. I didn't feel good about doing it, but felt I had no choice.

The three of them formed their own support group, but it only lasted a few months. I'm not sure why it fell apart, but I conjecture it was probably due to any lack of leadership or unity. In their quest for unity, one of them probably tried to be a leader and the others resented it, just as they had me. It took a lot of humility for me to finally realize that I was probably wrong in the way I handled the situation. I was right about my leadership and no cross talking, but I probably should have stayed and let it eventually work itself out, which it possibly may have. I feel sad about it now, but at the time I really felt I was doing the right thing by walking away, so I can't beat myself up over it. I also came to realize that my own love of harmony with others was a big contributing factor in my decision to leave. I hate arguing! I always say I am wrong a lot, because I would rather walk away from a fight than argue just so I could be right! I got uncomfortable with all the bickering between us and didn't know how to handle it. I gained not only some humility but some wisdom from that experience. One positive thing that came from our short time together was the *...fact is...* document, which they gave me input on.

...fact is...

We are the forsaken children of the world. Although we come from various ethnic and religious backgrounds and seemingly have little in common...fact is...there is a common thread woven through us. As children we stood by and watched helplessly as our worlds crumbled apart, depending on strangers to come to our rescue and decide our fate, a fate which many times was worse than what we were delivered from. We have a variety of stories to tell...some of appreciation for the caring people who took us into their homes, some of seeming indifference to our circumstances, and some of hatred toward foster parents who cared not for us, but only for the monetary and personal gain. Even though some of us were fortunate enough to have been placed in a better environment... fact is...many of us were placed in homes with people who simply were not equipped to deal with our special emotional needs stemming from the trauma we suffered from having been ripped away from our homes and families, however abusive and neglectful they may have been. Though our experiences are diverse, we share the same basic feelings of loss, isolation, shame, and pain. Our childhood wounds have left us feeling stigmatized. Many of us feel as though we have been nothing but a burden—unwanted by our parents and dumped off on society's doorstep to be still a further burden. Though we may strive mightily to belong in life's mainstream...fact is...we find ourselves more often on the fringes of life—homeless, incarcerated, and generally bankrupt. It may appear we walk the same roads as everyone else, but our shoes show the difference. Try as we may to find our way in this world, the search has often seemed futile. It is this search that has drawn us toward

CAROL LUCAS

another path, a path of our own choosing... ...We are tired of being angry, ashamed, and alone. We want to end our isolation. FACT brings us together to share our experiences, face our past, and walk a new path that will build a bridge to healing.

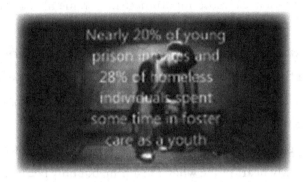

I hope FACT can reach these people

Although our time together as a **FACT** support group was short lived, I am grateful for the time we did have together and the input they gave me on the *...fact is...* document. *I believe part of the reason God allowed us this time together was for this purpose.* This was years ago, but I still remember Joe giving me the idea about the sentence *'it may appear we may walk the same roads as everyone else, but our shoes show the difference.'* I don't believe I could have said it better and told him so. Joe had a humility about him that was humbling. I learned some humility and gratitude from him, as my childhood seemed mild in comparison to his. I know it isn't good to compare trauma, but I am deeply humbled and grateful when I hear stories of people who were shuffled around from home to home, and never even knew their parents, as I know I could have had it so much worse! As a child I felt happy and relieved to be with some family, but what I feel today is a lot of gratitude for being rescued from strangers.

Since the FACT meetings didn't take off the way I planned, I just kept the website and gave FACT to God, knowing it would all work out in His way and His time, not mine. I was not concerned about it. My marriage and my home came first, and I was thoroughly happy with Larry. My time with him was what was most important to me. I remember always telling him that I wish I could stay with him forever in that precious moment, whether it was on the Harley, or being wrapped up in his arms. I never wanted our time together to end, and neither did he. They say time flies when you're having fun, and that must be true, as I now wonder where the time went. It went way too fast with him!

One thing I do know though, is that his memory will always live on in my heart. My heart broke when I lost him, but only because I have so many happy memories of us together. And I also know I will see him someday in Heaven!

Normal?

I was still trying to get pregnant until 2003, but my perspective on the dream of a child changed once I completely surrendered to my purpose of helping foster children. I came to realize that my dream child was largely a way to heal the hurt from my childhood. Though it may have helped some, in reality I would be living through that child instead of being a whole and healthy person. I believe another reason I wanted a family of my own was so I could feel normal like everyone else. Normal like everyone else? What is normal? I don't believe there is any such thing as normal. And I definitely don't want to be like the society norms I see around me today! Normal? *Normal is just a setting on a washing machine!*

A lot of that thinking had to do with my own fears of rejection, feeling like I had to be like others to be accepted. I felt different. Well, my experience was different! What can I say? I got what I got, and *it is what it is*, which is my quick version of the serenity prayer. I have grown so much since that time, both emotionally and spiritually. I do not need other people's acceptance today to feel ok with myself. It is always nice when people like me, but I like myself enough today to be ok when they don't. I don't take it personal today. *I get my self-worth from within as a child of God today, not from people.* The insecurities I had years ago largely seems like nonsense to me now. Larry had a positive influence on me in that way, as what people thought of him rolled right off his back. He knew who he was, and today I know who I am. That is true freedom! I heard other people talking about this issue when I was younger, but I just didn't get it then, but I do now. *Thank God!*

FACT...The Desire of My Heart

I realize now that helping foster children is more healing and rewarding for me than having a physical child could ever have been. There is no way one child of my own could give me the satisfaction I have gotten from knowing that many, many foster children can be helped from **FACT**. As **FACT** evolved into a book, I had a better sense of my purpose. I knew the **FACT** book was my real baby. *Most importantly, I realized that God in His Infinite wisdom knew the true desire of my heart long before I did! Wow! Hallelujah! I finally get it! God's ways are not our ways. He sees so much deeper and knows me so much better than I know myself, which today I am so grateful for!*

More importantly than even helping foster children, is the supreme joy I have from knowing that Jesus is happy with the work I have done. I rarely talk about my work, but when I do people look at me rather strangely, like they don't understand why I would want to do that. They sometimes look at me like I am an alien! It doesn't impress me much one way or the other what people think of my work because I know what I am doing, and I only need God's approval. I am both proud and humbled to be fulfilling God's purpose. I am proud because I know how much work I put into it, and humbled that God called me to do this work. I could have ignored the calling, but I didn't... "Here I am Lord, send me." My supreme joy is pleasing God. Everything else pales in comparison to that. Jesus is the one true love of my life, and I look forward to hearing Him say to me, "well done, my faithful servant."

I have sometimes said I know God called me to do this work, but I wish he would have called someone else! This certainly has not been an easy calling, not one I would have volunteered for, but He did call me and I decided to answer the call. *"Hello, this is God; would you please help my children?" "Yes, I will."*

A FACT Message from God

While visiting the Little Rose Chapel in December 1996, I was led to go outside and take a picture, of what I did not know, but it soon became apparent that God gave me a message about FACT. Look closely, and you will see ten lines. This happened three years before I even began forming FACT, and seven years before the completion of FACT and the Ten Stepping Stones. God knew long before I did what FACT would be, and that is a fact! God, You are so incredible! When I showed this to the woman at the Little Rose Chapel she told me nobody else had taken this picture before. Amazing! I was blown away by how amazing this was!

CAROL LUCAS

FACT Dormant

FACT had been dormant since 2000. It was a seed in the ground that would eventually grow into a beautiful flower. *I surrendered it to God and went about my busy life, trusting Him to work it out in His time and His way, which He did!*

In 1999 when we were forming *FACT*, Glen, Pam, and I came up with the *Seven Stones* for the format, but Glen wanted a 12-step program, which we argued about. I am normally an easy-going person, but I stood my ground on this issue. We agreed to disagree, and let it be. I wanted something unique. I wasn't happy with the *Seven Stones* or a 12-step format. *I surrendered FACT to God and knew that in His time and His way it would unfold beautifully and perfectly. GO WITH THE FLOW... THE FLOW IS LOVE....*

John Dunn and the Completion of FACT

In April 2004 I got an email from John Dunn, a young man from Canada who had heard about *FACT* and wanted to form meetings using a 12-step format, but instead of arguing about this issue like I did with my brother, I suggested we collaborate, which John agreed to. I did not want to see *FACT* divided. John and I became friends and talked on the phone, and after praying about it, I felt very strongly that *FACT* should be a step meeting, and that somehow the *Seven Stones* would be incorporated into the steps. My feeling was right. I prayed a lot about, as I really wanted *FACT* to be done right, and after much thought and prayer, I put together what is now the *Ten Stepping Stones*. I asked John if he would like to be a contributing founder of *FACT* since he was involved in forming this, which he humbly accepted.

John is a strong advocate in Canada where he lives, which I was very impressed by. He is very driven in his purpose.

It has never ceased to amaze me how things have worked out with FACT.

God has always worked things out for this work, which ultimately is His work.

The Ten Stepping Stones
On the Bridge to Healing

1. *We recognize we have been injured from our foster care experience, that we are powerless over our past and our lives are unmanageable.*

2. *Come to realize we cannot heal alone, that only a Power greater than ourselves could restore order, hope, and sanity to our lives.*

3. *Make a decision to turn our lives over to the care of God as we understand Him.*

4. *Make a searching and fearless emotional inventory of our foster care experience to discover the nature of the damage.*

5. *Share this inventory with God and another human being.*

6. *Work through our anger, hurt, and pain.*

7. *Become aware of how our injuries hurt others and accept responsibility for our responses to the trauma we suffered.*

8. *Continue to take personal inventory and become willing to let go of our resentments.*

9. *Seek through prayer and meditation to improve our relationship with God as we understand Him, praying only for knowledge of His will for us and the power to carry that out.*

10. *Having had a spiritual awakening as a result of these Stepping Stones, we reach out to other former foster children and practice these principles in our lives.*

CAROL LUCAS

On the Bridge to Healing

It was also during this time that the idea of On the Bridge to Healing came about. This idea came about through a Daily Word devotional I found while cleaning a woman's house. I happened to notice it on her bedside and picked it up to read the devotion for the day, which spoke of Jesus being the bridge over troubled waters, and I said, "wow!" God did it again! I am always surprised and amazed how things work out when I trust Him. It was perfect—foster children walking across the bridge to healing. While doing the original Seven Stones, my brother had the idea of foster children going through an arch made of seven stones, but that did not seem appropriate to me. I thought the idea of a bridge had a more natural flow to it, and apparently God did too!

Will We Ever Get Over It?

The subtitle on the **FACT** book, *Will We Ever Get Over It?* evolved as I was talking with people on the phone who were sharing stories. So many people sharing their story said to me, *"I don't think I will ever get over it,"* or *"do you think we ever really get over it?"* I always responded by saying, *"I'm not sure we ever really ever completely get over it, but we can get beyond it."* I hope my reply made as much sense to them as it did to me years ago in therapy when I asked Frank the same question. I didn't want to sound negative by saying, "no, you never get over it," so I left it as a question for people. Will we ever get over it? Maybe, maybe not, but having the *Bridge to Healing* as the main title certainly implies that there is hope for healing! **With God's Love guiding us across the bridge, there is always Hope!**

Busy, Busy, Busy...

From 2003 until 2010 I was busy finishing up with school. I was often up late doing homework because I wanted to spend time with Larry during the day. I was also still working and paying for my classes, which I know Larry appreciated since he had all the other financial responsibilities. He was supportive of my schooling and my involvement with *FACT*, and always encouraged me with both. I know he prayed for me a lot when I was taking difficult classes, especially Statistics and French. I am amazed I made it through those classes! I never once thought of giving up on school. I just kept persevering, one class at a time. My top priority was my marriage and home though, not school or *FACT*. I never wanted Larry to ever feel he wasn't the most important part of my life, because he was. His love was like the fuel I needed to keep forging ahead. It truly was.

Larry's Retirement

Larry retired in 2007, which we were both happy and relieved about. I noticed an immediate change in Larry once he retired, like a monkey was off his back. He was more relaxed and less stressed, which was good for both of us. Him being retired meant he was home, and we had more time together, which I loved! He even started taking me to school, which I appreciated. I hated the long ride all by myself, and I just loved being with Larry anytime and/or anywhere. We started going on long Harley rides now that he was retired, which was nice! Life got much more mellow for both of us. I felt less stressed knowing he was less stressed. I remember telling him that I was glad he was retiring, even if it meant less money. We would get by all right, and we would see more of each other. The saying, *'you can't buy love,'* is so true! We had more money when he was working, but we didn't get to see each other as much, so I was quite happy to see him retired. He meant more to me than the $ bill, and he knew it!

A Trip Down Memory Lane

Larry loved driving a lot, so we decided to take a trip to Illinois for a family visit, and I decided while we were there to take a trip down memory lane to visit ISSCS, the children's home I was in as a young girl. I left the home in 1963, and this was 2009, forty-six years later! I already knew the home had closed in 1979, as I had sent off for my state file from ISSCS while I was in therapy in 1997, so I was not all that surprised to see that the cottages were now various businesses, but what did surprise me was the immediate emotional reaction to the home, especially as I was walking down the sidewalks. Though *strange and surreal* do not adequately express how I felt while visiting my old *home*, they are the closest words I can find.

Everything came back to me, how I used to stare at the cracks in the sidewalks while I was walking, having such strong feelings of ambivalence about my mom, saying, *"step on a crack; you break your mother's back."* My immediate emotional reaction when I first started walking the grounds was sadness, deep sadness, for the little girl who felt so abandoned by her own mother, so lost and alone. What happened after this feeling of sadness was even more surprising, though it shouldn't have been, considering all I have written about suppressing my emotions as a child. Immediately after this feeling of sadness came over me and tears came to my eyes, I instantly shut them off and just kept on walking, which I realized was exactly what happened while I was a child there. I could not or would not let myself cry. I had to be strong! To be vulnerable and cry would mean I wouldn't make it, that I wouldn't survive. It is amazing what children do to survive trauma. It saddens me now to think of myself as that little girl who was so sad.

While I was at ISSCS I decided to visit the museum, which was interesting. I started talking with a woman there who informed me I could get the ISSCS book from a woman who had worked there, so I made plans to do that. I also found out there were reunions at the home, which Larry and I attended twice. I walked over to the playground where I had spent so much time as a young girl, but since I was only six when I was put in the home, I only vaguely remember playing there. I am sure the reason I only have vague memories of playing there is also because I was so emotionally detached. My coping mechanism was dissociation, which I believe I continually did while playing.

I use the words strange and surreal to describe how I felt on my trip down memory lane, because it felt so strange after all those years to be back there. I was placed there in 1961, and here it was 2009. It had been forty-eight years ago! It felt strange to be there as an adult, and to be in touch with the child who had been there. For the first time I felt like the adult and child connected, which was both sad and enlightening. I'm not sure I can adequately express what I felt, but I do know it was a turning point in my recovery.

As I was sadly walking along, I told myself, *"it's ok; I am here for you, and I will never abandon you."* I also thought how nice it would have been had I had an adult reassuring me as a young girl, preferably my own mother, which further saddened me. But I have learned in my recovery, that when little Carol is insecure and feeling lost and abandoned, I can be there for her. No, it isn't fair that I didn't get that emotional support when

I needed it as a child, but I must deal with my reality, which is that I was abandoned as a child by my mother, and now must find a way to resolve that, and this *adult to child self-therapy* works for me.

I also have Jesus, Who will never abandon me. I may have felt like there was nobody there for me as a child, but I know today that Jesus never abandoned me. He was there all the time, even though I could not see Him or touch Him. He sent me many human Angels along the way to love and care for me, when my own mother couldn't or wouldn't. He was there in the way I was provided for by the people at the home. No, I did not want to be there without my family, but who knows how much worse things could have gotten at home, and at least I was not in that awful foster home on Rose Hill! His hands and feet were the people who took care of me while I was there, which I am grateful for today. Thank You Jesus, for sending me human Angels!

It felt surreal to be there at the children's home after all those years. *Was I really here as a child? Did I really go through all that trauma when I was a six-year- old child? Maybe it was just a bad dream? No, it was not a bad dream, Carol. You were really here. I thought, how could I have survived this?*

I know today that I survived to the best of my ability as a young child. I could not have done any better than I did. I was just a child, way too young be able to reason or make sense out of the trauma. I did not even understand it was trauma then, but I most definitely do now. It was a trauma that no child should have to go through, but I did, and somehow survived. I recently talked with a trained therapist over the phone about my childhood, and she explained very well how as an adult I can now fully comprehend the trauma and deal with it, both emotionally and intellectually. She explained to me how the trauma and all the feelings attached to it were put in a safe place as a child, until I was old enough to deal with it. For instance, even though I do feel emotional while writing this, I also understand intellectually how the emotions are attached to the trauma, and why I felt the way I did. I had no way of understanding this as a child, but I can now as an adult. Wow! It is very strengthening and healing to be able to do this.

Although it was strange, surreal, and extremely sad to be back in my past at the children's home, it was also where the past met the present and the future. By being there, I was able to see just how far I had come from having such an unstable childhood, being thrown in foster care, and being a self-destructive young adult, to maturing into woman who was now living a very stable life with a stable man. That is amazing to me now! The past also brought me to the future, where I made more sound decisions, including doing the *FACT* book. I would never have dreamed years ago that I would have accomplished the things I have, and yet here I am writing another book. *For any former foster child reading my story, I want you to know that if there was hope for me, there is hope for you! But I believe our only true HOPE is with Our Heavenly Father.*

Write the Book Now!

I already had ideas about doing a book and had been praying about it, but was unsure as to the when and how, but God let me know in His way. While coming into my kitchen one Spring Day in 2009, I heard a voice say in my spirit, "write the book now." I was so shocked by what I heard, but then I heard the voice say again, "write the book now." Wow! OK God! I had always thought that there should be FACT meetings before a book was written, but apparently God had a better idea! No, I am not schizophrenic, but I do hear the voice of God sometimes, and I heard Him loud and clear that day! Why now? Well, why not now? It made perfect sense once I thought about it. The book would not only have all the material in it needed for former foster children to form their own meetings, but it would also have all the stories of former foster children in it for others to relate to. FACT meetings would much more likely be formed this way! It truly was Fostered Adult Children Together! Wow! God, You did it again! I am so amazed at how He works!

The Beginning of the FACT Book

When I first embarked on this venture, I was not even sure where to begin, but when I began praying about it and was led back to my childhood at ISSCS, my prayers were answered, and the book unfolded. I was informed of a book about ISSCS while I was visiting there, which I ordered through a woman who was involved with the book, who gave me the phone number of another woman involved with the book, who sent me the ISSCS reunion list. I got started on the **FACT** book in the Autumn of 2009, a few months after my visit to ISSCS. I started calling phone numbers on the list, which is how I got the first fifteen stories for the book.

I also had the pleasure of talking with a girl who had been in my cottage, and she remembered me! The reason we remembered each other so easily was because I defended her once when someone called her a bad name. I yelled, "don't you call her that; she's my friend!" I find that incredible, considering how shy and withdrawn I was during my time there. Although she chose not to share a story, it was nice taking a trip down memory lane with her!

I believe there is a special bond between children in foster care, something that is unspoken but apparent in the way we connect. We are all in the same boat trying to survive the storm and need each other to survive. Children often get more support from each other than they do from the parents even in functional homes, so it is easy to understand how it would be even more prevalent with foster children. Children can get support from their parents in normal homes, but foster children are not normal children in normal homes; they are in situations in which they often must fend for themselves, especially in children's home, where there are so many children in one cottage.

Although I didn't get all the love in foster care that I needed, I am grateful for what I did get. One thing about being in foster care, is that you are so used to receiving crumbs that you appreciate more if and/or when you are fortunate enough to get it. Nothing is taken for granted, at least I know it is that way with me. I know people who have had everything handed to them, yet they don't seem to fully appreciate it because it's all they know. As my husband told someone, "Carol came from humble beginnings." I know what it is like to have little, so I am grateful for everything! *I thank God for all His blessings!*

Being a Ghost Writer and Empath

What I became was a *ghost writer,* which a publisher told me is a rare gift. Wow! That was quite a compliment, considering the hours I spent on the phone talking to get stories. It took a lot of time, patience, and empathy, which I did not lack to do the stories for the **FACT** book.

I only recently realized that I am an **emotional empath,** which is a double-edged sword. I am glad I am compassionate and empathetic, but I am so empathetic that I tend to take on others pain as if it is my own, which is not healthy for me! I am now learning a lot about boundaries, so I don't harm myself emotionally. I am always needing to remind myself that although I can be empathetic, it is not my responsibility to take on another person's pain. *I can care, but I cannot carry! I have gained much wisdom about this since I wrote the FACT book, thank God!*

From the Autumn of 2009 until May 2010 when I graduated from college, was a busy, busy time for me. I was beginning the **FACT** book, and finishing up with school, which included an internship that I did at a girl's home. The last credit I had left was spent doing a research paper on *orphanages vs. foster care,* which was interesting since I spent time in both as a child. I was so happy to finally be done with school! I was probably more relieved to be done than proud of my accomplishment, but I was also proud. I think there was a part of me that thought I shouldn't be too proud about my success, but Larry put me right in my place about that!

Graduating from College!

When I told Larry I didn't want to attend the graduation ceremony, he insisted! He said, "Carol, if you don't go to the ceremony, you will regret it. You should be proud of yourself for what you did and take part in the ceremony." I always listened to Larry, so I ordered the cap and gown, and attended the ceremony. I am so glad now that I did. Larry was right; if I had not gone, I would have regrated it. It was quite memorable for me, having my name called out for graduating with high honors. Wow! Larry was in the audience watching me as I walked up to get my diploma, which made me feel good. I only wish my dad could have seen this too, as I know he would have been just as proud as Larry. The day ended with Larry taking me out to eat, which was nice. Larry really made me special that day. Wow! I really did it! I graduated from college! ***Thank God!***

Larry's Love

I always loved being with Larry, no matter what we did. Nobody has ever made me feel so loved and secure as he did, not even my dad, which is saying a lot. Larry gave me all the security I didn't receive as a child emotionally, spiritually, and monetarily. He was so protective of me. I miss that more than anything now that he is gone. I miss his presence in my life more than I can express. It is an ache in my heart and soul that I don't think time will ever mend. He told our friend that when he passed away, he didn't want me alone, that I need a man to take care of me. Now that he has been gone two years, I am beginning to feel the impact of those words. When he first passed away, I swore I would never marry again, but I am now beginning to believe I may have to eat those words. I wonder if I can ever love again, but it really is not a question of whether I can; it is a question of whether I will let myself open my heart again to love. Nobody will ever take Larry's place in my heart, but that doesn't mean I can't love someone else. Being with another man will never lessen my love for Larry. It will remain forever in my heart. The reason Larry was able to say that to our friend was because he knew that. Larry knew me better than anyone has even known me. He seen my heart and understood how broken it would be with him gone, but he also knew I would eventually want and need to share my love and life with another man. *If and/or when that happens is in God's Hands!*

Larry's Health Crisis

I wish I could rewind the clock and go back to February 2010, as this was the beginning of a health nightmare for Larry and me. Larry accidentally inhaled some smoke from a moldy piece of wood we were burning in our wood burning stove on the back porch, and got fungal pneumonia, which is usually fatal. Months went by without knowing what was wrong, which was incredibly stressful for both of us. From February until July, he was suffering from a health condition he didn't know he had, congestive heart failure. He went to three doctors who didn't diagnose him with it, even though he had all the symptoms of it. How inept can these doctors be?! I still get angry when I think of all the suffering he went through because of these stupid doctors! We were both praying diligently for answers, and finally one night while in prayer I felt led to tell Larry he should see a natural doctor we had seen before, so he went to the doctor, who probably saved his life by healing the fungal condition in his lungs, but he was still terribly ill. I was praying so hard for him, begging God for help, often late at night by his bedside. Our prayers were finally answered one day when Larry went to visit a friend, who told him he had all the symptoms of congestive heart failure. Larry read an article online that night that said, "if you have all these symptoms, go to ER right away or you won't make it through the night." The night this happened I went to bed begging God with all my might to please, please, help us! *God heard my plea!*

Larry called me the next morning to let me know he was at the hospital, and I freaked when he told me had congestive heart failure. I was so upset! He told me he was so bad he could barely make it out of the car and walk into the hospital, that people were all around him when they saw how bad he was. Lord, why didn't he wake me up?! I would have gladly taken him to the hospital! He was my husband, for crying out loud! He knew I had been losing sleep almost as much as he had been and didn't want to wake me up. I gave him a chewing out over that!

I will always remember that day at the hospital. I was so relieved he was finally getting the help he needed, but I had such a fear of losing him that I broke down in tears by his bedside, which I am sure he was quite touched by. He had to be transported to another hospital where there was a cardiac specialist, and I stayed with him the whole time. Because of my childhood, I was extremely sensitive to him needing emotional support from me during this time. I remember how alone I had felt as a child when I was sick in the hospital and didn't want him to feel that way.

A Turning Point in Our Marriage

This was a good turning point in our marriage. It might seem odd to say this, but it's true. Larry had always been in robust health up until now. Our life and marriage had been smooth sailing, but now we were faced with his health crisis that needed constant managing. I knew Larry would never manage this all this himself, so I did everything I could to help him eat the right foods, watch his water intake, and exercise, but it was still a struggle for him. I made Larry my top priority, even though I was doing the **FACT** book.

The reason I say this was a good turning point in our marriage, is because our love deepened throughout this time. I remember going to the hospital and crying by his bedside, which he was so touched by. I was so afraid of losing him. I stayed overnight with and even slept in bed with him, which he loved. My devotion to him stirred his heart toward me even more, knowing I was there for him, for better or for worse. All the Harley rides, Christmas gifts, my fancy wedding ring, didn't compare to holding him in my arms and telling him I loved him. It was like music to his ears! He used to say, "I love you, Dolly," which was like music to my ears!

One thing I know for certain, is that Larry knew I loved him. I took care of him like a mother hen, which he loved, loved, loved! I have a very nurturing spirit and gave him all the love he needed and wanted. I loved doing everything for him, and I especially loved our cuddle time together. I loved tucking Larry into bed and rubbing his back. He loved that so much, and I loved it too. I would often fall asleep myself while rubbing his back. There was a lot of physical closeness between us. We cuddled and snuggled a lot 😊

Writing the FACT Book

With school now behind me, I was able to devote my time to doing the *FACT* book, which I became passionate about to the point of being driven. I put the term *a purpose driven life* to a whole new level, which was both good and bad. It was good because I truly had a passion to do the book, but it was bad because I had poor boundaries at the time and didn't take care of myself physically or emotionally. Instead of taking my time like I have with this book, I was so driven that it felt like I was almost manic. I know now that I should have slowed down, relaxed more, taken some breaks when I needed to, and most importantly, I should have been getting some therapy while doing the book. I am so much of an empath that I was starting to internalize other people's trauma and pain as if it were mine, which was bad, bad, bad. I not only was doing story after story, but I was also working on my own story. That was way too much trauma for me all at once, but I didn't recognize the danger until it was too late. Larry tried to warn me to slow down, but I didn't listen. Today I better understand what happened. I was getting more and more anxious with each new story, and the anxiety was driving me. It reached a point where I felt compulsive, like I had to keep pushing myself. Normally I always listened to Larry, but I didn't this time, and paid the price. But I also learned a much needed and valuable lesson about boundaries, not only family boundaries, but emotional boundaries with myself. Why is it I always have to learn things the hard way!? What's important is that I did learn, and what doesn't kill you makes you stronger!

Boundaries

I now realize that the reason I had poor boundaries while doing the book, was because I never learned boundaries in my young life, especially in the first six years of my life. Boundaries, in a home with ten children and absent parents? Are you kidding?! There is no way I learned anything about boundaries in my original home. The lack of boundaries is so deeply ingrained in me, that I didn't realize how poor my boundaries were until I was almost drowning from lack of them. Where did I get the idea that I had to do all this work without taking care of myself? Where did I get the idea that I was responsible for taking on other people's pain? Where did I get the idea that I was not worth taking care of, that I had to sacrifice my own well-being for other people's benefit? It all came from my childhood.

Deep down, I felt like I was not worth taking care of. It has always been easier for me to care for others to care for myself, but not so much today. Today I am worth taking care of! And I am not responsible for other people's pain! They have their emotions, and I have mine, and I am only responsible for mine! I can care about people, but it is not my responsibility to carry them! It is not my load to carry! How incredibly freeing it is to finally get this, to really in my heart and soul get this! Wow! It may have taken me a long time to finally get it, but it was worth the wait! I am so much freer today! Boundaries are so important to me today, that I always say, *"if a boundary doesn't work, a wall will!"*

A Family Gathering with My Baby Brother

While writing my own story for the FACT book, I began to feel deep sadness about my family, so much so that my heart felt very heavy. The sadness was so deep that it felt unbearable. I know now that I was grieving the past, which would heal me more in the long run, but at the time it was awful. Then a miracle happened right out of the blue! Our family began communicating, which had rarely happened throughout the years. I thought God had answered my prayer! Maybe there is at least a glimmer of hope for our family! *God did answer my prayer, but not in the way I expected.*

In early March 2011, I got a surprise in the mail from my younger brother, a book called *In Cold Blood*, which is a true family murder story. My first initial reaction was surprise, then immediately following the surprise was a gut sense of uneasiness and anxiety. Why would my own brother send me such a book? It didn't make sense, but something started stirring in me that made me uncomfortable. I hadn't even heard from this brother in about ten years, and he sent me a book about a family that was murdered! When I eventually asked him why he sent the book, he said, "he was sending out books to everyone, and thought I might like this one." Really? Why would I enjoy reading a book about a family murder? I wanted to believe he meant no harm but was unsure of his intention. Was he trying to put fear in me, or was I being paranoid? I could not remember if I had ever told my brother that I had almost been murdered in Detroit, and he said he never knew about the attack when I asked him, but even if he didn't know, I still thought it was creepy to receive a book like that. Really creepy. **I believe today it was a message to our family.**

I call this a *family gathering* to be sarcastic, not sentimental. My brother told me on the phone that he decided to leave his wife and family and come back home to Illinois to live. I didn't know my brother well enough to foresee what he was up to, and apparently the rest of my family didn't either, or they would never have allowed them into their lives and homes. My dear young brother, the baby of our brood, ended up going through our family like a train wreck that a tornado had caused. He did so much damage throughout our family that it still hasn't recovered from it, and probably never will. The last thing our family needed was more division, hate, and chaos. What our family needed was healing, but instead it was rolling off the tracks, ready to crash.

My brother stayed with my sister in Illinois for a couple weeks, who gave him money that she didn't really have to give, and he in turn robbed her and her husband while he was there. He also went over to my nephew's house and did the same. My sister called and told me she couldn't handle our brother in her home anymore and wanted him out, so Larry and I decided to pick him up and bring him to our home. We were going to let him stay with us until he could get it together, but after only two days of him being in our home, I called my sister and told her I could not handle him here. She said, "I warned you!" And I said, "Yes, you did, and I should have listened!" The sign I have outside that says, *Family Welcome, Family By Appointment Only,* should have been there then! It takes me at least a week to get ready for a family visit, and another week to recuperate afterward!

While my brother was in our home, he managed to rob my husband of clothes, some expensive watches he owned, and an expensive gold and diamond bracelet Larry gave me, along with miscellaneous items. I forgive him today because I understand he was mentally off at the time; in fact, he later told me he can't remember stealing from us. I'm not sure if this is true or not, but I did read that memory loss is common with someone who is manic, and he was extremely manic at the time, so he could have been telling me the truth. God only knows for sure.

I heard him making a lot of noise the second night he was here, and when I got up to see what he was doing, I found all the lights on, and him standing in our kitchen eating peanut butter out of a jar. I told him to turn out the lights and go to bed, that we sleep in our home. He started crying when he went to lay on the couch, then he started acting like a young child wanting his mommy when I went over to console him, so I calmed him down like a mother soothing her child, which was rather strange. I remember him telling me that he sometimes wished he could leave this world, which saddened me. My brother has bi-polar disorder and decided before he left home that he no longer needed his medication, which was a huge mistake! He was so manic he was like a tornado looking for a place to land!

What was particularly disturbing to me about my brother was the way he stared at me. I can be naïve but thank God my husband wasn't! Larry told me later that he made sure I was never left alone with my brother while he was here. Thank God for Larry's protection! Considering the sexual abuse my brother went through in his past, I shouldn't be surprised that he had poor boundaries, but it was still unsettling for me, and very creepy.

We decided to take my brother back to Illinois and help him get settled in an apartment near my sister, so he got his stuff packed, but we should have checked his luggage before we left! On the way back to Illinois my brother was acting goofy, saying he knew how mentally ill he was. He was sitting in the back seat of our car making out a list of all the mental illnesses he had, and I added one more, telling him I thought he had an attachment disorder, which he was laughing about.

I will say, at least my brother knows he is mentally ill. He is not in denial; he just doesn't know what to do about his mental illness, and neither did any of us. I never even knew this brother well, so I was shocked at the severity of his mental illness. It broke my heart to see him like this, knowing it was all caused by the trauma he had gone through as a two-year-old child when he was taken away from our mom, put in foster care, and sexually abused by Jean after our dad died. It was sad for me to see him like this. I was honestly more sad than angry, which surprised some of my family, but I am the one in the family with the big compassionate heart. I can see beyond the surface of things and see into the heart of people the same way Jesus did, which was why I was able to forgive him.

My husband and I helped my brother find an apartment when we arrived in Illinois. He also got a job at a Sears store he had worked at as a young man years ago. My brother and I found the house we had lived in as young children while we were there and went inside to see it with the present owner's permission. I could not remember much about the house or living there, but my brother did for some reason, even though he was younger than me. I only have vague memories of my young years in that home, and I only had a vague sense of living there while I was visiting. It felt strange. Did I really live here as a young child?

We also went to Hammond and looked inside the house I lived in as a teenager. I remembered that house very well. While walking along with my brother and husband, I noticed that my brother kept trying to come between us, which I know is a trait of a child with an attachment order. We also had a nice visit with my sister. My sister, brother, and I were the three remaining at home when our dad died, so there was a rather special bond between us. After spending the night at my sister's, we dropped my brother off at his new apartment and came home to Michigan. We felt good about helping my brother and thought everything would be fine with him. Wrong! This was only the beginning of the train wreck. It was also the beginning of some serious PTSD for me.

Post Traumatic Stress Disorder

CAROL LUCAS

The Woodard Tornado Train Wreck

The train wreck got worse shortly after we got back home. There were so many family dynamics whirling around in this *Woodard tornado train wreck* that it is difficult to talk about, let alone write about, but I will do my best. Right before my younger brother decided to leave California to come back to Illinois, he had been in touch with our niece, who is the daughter of my brother who died tragically in 1990. I was on Facebook a lot back then, not so much for the social aspect but to find people who wanted to share stories in the FACT book, and decided to contact my niece, the one Steve had been in touch with on FB. The only time I had ever seen her was at a family reunion in 1977, when she was an infant, so I was happy to contact her. We talked on the phone a couple times, but I said something about my brother's death that upset her. I explained to her that I was only saying what had been told to me at the time of his death, which was true. We were able to smooth things over, but I knew she was upset over what I had said. I called her again not long after this, and that is when holy hell broke loose. This was the eye of the tornado! And it did a lot of damage in my family.

Apparently, my brother thought he would make the train wreck worse and told our niece that I had written something in the ***FACT*** book about my brother's death, which had my niece thoroughly angry at me. She threatened to sue me over this, which had me thoroughly upset and anxious. There went that budding relationship! It flew right out the window thanks to my brother, along with any trust for my brother. I called my brother and started yelling at him over what he did, that it was none of his business what I did! I was so angry at him over this! I felt I had a right to share my story in the most honest and truthful way possible, and I was angry that people interfered like that. It was *my* story!

My brother had stepped over a boundary, and I let him know it. I felt violated. I believe that my brother was purposely trying to stir up trouble in the family, which can be a trait of someone with an attachment disorder. He tried putting a guilt trip on his siblings, telling me that our whole family had kicked him to the curb, that he had it worse than anyone else in the family, which is nonsense. We were all kicked to the curb. None of us had it easy when we were put in foster care. He also blamed me and my sister for the evil sexual abuse that Jean dumped on him after our dad passed away, which was also nonsense. How could it have been our fault he was getting abused, when the abuse took place while we were gone? I told him he should have said something to us about the abuse and we would done something, gotten social services involved, but he insisted on blaming us. When I talked with my therapist about this, she reassured me I was not responsible, that I was only a 16-year-old girl, not an adult caregiver.

I may have known intellectually that the abuse was not my fault, but emotionally I was still upset over it. This is a good example of me being an emotional empath. I felt my brother's pain so much that I internalized it. As angry as I was for things he did to our family during this time, what I really felt more than anything was heartsick over how his childhood abuse destroyed him. I have a picture of me holding my brother as a baby, and it made me feel so sad. He even told me that he remembered me holding him as a baby, and that he always felt comfortable with me. He also told me I was his favorite sibling because of this. I was torn between being angry at him over the train wreck he caused in our family and being compassionate toward him. I told him I forgave him when we eventually talked again, but that he would have to regain my trust. One thing I know for certain though, is that it is necessary for me to have strong boundaries with him. I feel so sad that everything happened to him, but he is not a safe person for me to be around or even to be in touch with. But God bless him because I do love him.

Me holding my brother Steve

Sadly, because of all the turmoil my brother caused in our family, nobody wants anything to do with him except me, and I only have minimal contact through occasional emails and phone texts. I don't do this out of hatred; I do it out of love and respect for my own sanity. Today I have healthy boundaries. Yes, it is sad what happened to my brother, but I can't carry him or his past. There may be people who think I hate my family because I don't want them in my life a lot, but that isn't the case at all. It is because I love them that I can't handle them. I feel too much pain about our family because I am an emotional empath. I must respect my limitations and boundaries. Today I am very guarded with family because I love and respect myself.

I have my *Friends Welcome, Family by Appointment Only* sign in my yard for a good reason! I didn't have the luxury of taking a week to get ready for his visit, but I sure needed it! And with all the emotional trauma his visit caused, it took me a long time to recover. Boundaries, strong boundaries. And if a boundary doesn't work, a wall will!

An Avalanche

After having it out with my brother over causing turmoil in my life, I started having severe anxiety, so much so that I thought I should seek some therapy. I decided to stop by a church on the way from a job one day, to see if I could talk with the pastor. I thought maybe he could help, since I had talked with him in the past when I attended the church. The

CAROL LUCAS

anxiety was rising high, and I knew I needed help, someone who could calm me down. I was not doing well at all. I went into the church and briefly told the pastor I needed to talk with him, and a woman overheard us speaking and asked me to come with her. She led me into her office, and I unloaded on her, telling her everything that was happening with me and in our family. Then when I explained to her about my brother sending me the book *In Cold Blood,* and my close death experience in 1992, she said, "bingo!" I looked at her and said, "what do you mean, bingo?" She explained to me that she thought I was being triggered by the past trauma, which I didn't fully understand. It had happened so many years ago that I thought it was over, done and forgotten, but I was wrong, very wrong. This was the beginning of some serious PTSD for me, that I almost didn't recover from.

I started seeing this therapist on a regular basis after this, but I didn't take her advice early on about taking an anti-depressant for anxiety and insisted on no medication. That proved to be a mistake. I also didn't take her advice about slowing down on the book. That also proved to be a big mistake. She tried to make me understand that I needed to take better care of myself, but I didn't listen, which was a huge mistake. I thought I could handle all of this, but I was so very wrong.

I was on emotional overload but didn't realize how much until it was too late. Shortly after I met this therapist my 16-year-old dog Trucker died, who I had since the time he was a puppy, and I grieving over his loss. I also explained to her about Larry almost dying the year before, which triggered my deep-seated fear of abandonment. I was also disappointed about an adoption that didn't work out with a boy who shared his story in my book, which was mostly due to his attachment disorder. My whole body was off hormonally, not only from being menopausal but from the emotional stress that affected my adrenals. I am emotional enough without all this added stress! I was left wondering what came first, the chicken or the egg? Did all the stress cause the physical issues, or did physical issues cause the stress? The only thing I knew for sure, was that the stress had made me a mess! A big hot mess!

The mess I was in was particularly scary because not only was I on emotional overload, but I was emotionally regressing back into my childhood to the point of not feeling safe. My dear husband was my strong rock and helped me a lot, but I couldn't seem to get a grip emotionally. I felt like the waves were taking me under, and I was going to drown in my past. It was so, so scary. I remember thinking, I am never going to get through this. I am going to be in this messed up emotional state forever. That was really scary. I felt so vulnerable, just like the little six-year-old girl who was put in foster care.

I prayed a lot for God to help me, but somewhere in my lost emotional state, I felt like even He had abandoned me. Where are you, Lord? I felt like Peter calling out to Jesus to help him when they were in a storm, fearing he was going to drown, but Jesus didn't come walking on the waves to calm me. The scariest part of all was feeling like Almighty God, My Heavenly Father, had abandoned me. Why won't You help me, Lord? If You won't help me, who will? I remember my older brother telling me, "Carol Ann, God is allowing you to go through this to better help you do this work for foster children, to make you fully understand foster children who have had it even worse than you." It was only by God's grace, many prayers, and Larry's love, that I eventually made it back to shore. Jesus had not abandoned me after all. I now realize that what my brother said is true, that God allowed my suffering so that I could more fully understand and be there for other foster children.

This happened in 2011 and it is now 2023. I am in EMDR therapy, understanding more deeply how my childhood affected me, how vulnerable I felt as a little girl in foster care, and healing that trauma.

CAROL LUCAS

Healing of the Memories

It was during this time that Larry encouraged me to do something called *Healing of the Memories*, which is done through Jesus. He had gone through this himself as a young adult and thought I would also benefit greatly from it. At this point I was willing do anything, as I was tired of the pain and suffering. I wanted healing. I wanted peace. *I did not have any high expectations from doing this; it was purely an act of faith, believing that Jesus would heal me, even if I didn't understand how.* The woman who I went through this with had years of experience and gave me great reviews of others who had been healed of their past, and she convinced me I would also be healed. All I had to do was believe. I thought, what do I have to lose, other than my sanity, if I don't at least give it a try. *I decided to take a leap of faith and trust Jesus.*

I believe the healing largely came about through my willingness to let go of all my resentments toward others who had hurt me, especially my mom and the pervert who sexually abused me. I did not want to carry the heavy baggage anymore and was ready to let it go. It was while doing *Healing of the Memories* that I believe I was finally let go of my resentment toward my mom. This is when the sidewalk truly ended. *Thank God!*

Even though I didn't fully realize at the time that I was being healed, I believe now that I was. I didn't fully realize that Jesus had healed me until I had completely gone through the PTSD trauma. I don't believe God usually sends thunder and lightning to get our attention; He usually works in quieter and gentler ways.

I always liked what Larry said about the Holy Spirit, that it was a gentle, wooing spirit. I agree with him. The Holy Spirit's voice is so soft and gentle that it often goes unheard, but we will hear it if we listen. I know today when I hear that gentle voice, and I listen.

I often remind myself of the night I heard the Holy Spirit speak to me, "Go With the Flow; the Flow is LOVE." God is LOVE and it Flows on.

My Rededication to Jesus

It was also during this time that I rededicated my life to Jesus. In 2004 I began taking a meditation class through an Indian guru, which I thought nothing of at the time. I just thought it would be a nice way to get more centered, but the problem came when I began putting my focus on this man instead of Jesus. I never put him on a pedestal like so many others did, but I got swayed too much into the Eastern religion while doing this and lost my spiritual roots. I told the woman I did *Healing of the Memories* with about my involvement with this guru, and she highly suggested that I renounce it, which I agreed to. I went into the chapel at the church and got on my knees, while her and Larry prayed over me. *As I was rededicating myself to Jesus, I felt ashamed for drifting away from Him, and fully realized the error I had made.* I left the church feeling like a burden had been lifted off my shoulders and I was free again. *I got lost and Jesus found me, again! I have jokingly said that Jesus had to use His staff on me to get my attention and stop me from wandering!*

I had been a Christian for years, but I became a stronger one after this. *Jesus is the one and only one for me.* I told my husband about a year before he passed that the longer I was away from that Indian guru, the more I realized how deceptive and wrong that spiritual path was for me. Larry smiled at me when I said that, as he had been praying about this for seven years before I finally seen the light. He was happy to have me back as the Christian woman he had married. I thanked Larry for his prayers, and our bond as man and wife deepened after this, primarily because of the Holy Spirit but also because I was honoring him and respecting him more as being the Christian man and husband. I learned a lot spiritually from this experience. *It is so easy to be deceived in this world if we don't rely on Jesus and the Holy Spirit. Today I listen to the Holy Spirit, and only the Holy Spirit.*

Still Suffering

I wish I could say that my bout with PTSD was over after doing *Healing of the Memories* and rededicating my life to Jesus, and continuing therapy, but it didn't end yet; in fact, it got worse before it got better. I was still suffering from severe anxiety, which I couldn't seem to get a grip on. I think a lot of it was due to lack of sleep, but again, what came first, the chicken or the egg? Was the anxiety causing me not to sleep, or was the lack of sleep causing the anxiety? It was both at this point, but initially it was the anxiety that was causing me not to rest. If only I could sleep well! The lack of sleep was taking its toll on me physically and emotionally. I am a highly sensitive person who requires a lot of sleep, so going without it was the worst thing for me. And I love to sleep!

This anxiety went on for about three months, before I finally reached a breaking point. I felt like I just couldn't take it anymore. I had enough!

It was at this point that I started feeling a little suicidal, which was really scary. I know I didn't really want to commit suicide, but I felt desperate. I told Larry how I was feeling, and he encouraged me to go in the hospital so I could get some help and get some medication, so I agreed but then left after only two days. I know I should have stayed, but I just couldn't stand being away from Larry and my home.

I am Amazing?

I will never forget something that happened while I was there. While in group therapy talking about being attacked, and writing this book for foster children, a girl said to me, *"you mean to tell me you were almost murdered, and you are writing a book for foster children? You are an amazing woman!"* I don't think I said anything to her, but I was thinking, yeah, I am so amazing that I am sitting here with you in a psyche ward! Seriously, I was feeling anything but amazing. What I was feeling was hopelessly crazy. Real amazing. Still, when this PTSD episode was over, I remembered what she said and took comfort in it. It was really quite a compliment; I just couldn't appreciate it at the time. I also realize now that when people tell me I am amazing for doing this book after everything I have gone through, it validates the past trauma, which I would rather minimize. There is a whole of truth to the saying, *what doesn't kill you makes you stronger.* I can certainly relate to it!

I thought I would be ok when I left the hospital, but things got worse. It truly does get darkest before the dawn. I couldn't seem to get a grasp on my anxiety. I felt like I was losing control, which was really scary. I felt like I was in a dark tunnel forever, with no light at the end of it. I felt hopeless, and to make matters worse, I was beating myself up over my condition, feeling like I was a crazy mental case, which affected my self-esteem. I hated myself for not being stronger. It got so bad that Larry called Kim and she told him to put me back in the hospital before they lost me. I was so overwhelmed by the anxiety that I got catatonic. I had reached my limit. Having read books on trauma since this happened, I now understand completely what happened. Although it was awful, I do realize I did a lot of healing and I made it through.

I could hardly utter a prayer for help to God at this point, but He heard the cry in my heart and gave me help.

Getting Some Help

I was in the hospital this time for three weeks, until the anxiety was under control, and I could relax some. I was put on medication, but unfortunately, I was also put on others medication for other disorders that I didn't have. Yes, I needed an anti-depressant and a sleep aide, but one of the doctors in there put me on medication for bi-polar disorder and schizophrenia, which I do not have. I am extremely sensitive to drugs of any kind, so this medicine I didn't need made me feel like a zombie. I probably would have only been in there for about a week had I abided by rules for me to go to group therapy, but all I wanted to do was lay in bed and rest, so I had to stay longer. All I wanted was to be alone in my shell where I felt safe. I remember people coming into my room and asking me if I heard voices, and I replied, "only yours." One woman there seemed bound and determined to make me a schizophrenic, but I persisted in telling her I wasn't. I have PTSD! I was so happy to get out of that place!

I hate writing about this traumatic time, but I got through it by the Grace of God and my husband. God bless my husband for staying by my side. My biggest fear was of being abandoned, and Larry knew that. He came every day to visit me until visiting hours were over, and continually reassured me that I would be all right. I will never forget him saying to me over and over, *"we're in this together."* He brought me SO much comfort during that horrible time. I cannot thank him enough for being there for me. It made all the difference in the world for me at that time. I told Larry, "I don't think I would have made it through that time without your love and support." I also told my therapist that she was my Angel during that time. *Larry and Kim were both my Angels during this time! Thank God!*

Diagnosed with PTSD

I was still somewhat anxious after I returned home, though nothing like I had been before I went in there. I was relieved to have a follow up appointment with a psychiatrist, who took one look at me and said, "you're not bi-polar or schizophrenic; what you have is PTSD." Hallelujah! I finally have a doctor who knows what she is doing! Kim knew I had PTSD, so I don't know why the doctors didn't listen to her when I was in the hospital. Although I wasn't thrilled about being labeled with PTSD, it was a relief to finally know what was wrong with me.

I didn't particularly like being labeled with PTSD at first, but I got past the stigma and was not only ok with it but was grateful that at least now I understood why I had such anxiety. I suffered with anxiety years ago after the attack happened but didn't understand PTSD, so at least now I understand what I have and can deal with it. You cannot fix something unless you know it is broke. I also felt better about the PTSD diagnosis once I found out it is not a mental illness. I just recently read a book on PTSD that explained it by using the analogy of a broken leg. If a leg is harmed to the point of it breaking, the same thing can happen with your emotional/mental psyche; it can reach a breaking point. My psyche had been broken and it needed to mend. It makes perfect sense when I think of it like this. What I find both sad and alarming, is that expected myself to not be affected by trauma. For crying out loud, I have been through so much trauma, yet acted like it was no big deal. I finally realized that I was a human being with limits. Believe me, with all the personality and mental disorders out there that I could have, I will take PTSD any day!

I continued to see my therapist for a few months after I got out of the hospital, and when I told her I felt bad about getting myself in such a mess, she said, "Carol, don't be hard on yourself. You got hit with an avalanche of crap that most people wouldn't have handled as well as you did." That made me feel better, but I still had a hard time feeling ok with what happened. I guess my pride was hurt and I felt humiliated. It was without a doubt a humbling experience. I found out I was human!

Where did I get the idea that I could handle everything I had been hit with, without beginning to unravel? Somewhere in my unconscious mind was still that little girl that felt she had to be so strong all the time, like I should have been able to handle the avalanche with no problem. I know people mean well when they tell me I am so strong, but I was far from strong when I went through this PTSD trauma; I was extremely vulnerable. What I realize today about myself, is that I am both vulnerable and strong. I often tell people that I am only strong because I am so vulnerable. I once asked a male friend of mine if I seemed tough, and he said, "no, you aren't tough, you're strong because you are a survivor." So true.

Chilling Out

I was ready to toss the **FACT** book right in the garbage when I returned home. This book was not worth my sanity! I didn't toss the book in the garbage, but I did set it down for a few months, and just relaxed. Larry and I went for long rides, sat and watched television, anything that was relaxing. I was still feeling rather insecure for a few months, but I slowly healed from the trauma of this avalanche. I had always been rather thin, so I started eating better, which had a positive effect on my health.

I began to realize that something in me had changed, but I can't fully express it in words. As painful as it was going through this PTSD trauma, I believe it ultimately healed me more. I can now say with certainty that I am not the same person I was in 2011. *And Thank God I'm not!*

I strongly believe that *Healing of the Memories* did help me, even though I didn't know it at the time I was going through it. Larry smiled when I told him this, and said he knew it would. Another beautiful thing about going through this ordeal, was that there was an even stronger bond between Larry and me afterward. I always knew Larry loved me a lot, but to have him so wholeheartedly and devotedly be there for me when I was at my most vulnerable, put a whole new meaning and depth to our love. *My husband was one in a million, a Godsend from Heaven.* I never doubted his love for me, but he sure did prove it to me then, which only increased my love for him! I am convinced today that we had a unique and real love, something I don't believe the average couple has. We were blessed. *Thank You God, for Larry's Love!*

A Lesson in Boundaries

What did I learn the most from this experience? *BOUNDARIES!* My lack of boundaries was my main problem! I should have taken better care of myself. I should have respected my limits better, but unfortunately, I had no idea what my limits were until I went way beyond them.

I put up walls around me for a while, which Kim reassured me was not only ok but necessary at that time. I withdrew into my safe shell and had nothing to do with anybody in my family for a long time. I simply could not handle them. I have healthy boundaries today, and if a boundary doesn't work, a wall will! I am super protective of myself and my boundaries today. I came to realize that however horrible the experience had been, something had deeply changed in me. I had gone through the valley, and not only survived but began to thrive. I was much more at peace. My perspective on life changed. I was more humble, more human. I felt like I could put the traumatic memories on a shelf and live in the present. *I had grown emotionally and spiritually, but only by the Grace of God!*

Holden!

I lost my dog Trucker in May of 2011, which broke my heart. I had him since he was born, so there was an extra strong bond between us. He was like my baby. It hurt me so much to lose him. I don't even remember crying over the loss of Trucker. I felt sad, but I was not able to cry. Again, I was grieving and didn't even know it, just like I was grieving as a child and didn't know it.

Larry started encouraging me to get another dog not long after I was more stable, but I kept telling him that I wasn't ready yet, to give me a little time to relax and grieve. *He was looking online for dogs, but I told him, "when the time is right, God will bring the right dog to us," which He did.* I overheard a woman talking about working at the animal shelter while I was in the Walmart pharmacy line one day, and I asked her if she knew of any Husky dogs there. Lo and behold, she said, "yes, there is Husky Lab mix there right now." Wow! I called the shelter the next day and was told, "yes, there is a Husky Lab mix. His name is Holden, and he is extremely sweet." I told them I thought I wanted him, so the next day we went to visit him, took him for a walk, and decided to adopt him. We didn't take him that day because we wanted to get prepared for him at home, but we went back Monday to pick him up. I will never forget the way Holden looked at us all sad eyed when we left him the first day, like, aren't you going to take me? I reassured him we would be back to get him. I think dogs understand more than people give them credit for. I am a dog lover and communicate very well with them, often better than I do with people! Apparently, Larry felt the same way, as I found a video recently of him and Holden in the car, and he said, "the more I'm around people, the better I like my dog."

We brought Holden home and he attached himself to me, Larry, and our home like he had always been with us. Larry and I both thought because Holden was part Husky he would want to be outdoors. Wrong! We had everything ready like we had for Trucker—a heated pad, a heated water bowl, but we soon found out Holden was not Trucker. Trucker loved being outdoors, but he was mostly Husky, whereas Holden was mostly Lab. We put Holden outside for two nights and he howled and cried all night, keeping us awake. We tried the next night, and he did the same thing, so we both decided we would bring him inside but keep him in the basement. Larry had a flea infested home in the past, so he was against the idea of Holden being in our home at first. I remember Larry saying, "ok, he can come inside, but only in the basement, not in our home." Larry finally decided to let him come up stairs from the basement, just to visit some, and then he finally decided to let him come up to stay in our home, but said, "he can come up here, but I don't want him on the furniture." After he was permanently allowed in our home, he started coming up to us while we were sitting on the couch together, trying to nuzzle us and stick his paws on us rather shyly and sweetly, and before we knew it, he was sitting between us on the couch, just as happy and content as any dog could be. Larry and I just looked at each other, neither one of us having the heart to make him get down. I remember Larry saying to me, "it's ok if he is on the furniture, but he is NEVER allowed on our bed!" You know what happened! Yep, the next thing we knew, he wanted to come in our bedroom and lay down next to us, so I made him a soft bed with a comforter, complete with a pillow and a teddy bear, which he loved cuddling with. Then before we knew it, he managed to find his way on our bed! Not only did he find his way on our bed, but he managed to get in our bed in the mornings as we were waking up, snuggled up between us, all stretched out with his long Lab legs, like he was human! Not only did Holden love it, but so did we! We would hear him snoring, and snicker.

The reason I love writing about Holden is because he brought so much joy to our home and lives. *God knew exactly the dog we needed and brought Holden.* Larry and I both agreed he was the perfect dog for us. What was amazing was that Larry was not particularly a dog lover, but he absolutely 100% fell in love with Holden, and it didn't take long. Not even a week after we adopted him, I discovered Holden missing from the car after my therapy session with Kim, and found it was Larry who took him!

We were mommy and daddy to Holden. Holden would sit on the couch looking out the window waiting for Larry to come home when he was gone, then race down to the front door to greet him, which Larry loved! Daddy's home! Holden loved being with both of us and hated when either one of us was gone. Lucky for him, we took him just about everywhere with us, so he was rarely left alone. He was the sunshine in our life.

Holden had strong fears of abandonment, and of course I understand that issue and was sensitive to his needs. We loved going for long rides in the country, and Holden would lay in the back seat of our car sleeping while we were traveling, just as happy and content as can be. We realized Holden had us trained very well after we had him a few years. He even knew when it was time for his nightly treats! He would come to us on the couch and start begging, looking sweetly at us, as if to say, "it's time for my treats." I am so glad Larry had the opportunity to have this love connection with Holden, as I believe with all my heart that God knew he needed it. Larry even told me that he learned a lot about love from Holden. *God truly does know what we need and when we need it, if only we can trust in Him. I have so many happy memories of the three of us together that I treasure. Thank You, Lord, for blessing Larry and me with Holden!*

I have a saying on my refrigerator that says, '*until we love an animal, a part of your soul remains unawakened.*' I also have a pillow that says,' *a house is not a home without a dog.*' I am obviously an animal lover. I always say, "*God is Dog spelled backward!*" *God knew what he was doing when he gave us dogs!*

A Broken Leg

I had another health challenge in 2012, but this one was physical, not emotional. While trying to reach a corner wall when standing on a dresser (bad idea!), I fell onto my antique vanity table and fractured my leg. OH MY GOD!! I have never felt such pain in my life!! Larry heard me screaming and came upstairs immediately to see what was wrong. I was in such unbearable pain I was crying in anguish, not knowing how to deal with the pain. This happened rather late at night, so I had to wait until the next day to go to the doctor, and when I got there, the young intern told me I didn't break my leg! Really?! No, I didn't break it; I fractured it, which was even worse! Where do these inept doctors come from? This was a Monday, and I was only given enough pain medication for a few days until my appointment with the Orthopedic doctor, so I suffered terribly. I must have a strong mind, as I was able to block out the pain to a certain degree and sleep, which was my only escape from the pain.

I was told by the orthopedic doctor on Friday that I needed an operation for my leg to heal properly. He gave me more pain medication and I was operated on the following Monday. Larry sat with me while I was in the anesthesia preparation room, which was a great comfort. Nobody likes being put under, and I am no exception. It's scary. You have no control, and you are putting your trust in a doctor, which is even scarier! *But Larry and I prayed and trusted God to be with me throughout this ordeal, so I was at peace, plus my intuitive sense told me that I was in good hands with this doctor.* I remember making the anesthesiologist smile when I asked him if there was any possibility of the anesthesia not working, and me waking up during the operation. He reassured me that there was no way I could wake up during the operation, which was a comfort to me. He thought I was so silly! I was out within seconds of saying that! *The rest was in God's Hands.*

I was very disoriented when I woke up, almost forgetting where or why I was there, but the pain in my leg quickly reminded me! I hated having to stay the night in the hospital, but I got through it, and the pain, with heavy IV pain medication. I told the doctor I didn't want any pain medication, which of course he knew was ridiculous. I didn't like the idea of being all doped up, but he smiled and reassured me that I would be fine, but there was no way I could go without the pain medication. The pain wasn't too bad at first but got much worse, and I agreed with the doctor! How silly of me to think I could go without pain medication with a fractured leg! I was given a prescription for pain medication and Larry took me home, where I settled in for about four months. I have never been so settled in my whole life!

Larry was so good about taking care of me during this time. He waited on me hand and foot, fixing me meals, helping me with baths, etc. I couldn't do anything for myself during this time. I was completely dependent on Larry, which was both comforting and scary. It was scary at first because I had never been in this sort of situation before, but it was also comforting because I knew he loved me and would care for me. He never ever complained about anything, and I always thanked him and told him how grateful I was for him. I always said to him, "thank you so much, honey. I really do appreciate it." Holden was also a big comfort for me during this time. He sensed I was not feeling well and cuddled with me. All I did during this time was watch tv and eat. Larry set up the laptop for me so I could edit the *FACT* book, which was perfect timing.

My leg slowly and gradually mended, the pain lessened, the brace was removed, and I was up walking around with a walker, feeling like an old lady! Then one day in Spring I managed to go outside without the walker! Hallelujah! I have always loved walking, so not being able to walk was the worst possible thing for me, but now I was walking again! And I appreciated my legs even more after this experience! Holden was so happy to have his mama walk him again! *Praise God!* I am so thankful for my legs and being able to walk!

What did I learn from this experience? As much physical pain as I had been in, I would take physical pain any day over the emotional pain I had been in the year before. I remember calling Kim to request prayer for my healing, and she asked me, "Carol, what would you rather have, the emotional pain or the physical pain?" I told her without hesitation,

"I would take the physical pain over the emotional pain any day." She agreed.

The biggest thing I learned from this experience was that I could 100% depend on and trust Larry to always be there for me. I already knew this from having him be there for me when I had my bout with PTSD, but it was very humbling the way he took care of all my physical needs. I can't say enough for Larry. There aren't enough words to describe how I feel about his love and devotion to me. I kept thanking him for being there for me until his death. His famous words to me, *"we're in this together"* will stay with me forever. As he got older and depended on me more, I said the same words to him. We both meant the words in our marriage vows '*for better or for worse.*' We were truly *in this together.* **Thank You Lord, for giving me Larry! I am looking forward to us being 'in this together' in Heaven.**

Contented Years

My life became very settled with Larry and Holden and stayed that way for the rest of Larry's life. The years from 2012 through 2019 were the most contented years of our marriage. Our life together might have looked boring from someone else's perception, but we were not bored; we were just very contented. I remember asking Larry if he was bored with me, because we often fell asleep while sitting on the loveseat together, and his reply was, "no, I'm not bored; it's just that I feel so content with you that it relaxes me to the point where I fall asleep", and I told I understood because I felt the same way. We had both worked so hard for so many years that we just enjoyed relaxing with each other. I always told Larry that the best time of day for me was when we were all cuddled up in bed together or snuggling on the loveseat. Pure Heaven. When I asked Larry if he ever got bored with me, his reply was, "no Carol; you're just crazy enough to keep my life exciting!" I know he meant it, as Larry just told it like it was. He was a character. He could be so serious and funny at the same time.

The FACT Book Publication

It was while I was laid up with my broken leg that I decided to complete the **FACT** book. I had everything completed for the book, but it still needed editing for publication. I found out editing was very tedious and time consuming, which I am being reminded of now. I had to go through every story and all the other materials to correct punctuation and grammar errors, etc. It was a lot of work!

After I sent the manuscript to IUniverse publishing company, I was admonished by the publisher to make numerous revisions, which forced me to delete explicit material relevant to the stories to avoid a possible libel lawsuit in the future. Although I was disappointed about being forced to do this, I expressed myself in the Foreword by stating, *"It's a shame that the stories had to be watered down so far to protect the perpetrators that we couldn't express in actuality what really happened to us—we can't name the abusers, locations, or anything that links the abused to the abuser. Any readers who have been in the foster care system pretty much know what these issues are and should be able to fill the blanks in for themselves, where the material isn't lost, it's just hidden."* I hated having to water down the stories, but I had no choice. Larry was a very good writer and helped me write this. He also came up with the idea about the excerpts in the **FACT** book, which I thought was perfect! As I was editing this book in October 2023, it's been four and a half years since Larry passed, and wish he was here to help me.

CAROL LUCAS

It took me a few months to get everything ready for publication, as there was a lot of time delays due to communication between me and the publisher. I found out publishing a book is a lot more complicated and time consuming than I expected, but I was patient. *I just went with the flow, knowing it would be published in God's perfect time!*

Larry wanted to help me publish the book, and we trusted God that somehow the money would come through for us to do it, which of course it did. Larry was doing taxes that year for the years 2010, 2011, and 2012, which was enough for us to publish the book! I could not thank Larry enough for letting us do that. He knew how important the book was to me and he really wanted it to be a success, so he generously let us do this. We were both amazed how it all worked out. *God is so amazing!*

For anyone who thinks that I will get rich off the *FACT* book, let me reassure you that I will probably never get out of the book financially what I put into it. A woman I knew years ago accused me of writing the book for money, which offended me deeply. Really?! If she only knew the truth. I unfriended that friend real fast! Why is it so hard for people in the world to believe that some of us actually do have integrity? Not everyone does everything for financial gain, and I am one of them people. Writing the *FACT* book was never about money! I am driven by purpose and love, not money. *I am ultimately driven by God's love and purpose.*

The FACT book was officially published on July 9, 2013! All my hard work was finally in print, and it felt so good! I was both proud and humbled to have accomplished this. My only prayer now was for the book to reach former foster children who needed/wanted it. Larry was also proud of me, just like when I graduated. He took a picture of me holding the book right before he took me out to celebrate at a nice restaurant, which I will never forget! Wow! There have been people who've told me I am an amazing lady, but I say that the truly amazing one is God, not me. Humility is important.

It was after the book was finally published that I fully realized that this truly was my baby that I had finally given birth to. Years earlier I could not have imagined I would feel this way, but now I realized Father knows best! I learned a lot about surrendering to God from this experience. I realized His ways are not our ways, and His thoughts are much deeper and higher than we could ever imagine. Me doing the book was another way that God made beauty out of ashes with my life, but I could never have seen that without going through with the book, including all the upsets along the way.

Thank You, My Big Daddy, for knowing all along what your child wanted and needed! You are an awesome Father!

And now I am publishing my autobiography! When I look back on my past I am truly amazed. People tell me I am a living miracle, and they are right. I should be dead, but here I am alive and writing my story about how I survived. *And one thing I know for sure is I am only alive because of God.*

I want people reading my story to know that when I speak of God, I am not a fanatic! God works in so many ways, and often mysterious ways. I like what my therapist said, that usually when pray for help, God sends a person. When I was praying about EMDR therapy I was led to the perfect therapist.

Another Move?

Larry and I began considering the possibility of moving to Texas shortly after the **FACT** book was published. We were both upset over the way our country was looking and decided to move to Texas because they have different laws there with guns, etc. My husband was a strong supporter of the 2nd Amendment and there was NO WAY he was giving up those rights! We started looking online for a house there, but nothing appealed to us, so after a few months of looking we decided not to move there, but instead decided to look for a ranch home in our area. Our home is a tri-level with stairs, which we didn't want anymore. I will never forget the commercial for stair lifts that kept coming on tv right around the time we were considering moving. The man in the commercial said, "it is definitely more affordable than moving," which made us laugh. We would look at each other and say, "maybe we should consider this, honey?" *Although we were seriously contemplating moving, we put our trust in God for the outcome, knowing that He was Our Heavenly Father Who knows best. We knew when the hurricanes hit Texas a few years later that God definitely did know best!*

We kept looking around in the area for a ranch home we liked while our house was on the market, but never found one we liked, nor was our house selling. We even considered buying a manufactured home to put on our land but decided it was not affordable, nor was building on our land. *We had given up on that dream a few years prior, so the only thing for us to do was pray and give it to God. God did answer our prayer, but not in the way we intended. While we were searching for a physical home, I believe God was leading us to a loving spiritual home.*

Again, God's ways are not our ways. He sees much deeper than we do, and He sees much further ahead than we do. Trust in His Wisdom. His ways are higher and better than our own.

Another Health Crisis for Larry

Larry had another health crisis during our house hunting, which ended up being both bad and good. I came out to the car one evening while doing some work for a friend, and found him incoherent in his speech, which I quickly recognized as a stroke. He was able to drive home (I didn't know how to drive a stick shift), and I got an ambulance to take him to the hospital, where he spent a couple days. His speech was the only thing that had been affected, and it came back very easily, though he told me he was slower at gathering words in his mind, which was frustrating for him.

I spent time with him at the hospital like before, and told him, "we are not moving. We are staying where we are, and if you ever mention moving to me again, I might slap you! You are way more important to me than a new home." We both agreed that the stress of moving was getting to both of us, and that stress probably brought on his stroke. Our house went off the market after that and we were no longer even considering moving. No way! I also told him I honestly didn't think I wanted to move out of our home that I had lived in for so many years, and I don't think he did either. I remember telling him, "you built this house yourself and you have been here for forty-four years. It isn't that easy to just pack up and leave after that many years." I also teased him and reminded him that having to clean out the garage should be a good enough reason to stay!

What was the important lesson we both learned from this? That like Dorothy in the Wizard of Oz, we need look no further than our own home to find happiness. Larry and I had always been content in our home and became even more so after this experience. Our true home was in the love we shared, not just a physical home.

As I approach 2024, I face the possibility of moving out of my home of twenty-seven years, which won't be easy, but I will be courageous and trust God.

A Lesson About Love

What else did I learn about my love for Larry? A lot. Larry grew up believing he was not really loved by his parents. He never felt good enough, and nothing he did made his dad proud. He told me how he took his dad out to a building site where he was the top builder of a high school, hoping his dad would praise him, but all he said was, "look at all this mud." From that point on he never expected anything from his dad. He proved to himself that he could be successful without his dad's approval. My husband was a strong spiritual man, and I loved and respected him for that. He was the Godliest man I have ever known, or no doubt will ever know. *I pray all the time for God to bless him in Heaven.*

When Larry married his first wife and was building this house, and asked her what she wanted, she never gave him any input, then complained afterward and said, "you built this house for another woman." Larry and I both agreed that she was right. I told Larry, "yes, you built this home for me and I am perfectly happy with it!" We had a lot of laughs over that! He was also briefly married to a woman who was not any better than his first wife. Larry felt like he couldn't please anyone.

All his life Larry felt like he was not enough, that nobody really loved and appreciated him. Then he married me, and I appreciated everything he ever did for me. I made him feel like he was enough. He was enough. He was more than enough. I'm not even sure Larry realized fully what he meant to me. He was just being himself and didn't realize what a huge blessing he was in my life. He changed my whole life. I always say, "I wouldn't even have this home without Larry." And now that he is gone, I feel like this home is not really a home without him. Not long before he passed away, I told him, *"we will build our dream home together in Heaven. And I know it will be the most beautiful Home ever, better than anything we could have built here! It will be perfect and we won't ever have to make repairs. God will bless that Home forever!" Larry just smiled at me.*

What I realize more than ever now that he is gone, is that Larry knew wholeheartedly my love for him when I told him he was more important to me than a new home. Building a new home out in the country seemed so important when we first met, but as time passed and our love grew, the dream home became less and less important. What became more important was the love we shared. It was priceless. Love is about giving, and what I gave to him by expressing this to him was a loud affirmation that he was the most important thing to me, which Larry needed to hear. He waited a long time to get that kind of love, and he finally got it from me. The words he expressed in the last anniversary card we gave each other weren't just flowery words; he meant them—*"Thank you for the years of love. I will always love you."*

Other than a few family upsets, the years from 2014-2019 were very mellow and contented years for me and Larry. We spent a lot of time together, going for Harley rides in the nice weather, but mostly car rides with Holden because we couldn't fit him on the bike! Larry and I were joined at the hip, and we liked it that way. It might seem too codependent to others, but I say that is love, at least the kind of love we had. We were very close. We spent so much time together that I rarely even drove a car anymore, which I didn't mind at all. Larry loved driving a lot and I was perfectly happy to be sitting next to him in the car while he drove. I spent years in my own car, going to jobs, going to school, running errands, etc., so it felt nice to just take it easy and enjoy the ride. Things change as you grow older, at least they have for me, and I know they did for Larry too. We were gracefully growing old together, which was a beautiful thing. Now with him gone I am growing old gracefully alone, but I sure do miss him with me. He will always live in my heart and memories, but what I wouldn't give to hold him in my arms again.

As I sit writing it appears there is change in the air and I won't be growing alone after all. There is a man in my life who I will be marrying. My husband told a friend of ours he didn't want me alone, and he got his wish.

Thank you God!

My Sister's Death

One sad thing that happened in 2015 was the death of my older sister, the one who had been my caretaker as a child. I lost touch with her through the years and didn't know her address but found out while I was visiting in Illinois and went to see her, which was both a happy and sad visit. I hadn't seen her since 1986, and we hadn't spoken since 1999. She was so overwhelmed with happiness to see me that she started crying, which of course made me emotional.

I was so happy to see her, but very unhappy and sad about her condition. My sister had always been pretty and well-groomed, but the woman I looked at did not look like my sister. She had gained a lot of weight, she wore no makeup, her hair was a mess, and she was hooked up to an oxygen machine. Not only was she a mess but so was her house. It was very dirty and messy, with holes in the walls, and the worst part of all was the cock roaches all over her house, which she was either oblivious to or unconcerned about. I didn't judge her over this; I just felt sad that her life had so deteriorated to this point. What happened to my sister?

What happened to my sister was that she never got help for her alcoholism, and she never dealt with her past. My sister had five children (maybe six) and lost all of them due to her neglect, as she was more concerned about drinking than she was about taking proper care of her children. Her first husband got custody of her first two children when he found out my niece was being sexually abused by a man my sister was involved with, then when she remarried and had three more children, she didn't take proper care of them either, so social services put them into foster care. I heard rumors that she was pregnant while under the jurisdiction of the court, and the state took the baby. My sister denied this, but who knows for sure?

My sister could have gotten her children back if she had been compliant with the court, but my niece said she didn't even show up for the court date. Like our own mother, she apparently did not care enough to get her children back. I'm sure she loved her children, but not enough to get it together. I have a gift for analyzing people, so it was easy to figure my sister out. She was the oldest of my sisters who were exposed to the pervert, and my sister told me herself what happened with him, so I know she was messed up from that. I also believe the uncle she lived with was abusive. She turned to alcohol and became very promiscuous, which is common for sexually abused people. She got lost. She never dealt with anything from her past; she just buried herself in the bottle, and along the way happened to have five or six children, which she was not mature enough to take proper care of.

I went back to see my sister the following day, bearing a few gifts for her, which she was happy to get. I prayed for her while I was visiting. I wanted so much to bless her, to let her know at least one of her siblings

CAROL LUCAS

cared about her. Most of my family shunned her, and even her own children, except one daughter, would have anything to do with her. I tried explaining to my niece that my sister had her own issues from her own childhood, but she wouldn't get out of herself enough to at least try to understand that. My sister was a very damaged person. I believe she was probably abused the most by the perverted candy man.

She had started going to church and had been sober for five years, but she still had an addiction to cigarettes that she was battling with, which was killing her. We promised to keep in touch when I left, which we did through phone calls and letters. She died in February of 2015, but I was unable to attend her funeral due to a severe blizzard. I have three sisters who live in Illinois, and only one attended. My brother told me once that the only time our family would get together was over somebody's casket, but sadly we can't even do that. I was sad about her death but happy to have reconnected with her before she passed away. I was also relieved she wouldn't be suffering any longer. *My sister had a rough life that she was now free of, praise God!*

Stepfamily

Another upsetting family situation that occurred around this time concerned my husband's son, who should be referred to as a stepson, but that wouldn't be honest, as it would imply a relationship that we didn't have. He contacted my husband while he was here, wanting to go out for breakfast, which Larry agreed to. My husband told me that his son was acting edgy, like he was afraid to speak up about something important to him, then he finally told Larry that I wasn't invited to his upcoming wedding, which of course Larry didn't like. This put Larry in a position to have to choose between me or his son, which he resented, and he resented his son for doing this. He especially resented the fact that his son didn't respect our marriage yet expected Larry to respect his.

If I remember correctly, this was not resolved during their breakfast. Larry came home and told me about it, and I told Larry to do whatever he wanted. I told him I wouldn't be happy about it, but that I would understand if he wanted to go to the wedding without me; after all, it was his son's wedding. But Larry made the final decision not to go. He told his son that if he could not respect our marriage, that he was not going to respect his either. My husband always put me first, which I respected. When I say I never doubted Larry's love for me, it was things like this that proved it. One of Larry's friends told me that he told him, "if my children won't accept Carol, then I won't accept them."

I can't mention this incident without fully explaining the whole situation with his estranged family. My husband was very unhappily married with the mother of his children, and she continued to poison her children's minds against him even after the divorce. His children seemed fine with me when I first met them, but over time they became increasingly negative toward me. I never did anything to encourage this at all; they simply would not accept me. I even talked with them in the beginning and told them they didn't need to think of me as a stepmom; in fact, I preferred they didn't. All I wanted was to be accepted and respected as the wife of their dad, but they couldn't even give me that much. I was treated with total disrespect and so was our marriage.

For instance, shortly after Larry had his health crisis in 2010, his daughter came to Michigan with her three girls so Larry could see his grandchildren, under the condition that he came without me. Although I was hurt that I wasn't invited, I told Larry that it was all right with me, as I really wanted him to see his grand girls. The relationship was so bad between Larry and his daughter that while she lived in Michigan, he couldn't even go inside her house to visit when she had her first two children. He had to leave presents on the front porch, which angered my husband to the point that he simply refused to go over there anymore. The relationship completely deteriorated once she moved out of state, which Larry accepted. My husband knew there wasn't anything that could be done about the relationship and accepted it, so when his daughter came to visit him in 2010, he seized the opportunity for reconciliation, but what happened while visiting her only fueled more animosity between the two of them. This meeting was organized and held at Larry's sister's house. When Larry got home and I asked him how it went, he told me he enjoyed seeing his three grand girls but that when he got up to leave and asked his daughter, "is this the way it is always going to be, without Carol?" she replied "yes." He then told his daughter, "if this is the way it's going to be, then there won't be another time," and he left. That was it. Other than one Christmas card that she sent about a year before he passed that he refused and sent back because my name wasn't on it, there was no communication between 2010 and 2019.

I will never forget the day he went to visit with his daughter and grandchildren. I sat outside enjoying the warm weather, feeling rather sad and lonely, nearly in tears because I was not even welcome in my husband's family. It hurt some, which my husband knew, even though I acted superficially fine with the whole thing. I remember asking myself, what did I do to deserve this awful treatment? And the only answer was that I didn't do anything to deserve it. I married a man who had had a very unhappy and dysfunctional marriage that involved three children, who not only had issues with their mom and dad, but now with me also. That's it. Ironically though, the worse they treated us the stronger our love became, which only made them dislike us more. Larry and I both knew we couldn't win and walked away in grace. *If God was trying to teach me grace, he certainly gave me the perfect situation! I could have become bitter, but I chose grace, by the Grace of God!*

I told my husband that he could have whatever relationship he wanted with his kids, but please leave me out of it. I told him I knew I couldn't win. I was damned if I did and damned if I didn't. They resented it if I was nice, and they judged me if I was aloof. What they wanted was to use me as a scapegoat for their own issues, which I refused to be. They had issues with their own mother and projected those feeling toward me instead of dealing with their own issues. I was told by a friend who went to the memorial my ex-sister-in-law had, that Larry's children who showed up (one did not) didn't even sit with their mom, which is very telling.

There was another incident while he was visiting with his sister, which added more fuel to the fire. As Larry was leaving, his sister told him not to yet, that his son was coming over to visit with him, but he told his sister he wasn't interested in seeing his son and left. What his son did by not respecting our marriage left a huge wedge between the two of them that never was mended. His sister was never his favorite person in the world, and she became even less favored after this. She had no business meddling, and I told her so after Larry passed. His sister was so jealous of me she would go to any extreme to hurt me.

The reason I bring this family issue up is because through the pain this caused me, not only did our love grow for each other, but my love for myself did. It made me realize that I don't have to take people's unacceptance of me personally, which made me feel stronger. All I wanted when I first met my husband's family was to be accepted by them, but as time passed and I realized a lot of them didn't accept me, it forced me to look more deeply into myself. **What evil meant for harm, God used for my own good!**

What I realize today, is that you are wasting your time if you expect everyone to like you, because there will always be people who don't like you. Today I choose to a be ok with ones who do like me, and I choose to be ok with the ones who don't. I realize now that I am older and wiser that it just isn't that important to me anymore, because I like me! It is my firm belief that someone's dislike of me is often due to jealousy, so now instead of being hurt, I take it as a compliment that I have something to be jealous of and pray for that person. *God bless them!*

Now when I have a moment of insecurity, I pause and ask myself, "is this about me or is this about the other person?" The answer to that question is that it is not about me! I know who I am today and am comfortable in my own skin. Nobody can seriously affect that unless I let them, which I refuse to let them do today! It took me a long time to get there, but I finally got there! How freeing that is!

My worth today is not dependent on others; it is dependent on God's worth. The most important thing I realize is that I am made whole by the Grace of God because I am His Child! Hallelujah!

Losing Hope for Larry?

The next few years, from 2016-2019 were spent peacefully with my husband, with no major upsets, other than one more trip to the hospital for Larry's lungs. We knew he had congestive heart failure, which we were controlling with diet and medication, but he had another breathing issue that he had to get help for once. The issue with his lungs in 2010 had apparently affected his health more than he realized. I believe the doctors had my husband believing that if he took his medication and watched his diet, he would be all right, but I found out differently after Larry passed. While spending time at the beach in 2019, I got into a conversation with a cardiac nurse who explained to me that congestive heart progressively moves from the left to the right side of the heart, which causes the heart to fail. I was angry at the doctors for not being honest with my husband and giving him false hope. Needless to say, I do not have a high opinion of doctors at all. *I ultimately put my faith in God, not doctors! God is my doctor!*

I believe something gave in me after seeing him in the hospital again. I felt a sense of hopelessness, but instead of dealing with my fear and facing the inevitable, I think I unconsciously went into denial. I simply could not and did not want to face the possibility of losing my husband and living my life without him. I told him so many times that I didn't know what I would do without him, and he told me the same about me. We were so close that neither one of us wanted to lose the other. *I told him shortly before he passed that I never wanted to be here alone without him in this dysfunctional world, that if it were not for him, I would be happy to be with Jesus in Heaven. But here I am alone without him in this dysfunctional world that seems to be getting more dysfunctional by the hour, and all I know to do is take it one day at a time while trusting God. Everything in my life is in His Hands.*

Whenever I went for a walk and was gone too long, Larry would call me on my phone or come looking for me, and if he were gone too long on his own, I would call him to make sure he was ok. They say we all have regrets when a loved one dies, so I know it is normal, but I wish I had been more understanding of his illness. Because the doctors were not honest with him, and because Larry and I both had some denial about the seriousness of his health, I didn't see the truth. Larry would sometimes tell me that it was frustrating for him because he couldn't seem to gather words like he used to, and he would always be far behind me while we were walking and taking sitting breaks on a bench, which I was totally understanding of, but I still did not see how bad he was until the end. In retrospect I realize he was gradually declining from the years 2010-2019, but it was so gradual that we didn't notice. One of the hardest things to face is the reality of losing a loved one, especially a spouse you are so close to. Most people go into denial and pretend everything is ok, even when the facts speak otherwise. The time was coming when I would have to say goodbye to my soul mate, and it would be heart wrenching.

As Larry's health gradually declined, I was very understanding of his needs, and would always run upstairs to get things for him because I knew he was having more and more trouble climbing the stairs, but I still did not think he would die that soon. I knew Larry was feeling bad about having to depend on me more, but I always reassured him that he was never a burden to me, that I loved waiting on him because I loved him, and it gave my life purpose. I loved taking care of my husband; in fact, it is one of thing things I miss the most. I know it brought him a lot of joy to know that I loved taking care of him, which brought me joy also. One thing I can say with certainty, is that Larry knew I loved him very much. Not a day went by that I didn't tell him that, and how grateful I was for him.

Losing my Husband Larry

On March 29, 2019, Larry and I took one last trip to an Amish community that is about three hours from home. We loved going for long rides and loved the Amish country with the hospitable and simple folks who gave us such great food deals. I told Larry that I considered that my anniversary gift because I so loved the ride and all the bargains we got. I remember coming home and telling him to let me get him dinner because he was tired from all the driving, so I got him dinner. The reason I bring this up is because of the look on his face when I rushed in the door and got him dinner immediately. He knew I was putting him first—not unpacking the groceries or anything else, but him, which he was impressed with and loved. All Larry wanted was a woman who would love him, which I did, and as unconditionally as humanly possible.

He started having some problems with his urination and had gotten some medicine from the doctor about a week before, which I didn't feel good about, and I don't think he did either, but he thought he needed to do something, as the natural remedies weren't working. He wasn't sleeping well, which had him concerned, and when I asked him if he was having problems with breathing while lying down, he said "no," but I found him on his knees a lot during the last three weeks of his life, which he had done in the past when he was having problems breathing, so I wondered. My intuition tells me that he was more comfortable physically, but I also believe he was praying. In retrospect, I believe Larry was not only praying about his health and possible death, but also about me, for God to take care of me after he was gone.

On April 1, 2019, Larry and I celebrated our 23rd anniversary. We had two anniversaries since we were also married on September 21, but we mostly celebrated the one in April since it was our first marriage, and only acknowledged the second one. I went to get an anniversary card and picked out one card that we could both give to each other, just because I really liked what the card said on the front. It read *Time has a way of making love more beautiful,* which of course I thought was not only beautiful, but absolutely true of our relationship. A man I know who isn't happily married was talking about relationships, and I told him that love must be cared for like a rose. If you nurture it, it will grow. That is real love. Inside the card it read *Love…is the perfect bond of unity… Collossians 3:14,* which really impressed me, as I have a candle that I made for our chapel wedding on September 21st that says something about unity. We truly did become as one, and that is partly why his death was so hard for me. Where is my other half? I felt like a big part of me left with him, but I do know I will see him again. As I approach the 2023 holiday season, I am considering going back to Grief Share to help ease some of my loneliness, which is more pronounced during this time.

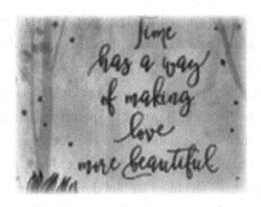

I wrote in the card to him, Larry, "I wouldn't trade in our time together for any before that. Love, your wife, Carol." I thought that really said it all, as he gave me the happiest years of my life. To me, he wrote, "Carol, though time has passed and we are still loving each other, each day is an adventure and gives us the ability to enjoy each other. Thank you for the years of love. I'll always love you, Larry."

When I asked him if he noticed the passage about 'Love is the perfect bond of unity,' he said, "yes," and I looked at him and said, "you know, you really do become as one." He smiled at me with such a look of love and tenderness, both of us understanding that it was true. As time passed through the years, we became one, bound not only by the Holy Spirit, but by our love for each other. I was so truly blessed to have shared 23 years of marriage with Larry, and I look forward to spending eternity with him.

I noticed a change come over him about a week before he passed away. There was a sadness about him that I had never noticed before, but it was so subtle that I didn't fully notice it. He seemed almost childlike in his need for me and my love, but I was so afraid of losing him that I feel I was not fully present, which I just feel terrible about now. I know he understood how hard it would be for me to lose him, but I wish now I could have faced my fear and fully embraced his passing. It is something

I have had to live with and will always regret. I remember telling Larry about a week before he passed away, "if I seem emotionally distant from you, please understand that it's just that I am concerned about you, and I don't know what I will do without you if you go." I was very honest with him about my feelings, which I know he appreciated, but I so wish I had been stronger about this situation. I just could not face the prospect of my life without him, which was a compliment to him about how much he meant to me, but I feel like I let him down when he needed me the most. I was praying for him a lot and hoping he would feel better, but his physical condition was getting worse, and we were both concerned. I felt so helpless. I hated seeing him suffer physically. He had been trying to exercise to better his health, and when I asked one day if he got on our treadmill, he said "yes, but I couldn't even do the slowest speed." When he told me that I had a bad feeling that his life force was leaving his body.

I believe my husband knew his time for leaving this earth was near and chose to pass away here in our home with me near him. I also believe that although he felt sad about leaving me, he was tired of suffering. He did not want to be a half man who couldn't do the things he enjoyed, like riding his Harley with me, and working around the house, etc. He was trying everything to make himself better, but the congestive heart failure had finally taken its toll on his body, and he just couldn't fight it anymore. He knew it and surrendered. And as much as I miss my Larry, I would not want him suffering. *I know he is with the Lord in a much better place than this world, and I will see him again in Heaven.*

Larry had an appointment with the doctor on April 9th, the day before he died. He had not slept well the night before and I offered to take him to the doctor because I didn't want him driving while so tired. I also wanted to be there for him. The doctor visit went well, and Larry was hopeful that he would be ok. He came out the door looking so happy to see me waiting there in the car for him, asking him how the visit went. He handed me a paper the doctor gave him about sleeping habits, etc., since he had not been sleeping well. More than anything I felt like Larry was so happy that I was there for him. All Larry ever really wanted was love. His face would always light up when I expressed love for him, which lit up my face also.

A Sad and Memorable Ride in the Country

I suggested that we go for a ride in the country with the dog after we returned home, which he happily agreed to. We always loved going for rides, and this was no exception, but something was different about this one. I can't quite express in words what I want to convey, but there was a sadness in the car. I remember saying to him, "sometimes I wish we would have had a child together," and he looked over at me with such a look of love and compassion that I had never seen him have before. Larry was fully aware of my deep-seated fear of abandonment from my childhood and knew I would be deeply affected by the loss. I know Larry felt terrible about me leaving me here all alone, just terrible.

I always told Larry I hoped I would go before him because I didn't want to be here alone without him, but now I am glad he went first, because I would not want him to suffer the way I have since he has been gone. I love him too much for that, so as much as I hate being without him, I would rather have it be me suffering than him. It worked out the way it was meant to. But when he first passed I said, "I know Larry is in Heaven, but I am in hell without him." Grief gets easier over time.

I know my husband does not want me to be alone, that he wants me remarried, but time will tell. He told our neighbor friend, "when I pass away, I don't want Carol to be alone. She needs a man to take care of her." He also told him, "Carol changed my world," and expressed how much he loved me. This friend came to Larry's memorial I had for him here in my home and had tears in his eyes when he talked about how much Larry loved me. He said to me, "Carol, that man really loved you."

There was not just a sadness in the car while going for this long four-hour drive in the country, but a third presence, which I believe was the presence was us becoming one. I remember looking over at Larry while he was driving and saying, "I love you, Larry," with total love and tenderness that came from the deepest part of my heart and soul. It was one of the quietest rides we ever had, with very few words spoken. I believe we both knew deep down that this was the end, but we didn't have the words to express how we felt about it to each other. The saying *silence is golden* best describes this, as the words were best expressed by our silence. Our love was in the silence. I will always treasure that ride. And I will always treasure Larry.

Our Last Day Together

The next day Larry came down in the basement to see me when I was working out. He seemed lonely and wanted my company. I mentioned something about a man I knew who had overdosed on drugs, and that I realized the reason I was so upset about his death was because our childhoods were so similar, then I said, "you never really get over your childhood." The reason I mention this is because when I said this, my husband said, "no, you don't." I waited a long time to hear him say that. What he was saying was that he still carried some hurt from his childhood. My husband went through **Healing of the Memories** long before I did because he had his own childhood wounds that needed healing. Larry loved talking about Bill, a neighbor man who lived next door to him while he was growing up, who loved him a lot and treated him more like a real son than his own dad did. I nurtured Larry's inner child.

My husband was physically abused throughout his childhood, which I believe is why he struggled with his weight. People who have been physically or sexually abused often turn to food to not only get comfort for the lack of love, but to physically protect themselves. The day he died I found him lying on our couch in the family room, and he reacted like I was going to hurt him when I bent down to kiss him on the cheek, which saddened me. He had the look of a child who was afraid of being hurt, so I reassured him it was only me and that I loved him. I had never seen him look so vulnerable, and it touched my heart.

It is so sad how this stuff affects you for life. It was so sad for me to see him react like that to me. It hurt my heart to see such a childlike look on his face. He was such a good man with a big heart, and it hurts me to think of him being abused as a child. It hurts me to think of any child being abused. I believe that the last few days of my husband's life were sad for him, which saddened me.

The last day of Larry's life started out with me making him breakfast as usual. I got up talking about Jesus and how much I loved him, of how beautiful Heaven was, and that anyone who has ever been there has never wanted to come back here, including me. After his death, I thought it was strange that I got up and immediately started talking about Heaven, but that is the way the Holy Spirit works. I believe He was uttering things through me for Larry to hear. God knew Larry's time was near and that he needed to hear those words about Heaven. I remember him looking over at me as I spoke those words, and smiling at me, as if I were an Angel who had spoken beautiful words of hope for him.

Later that day I suggested we go for a short ride in the country before dinner, which of course happily agreed to. Larry had not been sleeping well and I knew rides in the country relaxed him. He loved it when I suggested us doing things together because he knew I was wanting to be with him, which he loved. One thing I know about my husband is that he wanted love more than anything. He loved that I loved being with him.

When I first started dating Larry, I asked him why he wanted me when there were so many other women he worked with at Ford who had good jobs that he could have been better off financially with, and he said, "I don't like them women there. I want a woman in my home, not a career driven woman." I was living on the fringes of life when I met my husband, but he wanted me. Why? He wanted me because he knew my heart and knew I would love him the way he wanted and needed. In the beginning I felt bad about not having much money, but over time I realized that he picked me, not despite who I was but because of who I was. He found love. He found the woman and wife of his dreams. And I found the man and husband of my dreams. *God, thank you so very much from the bottom of my heart for blessing me and Larry with a beautiful love for each other!*

Larry and went for a short ride in the country that day, then I made him his last meal when we returned home. I made him a sandwich with homemade pickles, which he loved. He was very tired and was relaxing on our loveseat as I was getting ready to go for a walk with Holden. I remember going by him numerous times and saying, "I love you sweetheart." I kept saying it, as if I knew he needed to hear it. I believe I subconsciously knew his end was near, and all I knew what to do was tell him I loved him. I sensed sadness on the last day of his life, and perhaps a resolve of letting go, but he did not want to say goodbye to me. We loved each other very much. How do you say goodbye to your soul mate, your spiritual soul mate? I felt like I was losing half of me and part of my heart and soul. I know it felt that way for both of us, but we were both so overwhelmed by our sadness that we couldn't express it. I wish I could express better how it was for us at the end, but there is no way I can. It was too personal, too emotional.

My Last Words to Larry

I will never forget what happened as I left to go for a walk. It was about 7:00 and I wanted to enjoy the sunset as I always do, and as I was leaving, I walked by Larry resting on the loveseat and noticed that he was rather slumped over on the couch with his head hanging to the side, as if he wished he was resting his head on my shoulder. Before I left, I said to him, *"here sweetheart; here is a pillow for your head. It isn't good for you to have your head over like that. It isn't good for your neck. You need to get some rest. I'll be back in an hour."* Those were the last words I ever spoke to my beloved husband, Larry.

The words I spoke to him, "you need to get some rest," resonated within me after he passed. I believe the Lord heard my words and gave him rest. There is no doubt that my husband is in Heaven with Jesus, resting in His precious love. I pray all the time for God to bless Larry in Heaven.

Regret

I know my husband was still alive when I left because he gave out a slight sound when I put the pillow on his neck and kissed him on the cheek. I have regrets now about going for a walk and not staying there with him, like I believe he wished I would have. If I could go back in time and change that evening, I would have sat next to him on the loveseat like we always did together and hold him next to me and let him die peacefully in my arms while I told him how much I loved him. I have had a hard time forgiving myself for this. I have such a high standard for myself for being a loving human being that is hard for me to acknowledge that I wasn't there with him when he passed on. I have had to forgive myself for not being perfect. I just did not know how to say goodbye. I always say I don't do goodbyes well. I don't, which is partly due to my sensitive nature, and largely due to being forced to say goodbye to my family as a child. Goodbyes suck.

I didn't go through the family room when I came home from my walk because I didn't want to wake Larry. He hated being woke up from his sleep and would get grouchy if he did, so I took special care not to, especially since he had been so sleep deprived. I went upstairs on our back porch to do my prayers and meditation, then watched some tv. The about 10:00 I opened the family room door to check on him and see if he was awake. If the tv was on I knew he was awake, but it wasn't, so I went back on the porch and watched tv, then about 11:00 I checked on him again, but the tv still wasn't on, so I went back on the porch. I wasn't concerned yet, as I had known him to sleep for hours and hours in the past when he had been sleep deprived from working overtime at Ford.

Shocked!

Around midnight I decided to go downstairs to get my meds that I left on my stand by the couch where he was sleeping, and as I opened the door to the family room I sensed something wasn't right and was somewhat hesitant to go downstairs, but I turned on the light and went. When I got down to the bottom of the stairs and looked over at him, I noticed something about him didn't look right, but I still didn't think he was dead. I said, "Larry? Are you all right?" but he didn't answer back, so I said it again louder. I could feel the anxiety rising in me, then when I got up real close to him, I noticed his skin was grayish colored and his mouth was hanging open with his tongue hanging out, and his skin was cold when I touched him. That's when I knew he was gone, and I went into complete panic and shock. I started slapping him and yelling, "wake up honey, wake up!" But he didn't wake up. I have said that the only time I ever slapped my husband was when he was dead, trying to be funny, but it was not funny at all to me then. It was shocking to find my husband dead in our family room.

I was in so much shock I didn't know what to do. I started yelling and crying. I was in a panic, and the only thing I knew to do was go down to his sister's and wake her up, but I went to the wrong house, then decided to go home. I just wanted to pretend none of this was happening, but it was, and somehow I had to deal with it, so I went over to my neighbors and told them what happened and they helped me make arrangements. I didn't know what to do. I remember sitting in their living room in shock, saying over and over, *"oh God, how am I ever going to go on without him?"* I was falling apart. I hadn't drank in thirty-three years, but I remember having a fleeting thought of picking up a beer they had in their fridge, but of course I didn't. I remember asking my neighbor to hug me because I was so distraught.

The paramedics came to my house and tried to revive him, but he was too far gone. As I waited for the funeral home to come pick up his body, I lay next to him on the floor where they had laid him, resting my head on his shoulder, and telling him how much I loved him. It didn't bother me that he was dead. To me it was him and I was perfectly comfortable doing it. Sometime shortly after midnight the funeral home came to pick his body up and I said goodbye to my Larry. It was the hardest thing I have ever done in my life.

How I went through the first few days, weeks, and months of his passing are a mystery to me. It took every ounce of strength I had to function. I was in shock and grief beyond anything I could ever have imagined, but somehow I managed to take care of the arrangements at the funeral home and all the other business that needed to be taken care of. It all seems like a big blur to me now.

One thing I did right away was buy a cemetery plot and make a memorial plaque for us. I know that we will be *Together in Heaven*. I also bought a Jesus statue and two angels, which are with the plaque. What is amazing is that when I went in search of a stone for our memorial plaque, I found one that was almost perfectly shaped like a heart! *It never ceases to amaze me how God gives me exactly what I need and often what I want!*

I live right around the corner from the cemetery and often walk through there with my dog Opie. I look at the stone and remind myself that although we are separated physically, our spirits will reunite in Heaven someday.

My Last Kiss for Larry

I called my ex-sister-in-law to let her know Larry had passed away, and she came down to the funeral home with me. As I was sitting there with her and the funeral director, his sister decided she wanted to see Larry's body to make closure, so she paid some money to have his body brought out, as they already had him ready to be cremated. When she came back to the room, she told me she thought I should go see him, that there was a look on his face that she thought I should see, so I did. I was not going to at first because I felt like I had already said my goodbye at home, and I would have rather remembered him at our home than in a funeral home, but since she coaxed me, I decided to go see him, which I am glad now that I did. *He looked like a different man, and not because he was dead but because of the look on his face. It was as if his face had been spiritually transformed. He not only looked more peaceful but his mouth and his eyes both were upturned in a happy way. I am very spiritually discerning, so I know it was not just a physical thing; it was spiritual. He was with the Lord and there had been a spiritual transformation that I so strongly felt. I looked at him for a few minutes, then I tenderly put my hands on his cheeks and kissed him on the mouth, and said, "I love you, sweetheart. I will see you in Heaven someday." I am so glad now I seen him there and did that. It was a spiritual moment for both of us, and even though he was gone from his body, I felt his spirit there and knew he was aware of my presence. I have a picture of him on my phone that was taken there, and I often look at it when I feel sad, just to remind myself that he is in Heaven, and I will see him again someday. I pray every day for God to bless my husband in Heaven, which I am sure He is doing.*

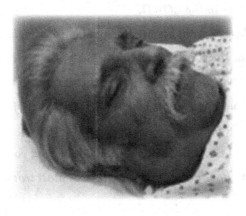

God Carrying Me

The next few days and weeks are somewhat of a blur to me because of the intense shock and grief I was going through. *It is only through the Grace of God that I made it through. The poem, Footprints in the Sand, perfectly describes this time for me, as God was carrying me.*

One night a man had a dream. He dreamed he was walking along the beach with the LORD. Across the sky flashed scenes from his life. For each scene, he noticed two sets of footprints in the sand: one belonged to him, and the other to the LORD.

When the last scene of his life flashed before him, he looked back at the footprints in the sand. He noticed that many times along the path of his life there was only one set of footprints. He also noticed that it happened a the very lowest and saddest times in his life.

This really bothered him and he questioned the LORD about it. "LORD, you said that once I decided to follow you, you'd walk with me all the way. But I have noticed that during the most troublesome times in my life, there is only one set of footprints. I don't understand why when I needed you most you would leave me."

The LORD replied, "My precious, precious child, I love you and I would never leave you. During your times of trial and suffering, when you see only one set of footprints, it was then that I carried you.

I just put one foot in front of the other, but it was extremely difficult for me. I felt like I was not going to make it. I felt stuck between wanting to fall apart and being strong. I wanted to cry but felt unable to because I felt like I had to be strong to survive, just like when I was in foster care. I thought I would just fall apart and not make it if I cried, so there weren't many tears in the beginning, only shock. The few times I cried was when someone who cared about me allowed me to. I was getting a lot of hugs though. It is a good thing Covid was not going on then, or I would have really been hurting! The thought of living without my husband was incomprehensible to me. I felt like it was just way too much for me, but somehow I managed to get up even when I was not sleeping well and take care of everything I needed to. *One day at a time* took on a whole new meaning. It was often *one moment at a time*. **It truly was only by the Grace of God carrying me that I was able to make it through this time.**

The first few months were honestly just mostly a blur. I can remember walking down the street with Holden and just feeling nothing. I was numb. I didn't feel much emotion in the beginning. That would some later, but I had too much business to take care of in the beginning to fall apart.

They say grief comes in waves, and I had a few waves in the beginning, but they were only short moments of anguish. I was afraid the waves would take me under, so I remained strong. I could not afford to be so vulnerable at this time, and I knew it. I am survivor at heart and I certainly proved that to myself during this time.

It truly was only by the Grace of God carrying me that I was able to make it through this time.

A Miracle Message

What a huge blessing this was in the midst of my grief

I had something happen two days after my husband's passing that was such a blessing from God that I must share it. I went to a doctor's appointment I had already made before Larry's passing, and afterward went to a restaurant next door for a burrito, and as I was standing there crying, the owner of the restaurant walked over to me with tears in her eyes and said, "I feel compelled to tell you that your husband loved you very much, and I know you think you aren't going to be all right, but you are," then she gave me a great big hug. When she gave me my burrito box, on the front of it was written *you have this*, with a heart shape next to it. I saved that box as a reminder of that day. I doubt if she knows how much she blessed me that day, but I have been back to the restaurant numerous times and told her how much she helped me. It meant the world to me that day to hear those words, as I really did not think I was going to make it. *God knew exactly what I needed at that moment and provided love and comfort through a woman I had never even met before. Thank You, Lord, for bringing this kind woman into my life when I so desperately needed it! Thank You, Lord, for your love and kindness! God knew exactly what I needed and provided love and comfort through a woman I had never even met before.*

A Family Visit

I called my older brother the night of my husband's death, urging him to please come up and see me, as I was in desperate need of some family support, so he came up immediately and stayed almost a week. The visit did not go as well as I would have liked, but I am still grateful he came to visit. He didn't show much empathy toward me, but at least he was honest about not being able to really understand, which I appreciated.

Having his company had a grounding effect on me, which I so desperately needed at the time, but I also had to be careful I didn't allow myself to be drawn into my insecure and vulnerable child around him, which can happen so easily because of the emotional dynamics between us.

When we were in foster care we were always together. Where he went, I went. He is five years older than me, so as a child I depended on him and looked up to him. As a young child in foster care, I felt like he was all I had at times, especially when we were in the children's home. The emotional dynamic between us is not always healthy for me because of this.

Initially I felt myself being drawn into the six-year-old girl who needed him when he came to visit, but I recognized it immediately and put a stop to it. He wanted to drive my car and I told him, "no." First of all, I don't want anyone driving my car, and secondly, I needed to feel in control as an adult. He made some remarks about my husband leaving me with such a mess, and I reminded him that everyone has a certain amount of mess when someone passes, and I was no exception. More importantly though, was that I recognized how vulnerable I felt and knew that if everything had been perfectly in order, I would not have had to rise with all my adult strength against the child in me and make adult decisions, which ultimately made me feel strong and in control. *I believe that God, in His infinite wisdom, knew this and allowed all this mess for me to grow, and to prevent me from heavy grief that I wasn't ready for.* If I hadn't had all the business to take care of, my grief would have swallowed me up and I wouldn't have done so well. Was it stressful? Very. But I grew from it, and I learned a lot about banking and business that I needed to know. *Most importantly, I grew with the Lord, having faith that he would provide me with all the help I needed to get through this mess, which He did.* I got help with everything I needed help with. It has been almost three years now since my husband passed, and I feel more competent than ever that I can manage things on my own, which is a good feeling. I am a grown woman making wise decisions, including about this book.

Just to make a point about how distraught I was when Larry first passed—I actually asked my brother is he wanted to come live with me! Really, Carol? What are you thinking? Even my brother didn't like that idea and told me he knew I was just fearful about being alone, which was true. My fears of abandonment were very strong when Larry first passed. The first night my brother was visiting I asked him if he would come sleep in my bed and he said, "no Carol Ann; you are just scared but you will be all right." When my brother and I were in the Rose Hill foster home together we slept in the same bed, so I was being triggered back to that time.

It astonishes me how quickly I regressed back into my childhood. It is now 2023, and I am in EMDR therapy. I have been in therapy throughout my life, but never like this before. My therapist is a trauma therapist, so he has helped me realize more things about myself and the trauma I endured as a child. He has taught me so much about trauma and the brain. He has made me realize that the reason I was dissociating was because it was my brain's way of coping with the trauma, and that this was a normal thing for me to do as a child since I was going through trauma. On October 11, 2023, I had my first EMDR session and feel calmer.

I have been blessed with the best therapy ever, thank God!

Friends Welcome, Family by Appointment Only!

There is a good reason my sign reading *Friends Welcome, Family By Appointment Only* is in my front yard! I truly do need time to get myself emotionally prepared for anyone in my family! I get triggered too easily into my past, which is not healthy for me at all. I want to live in the present today, not in the past. I want love and light today, not hate and darkness. I want peace, and it is hard for me to have that with my family, but I don't blame them anymore than I blame myself for that. It is what it is. Does it sadden me today? A little, but not much. I feel as though I have grown beyond that to a place spiritually and emotionally where it doesn't matter much to me anymore. Blood family in my opinion isn't what it's all cracked up to be. Many people have more problems and headaches with family than anyone else. I love all my family, but from a distance and with very firm boundaries. It is the only thing that works for me, and today I need to do what is best for me. And boundaries are best for me.

It took me a long time to get to this point, but I now fully understand that I am the most important person in my life today. I have learned to love and nurture myself in a healthy way, and as I do that, I am more able to reach out to others to love and nurture them when the opportunity arises. I feel much more whole within myself today, which is a good feeling. I am very comfortable in my own skin and like my own company. There is song, *The Greatest Love*, that perfectly illustrates this… '*the greatest love of all, is happening to me, learning to love yourself, it is the greatest love of all.*' What an awesome feeling! **To me, the greatest love comes from God, and when His Holy Spirit lives within you, that is the Greatest Love. Thank You Lord, for filling me with Your Holy Spirit!**

To me, the greatest love comes from God, and when His Holy Spirit lives within you, that is the Greatest Love.

When I think of the first few days, weeks, and months after my husband's passing, I am utterly amazed how God's Grace sustained me. I found a strength in me that I never knew existed. I always knew I was spiritual and had faith, but it is when your world is falling apart that you truly find your strength, not when things are smooth. I always say, "faith is not knowing." I didn't know what was going to happen, but I had faith that God knew. He did know, and things worked out amazingly and beautifully for me.

There was SO much to take care of! I had to take care of the cremation. I had to get multiple death certificates to prove his death for various banks, etc. There was SO much business! I had four banks to deal with, life insurance, getting everything solely in my name, etc. My biggest concern was my home. My husband always took care of all the business, so I knew little about anything. About a month before he passed away, I asked him if everything would be ok when he was gone, and he just looked at me and said, *"don't worry, you will be ok. Everything is yours."* I recall my husband years ago discussing whether to do a will or a trust, but I never knew what he did because we never discussed it. I assumed that he had a will but discovered otherwise when I went to the clerk's office, which upset me. Knowing how much my husband loved me, it didn't make any sense, but it made perfect sense to me after talking with my lawyer.

I contacted Ford Legal Services, which was free for me (I only paid for paperwork, which was a minimal cost), and I was assigned a lawyer here in town. While discussing the situation with her and expressing my concern over the lack of a will, I asked her if people often contest wills, and she said, "yes, all the time." That is when the light bulb went on and I understood why my husband chose not to have a will. He did it to protect me, not to hurt me. He knew that his greedy children would try to contest a will, so he made it easy for me. He could have done a trust, but it wasn't necessary and would have been much more expensive. Larry knew that

I knew he had free Ford legal services and they would take care of the legalities. All I had to do was go to a lawyer who put it through probate, and the house was mine. It was easy. ***Thank God!***

His oldest son would have definitely tried to contest the will. My husband was a very smart man about legal things and knew exactly what he was doing. Thank you, honey! ***And thank You, God!*** The house was legally in my name within three weeks of me seeing the lawyer. That was the biggest hurdle I had to get through. When that was settled, I felt like I was more secure. Losing my home was my biggest fear, and it is no wonder why, considering my past. Security is ESPECIALLY important to me. My home means everything to me. I LOVE MY HOME. As Dorothy said in the Wizard of Oz, "there's no place like home." ***I thank God for my home every day!***

Backstabbed by Larry's Family

I wish I could say that my husband's family was great during this time, but it wouldn't be the truth. Larry's only surviving sibling stabbed me in the back, bigtime. She and I had agreed that she would put together a memorial for Larry because I wasn't up to it. I was not planning on going to this memorial because I didn't want to be around his kids or ex-wife, nor would Larry want me to be. He would not have wanted his ex-wife to even be there at the memorial, but I knew she was too narcissistic not to be. I was already on emotional overload. I definitely did not need or want more emotional drama or trauma. I told her that I had already decided to have my own memorial at my home on our anniversary, September 21st. She asked me if she could come to it, and I said, "of course; you're his sister."

She came down to my house a few days after Larry passed with her niece and told me that she really wanted me to feel like part of the family. What a lie that was! She put on a good act in front of her niece, but she didn't mean a word of it. She had always been very jealous and negative toward me, so why should I believe her now? I wanted to believe her because I so desperately needed family at the time, or so I thought. Emotionally I was on very shaky ground, feeling very vulnerable and needy, so of course I wanted to believe she was sincere, but I soon found out she wasn't.

I called her up a day later and asked her if she would please say a few words for me at the memorial, and her reply to me in a very curt voice was, "no! I won't do that! There aren't going to be any eulogies at the memorial, only a movie of his life." I knew she was a narcissist, but this shocked me; after all, I am his widow, who should have been given the most respect at the memorial. But since she is a narcissist, she made the memorial about her. A good friend of mine went to the memorial, and later told me that there were four or five people who got up and spoke about Larry, yet she refused his own wife, who was the love of his life, the due respect of even a written eulogy. I was going to write something down on a piece of paper for her to read on my behalf, but she wouldn't even do that much. I also found out from my friend that she barely even mentioned me at the memorial, which didn't surprise me, given her narcissistic jealousy. She disrespected both me and my husband. If she really loved her brother, she would have honored him by honoring his wife. How disrespectful! I soon found out she could be even more disrespectful than that!

While sitting in church on Memorial Day weekend when his memorial had taken place, a friend of mine handed me the Fowlerville paper, letting me know that Larry's obituary was in there, so I started reading the obituary, and the first thing I seen was the mention of his ex-wife, followed by me! What the hell?! I was sitting in church, more distraught than you can imagine, so grief stricken at this point that I felt like I couldn't emotionally cope, when I read this obituary! Really?! *Oh God help me!*

As I got up from my seat and told my friend that I had to leave, she asked me if I was ok. "No, I am not okay at all. I need to leave," I replied. She followed me out of the church and walked me to my car. She heard me cussing in the hallway of the church, so she knew I was extremely angry about something! I was hyperventilating I was so angry. I was beyond anger; I was enraged. She asked me again if I was going to be ok, and I just asked her to please pray for me, because I felt like I was going to lose it. I have never been so angry in my life. Never. If she had been standing in front of me at the time, I would have decked her! I felt like going down to her house and having it out with her but knew better. I was so furious with her that I didn't trust myself around her. I might have ended up arrested and on the news! I can laugh about this now, but at the time it was anything but funny.

I got in my car and asked God to please help me calm down, then I went home, took some deep breaths, and prayed some more, asking for God's guidance. Within a few minutes of getting myself calmer, I got on my phone and called my ex-sister-in-law and spoke my mind, without even using one cuss word, which was amazing. It took three phone messages to voice myself, but I let her know what I thought of her disrespectful behavior, refusing to honor Larry's own widow by not allowing a eulogy from me, and putting this obituary in the paper. She did it to hurt me, and I knew that. Not only is it improper to mention an ex-wife, but she did this knowing that Larry loathed his ex. His exact words to me about her were, "I loathe that woman. If I had it to do all over again, I would never have married her. I feel like I wasted twenty-seven years of my life with her." His sister told me in the past that she didn't even like her, but still chose to invite her to the memorial and put her name in the obituary, just to hurt me.

She is extremely jealous of me, and I know jealous people can be evil, but this to me was the lowest thing anyone could do to me, especially at this time of deep and agonizing grief. But I asserted myself and let her know exactly what I thought of her, and that Larry would be livid if he knew what she had done. I believe she not only wanted to hurt me but also Larry. They did not have a close relationship and he told me numerous times that he wished if God had to take one of his sisters, he wished He would have taken her and not the other sister who had died years earlier. She hated me because she had a distorted idea about their relationship and expected him to act like her husband, which he hated and refused. She had started telling him how much she loved him, and he finally told her, "the only woman I want telling me that is my wife, Carol," so she quit doing it, but she resented me because my husband loved me so much.

She is a true narcissist, and all her true colors toward me came out after he passed. What I thought was particularly evil about her behavior, was that she knew she could be nasty to me without Larry being able to put her in her place or defend me. She took advantage of me when I was the most vulnerable, without any empathy whatsoever for me. Being family, she could have and should have been a source of comfort for me, but instead I got stabbed in the back. Not only did she not want me in her life, but she didn't want her extended family to welcome me either. Why didn't she want to welcome me? I am convinced the reason she didn't want me around her family was because they would eventually find out what she was like with me and Larry. They would find out that we hadn't been having Christmas with her over the past ten years because she was upset over a gift we gave her that didn't live up to her standards, and told us that she wasn't going to exchange gifts with us anymore. She is a phony hypocrite who likes to look nice to certain people who will support her ego.

I told her in the phone message, "if you ever come down to my house again, you're going to get a shot gun in your face. I don't ever want to see you again or have anything to do with you." She has probably gone around telling people I threatened her life. No, I did not! If I were going to threaten her life I would have said, "don't ever come down here, or I will kill you!" If she ever came down here, I would point the rifle at her face, and then I would point it at her back as she was leaving! She is wicked and evil woman of the worst kind, who wants to cover her own evil by making others look bad. How did I resolve this situation?

I was so upset all weekend after this happened that I was unable to let my anger and hurt go, so I began praying and asking God to please help me let it go. I was outside doing some yard work when the answer came to me. I felt like God spoke right to me and said, "do your own obituary!" Well, of course! Why didn't I think of that sooner, God? When I get upset, I often get so emotional that I can't think straight and rational at first, but when the light bulb finally came on, I decided to go to the funeral home and put my own obituary in the Livingston County Press, with my favorite picture of Larry on it and everything about his life with me, and left my ex-sister-in-law out of it as a surviving sibling. She didn't deserve to be mentioned after what she did, and I knew my husband better than anyone, and knew he would have been happy with what I did. He would have zero respect for her after the way she disrespected us.

When I got to the funeral home and told them what happened, I asked the older woman working there, "am I being too sensitive about this? Is it normal for people to do what she did?" She said, "no, you are not being too sensitive about this. What she did was not normal or appropriate and it was very wrong for her to do that to you." She told me that it is rare for an ex-spouse to be mentioned, and if it does happen, it only under special circumstances with the spouse's (me) permission. She felt so bad for me that she hugged me and said, "I am so sorry this happened to you. You are doing the right thing now by putting this obituary in the paper. It will be done the way you and your husband want, and you'll feel better." And she was right; I did feel better. I am sure my ex-sister-in-law seen the obituary I put in the paper and hated me even more, but that is her problem. She has always hated me. I don't care how she feels about me anymore, or any other people who support her in her actions, because I know that God knows her heart and knows she is evil. I also know that **what goes around comes around,** and she will pay for what she did. Karma is a bitch!

My Sorrow is My Strength

What did I learn from this? Sadly, I learned that I was all alone, that I had no family around to support me in my time of need. As painful as it was though, it made me even stronger. A spiritual friend of mine said, *"your sorrow is your strength right now."* This may sound strange to the average person, but it makes perfect sense to me. My sorrow HAS been my strength.

I took all my hurt, pain, sorrow, and grief and forged ahead, republishing my **FACT** book with GoldTouchPress, and now doing this autobiography. I was not going to let my grief swallow me up or land me on the pity pot forever. If I were on my way to being flushed down the toilet, who would help me? Nobody. I had to find a way to make it through my sorrow, and this was one of the ways I did it. Just as forming **FACT** and writing the book were positive outcomes to my past, so was republishing the **FACT** book and writing my autobiography to my grief and sorrow about losing my husband. I also know my husband would want me to move forward in this way, which motivated me.

I know how deep my grief goes. It goes way back to the time I was a child and had nobody there for me. I was a survivor then and I am a survivor now. I hate losing my husband and I hate the way I was treated, but I refuse to let my ex-sister- in- law have that much power over me. I stood up to her and I moved on. As much as she hates me, I don't hate her; I just don't want her in my life. I don't just have a boundary with her; I have a wall. We were never close when I was married to Larry, so it really is no big deal to me that I have a wall with her. She just doesn't mean anything to me.

I learned in AA years ago that resentment is not good for me, and that I need to pray for those who hurt me, so I prayed for her. She is not worth me hurting over. I would be hurting myself more than her by holding on to a resentment, and I don't want to hurt. And truthfully, I pity her more than anything else, because she doesn't truly have the ability to love, which is sad. She really hurt herself a lot more than she did me. She is a narcissist who doesn't really know how to love, which is very sad. Karma always comes back to the narcissist, and she is no exception.

God bless her.

More Family Drama

Sadly, Larry's sister was not the only one in his family who gave me problems. His oldest son also tried harassing me not long after this. I was talking with a friend, who told, "I don't want to scare you, Carol, as I know you are going through a lot right now, but Larry's oldest son called here and told me that he knew where Larry hid his guns (like I didn't know myself!), and that he was going to break into your home and steal them." My friend put him in his place, but just the threat of something like that happening put me on edge. I wasn't overly concerned since he lives in Texas, but this threat took place before the memorial, so I was concerned about him coming here at that time, or maybe having a friend of his doing it for him. I know now that he was probably just being nasty and would never even attempt to break in, but for someone like me who has PTSD from serious trauma, it felt threatening. I talked with my husband's neighbor friend about the situation, and he called Larry's son and put some serious fear in him.

While picking up Larry's ashes from the funeral home I was informed that his son also called the funeral home demanding my husband's ashes, and when he was told he had no right to them, that I was the one who would be getting them, he cussed the funeral director out over the phone. I called his son from the funeral home, and he started cussing me out! He is another narcissist who thinks everything revolves around him, but he was very firmly put in his place by me and others. I went over to visit a good Christian friend after I left the funeral home and happened to see there was a new message on my phone while I was sitting in her home, which was from Larry's son, cussing me out and saying the most vulgar things you can imagine, like burn in hell, you ugly bitch! I didn't even respond to it because I knew better. If I did respond, I would have said, "I think you got me mixed up with your mom!" He was projecting the anger he had toward his own mother onto me. I didn't take it personal at all. The only thing that bothered me was the threat of breaking into my home. *But I know God watches over me and my home!*

Larry's other two younger children were not a serious problem, but a friend of Larry's did tell me his other son called him wanting my phone number, that he wanted to see if I needed anything. Really? He treated me like crap all those years, and now he is concerned? I may be trusting, but I am not so naïve as to believe it was genuine concern. He was probably more concerned over whatever he thought he might get materially, like my husband's Harley, etc. He could care less about me, and I knew that. As far I was concerned it was only *a foot in the door* that I was not about to let in. Thankfully, my friend didn't give out my phone number to him, so I never did have to confront him or deal with him.

I didn't really have to deal with his daughter, either. She contacted me on Facebook and said, "in light of my dad's death, I would like to talk with you." Really? Why? Again, why after all these years of treating me like crap, did she suddenly want to talk with me? I did not trust her. I emailed her back and told her I wasn't ready to talk with her, that I was too emotional over the loss of my husband and couldn't handle it. Despite the way she treated me, I was quite gracious toward her in the email. I told her that her dad told me he loved her and always wanted to be a dad to her while she was growing up, but her mom did everything in her power to discourage it, which was true. I wished her well, and I let it go. I'm not sure why she contacted me, and I don't care. I just wanted to be left alone in peace, and still do. If they should ever contact me again, I would firmly but politely tell them to leave me alone, that the door is shut on them. I don't just have a boundary with his children; I have a wall.

What I did care about was having peace in my spirit and doing the right thing as a Christian. While speaking with my friend (Larry's friend), who had gotten the threatening phone call from his son, I made a comment about wanting to do the Christian thing with his children, and he said to me, "Carol, DO NOT have anything to do with his children! You CAN NOT trust them! Listen to me, please! Larry would not want you to have anything to do with his children! He knows what they are like and the way they have treated you. Let it go! Larry is gone and you have no reason to be close to them or have anything to do with them, and you don't have any responsibility toward them." **Thank God for my friend!** My friend and I discussed this a few times over the phone, and I had to reassure him that I would have no contact with any of his children. I remember telling him, "don't worry. I am not going to have anything to do with them." It was one of those times when I would have to let my head rule my heart, instead of the other way around. I am so glad I listened to his friend. His friend also told me that Larry told him, "if my children don't accept Carol, then I don't accept them." My husband refused to accept their abuse toward me and told them so, which I respect him for. If his children ever tried to make amends, I would simply say, "I appreciate your amends, but it doesn't mean anything to me now. It is way too little, too late. I don't care what you think of me. The one you need to make amends with is gone." I believe the only reason they would want to make amends, would be to get forgiveness from me to ease their own conscience, which I can't and won't do. They need to get their forgiveness from God, not me.

I always say that *karma is a bitch*. They have to live with what they did to us. My husband told me the day he died, that the last thing his son said to him was, "dad, I never needed you for anything. I don't need you now, and I never will." What an incredibly cruel and heartless thing to say to your own father. I hope he can live with those words for the rest of his life. Just living with that should be karma enough.

Yes, we reap what we sow. Karma truly is a bitch! God and I don't need to punish them; whatever karma come to them is their own doing.

Life is all about
"KARMA"
It always gives you back
what you give to others.

No need for Revenge.
Those who hurt you, will eventually screw
themselves up. And if you are lucky,
God will let you watch. Keep faith.

Taking Care of Business

Because I didn't trust his children, especially his sons, I took the major things Larry owned—his truck, his Harley, his two trailers, and his tractor, and I had friends and neighbors put them on their property so they couldn't get them. My husband always told me to sell everything of worth when he passed, that I would need the money. *I am amazed how it all worked out, praise God!* I was having a garage sale to get rid of some things, and a long time Christian friend of Larry's told me he wanted to buy Larry's Harley, then he told me he wanted to buy his truck, then he wanted to buy the flatbed trailer! *I trusted God and look what happened!* I got my financial needs met, and not only that, but I didn't have to worry anymore about his children butting into my business. With the house in my name and some money in the bank, I felt more secure. The stress was easing some, but not completely. I was still dealing with a lot of business, and one of the main things I still had to take care of was Larry's guns. I was clueless about guns, but it all worked out. *I was in store for another miracle! Thank You Lord!*

GUNS!

I still had my husband's guns to sell, and I didn't know a thing about guns or how to sell them, but my friend who advised me about Larry's children told me how to get the serial number, make, and model off the guns to tag them, and how to clean them. *I got on the computer and researched GunBroker to get the costs of the guns, averaged out some prices, tagged the guns, and put the rest in God's hands. And God was more than faithful!*

I sold about half of the guns to a few of Larry's friends and was wondering what to do with the rest of them, when a friend at AA told me about an ad in the paper for a gun dealer looking for guns, so I called him. He came to my home a few days later, then came back a couple days later and took the guns. He also bought all my ammunition, which I was relieved about. He was a very smart gun dealer and made some good money on my guns! *Praise the Lord again!*

Not only did he sell the guns, but he did his best to sell them as quickly as possible because he knew my situation and really cared about me. He sold them on *GunBroker*, where he did his business, which just so happened to be where I did my research. Wow! I always told him how much I appreciated him getting the guns out of my home and selling them for me. I hated having the guns in my home! Word gets around, and I was afraid someone would try to break in and steal them. I told the gun dealer that he took a huge emotional burden off me. One day when we were talking on the phone to make arrangements for him to give me money for the sale of some of my guns, I told him, "at this point I was so sick of having these guns in my home, I would have just given them to you! Get them out of here!" He laughed when I said that, but it was true. Now that they are sold, I am glad I got the money, but at the time I truly felt like the guns were not worth the stress they were causing me.

Not only did the gun dealer sell my guns, but he also encouraged me to get the *SimpliSafe Alarm System*, which I did. That makes me feel much safer. I know God has supernatural Angels watching over me, but it doesn't hurt to have some human ones too! Now when I leave my home, I don't have to worry about someone breaking in without being caught, and I also feel much safer at night. Not feeling safe was one of the biggest issues I have dealt with since Larry passed away. I feel much more vulnerable without his protection, so it only makes sense to do what I can to reassure my safety. ***Thank God again!***

What I also found amazing about the gun dealer was his personality resemblance to Larry's. I was always telling him how much he reminded me of Larry. I don't believe it was an accident that he came along when he did. ***I believe God knew exactly what I needed at the time and brought him into my life, not only to sell my guns, but to be a source of comfort for me.*** I felt safe and secure when I was around him, just like I did with Larry. I am very intuitive and could tell he really cared about me, that he went beyond the call of duty to help me. I remember telling my grief counselor at the time that I felt like he would have even done more for me had he not been married.

He was so much like my husband that I told him it was too bad he was already married (though not happily). I always told my husband I would never remarry because I would never meet another man like him, then I met this man who is so much like him. ***I do not believe in accidents, so I believe it was a sign from God that I would meet another man like my husband. I know my husband wants me to. I know that God will bring the right man for me someday if that is what He wants for me. All I need to do is trust Him, which I do! Thank You God, for bringing this man my way and giving me hope!***

As of 2023 I have come to the conclusion that I am perfectly okay with being alone if that is what God wants for me.

My Husband's Memorial

I had my husband's memorial in our on our wedding anniversary, September 21, 2019. I was planning on having it outdoors, but rainy weather forced me to have it inside, which I was initially upset about. I kept praying for the rain clouds to go away and got upset when God didn't answer my prayer. As the time was approaching for the memorial, I seen the stormy clouds overhead and wasn't sure what to do, then as people started arriving along with the rain, I decided to bring it inside. I bring this up to make a point about going with the flow of things. *I thought I knew what was best, but God had a better idea, and I am thankful He did!* As people were helping me bring things in from the rain, it suddenly dawned on me that this was exactly what Larry would have wanted! He always said he wished that his friends would stop and see him more often in his home, and now here they were. The memorial was simple and beautiful, with people sharing stories of his life. His friend Rick looked at me with tears in his eyes when he spoke of Larry's love for me. He said, "Carol, that man really loved you." I played my song for Larry, *Because You Loved Me*, by Celine Dion. Larry knew this was my song for him, and it truly did express what I felt in my heart for him.

For all those times you stood by me, For all the truth that you made me see, For all the joy you brought to my life, For all the wrong that you made right, For every dream you made come true, For all the love I found in you, I'll be forever thankful baby, You're the one who held me up, never let me fall, You're the one who saw me through, through it all, You were my strength when I was weak, You were my voice when I couldn't speak, You were my eyes when I couldn't see, You saw the best there was in me, Lifted me up when I couldn't reach, You gave me faith 'cause you believed, I'm everything I am because you loved me, You gave me wings and made me fly, You touched my hand, I could touch the sky, I lost my faith, You gave it back to me, You said no star was out of reach, You stood by me and I stood tall, I had your love, I had it all, I'm grateful for each day you gave me, Maybe I don't know that much, but I know this much is true, I was blessed because I was loved by you, You were always there, The tender wind that carried me, A light in the dark, shining your love into my light, You've been my inspiration, Through the lies you were the truth, My world is a better place because of you!

My husband healed me from my past. That God brought this man into my life is a miracle that I will always thank Him for. No words can adequately express what I feel in my heart and soul for God and Larry. Thank you both!

It is because God brought Larry into my life, who gave me a better life, that I was able to form FACT and do this work for former foster children. I felt that God blessed me, and I in turn wanted to bless other former foster children. What goes around, comes around, and I felt it was my turn to give back what God blessed me with. Love.

Grief Counseling

I was referred by someone to a grief counselor, who I seen from April-December 2019. She was ok, but I never felt like I was in real therapy with her. We always ended up talking about superficial things, and sometimes even about her own issues, which I think I preferred over having to deal with my intense grief. It was a good distraction for me at the time. I believe we deal with things when we are ready, and I wasn't ready to deal with my overwhelming feelings about the loss of my husband. Our relationship was more of a friendly one than a professional one, but it was nice while it lasted. I will always remember one thing she said to me that was worth the time spent with her. When I expressed how hard losing my husband was, she said, "this is no walk in the park." She validated my pain, which is what I needed more than anything. I am grateful for her understanding and empathy at a time when I so desperately needed it. She was also a Christian, which I was so grateful for.

She reminded me that I would see Larry in Heaven someday, which I needed to hear. Thank You Lord!

Yes, I know I will Larry someday, but right now I am here alone without him and I miss him terribly. I said at one point, "Larry's in Heaven, but I am in hell without him!" My grief truly was so overwhelming at this time that it felt like hell.

A Huge Blast of Grief

God help me!

It was during the holiday season of 2019 that my grief finally hit me, and it hit me like a huge blast. I started crying a lot during this time, and the grief was so deep I felt like I didn't know where to begin. *Most days I got up and got on my knees out of desperation, and just started begging God for help. I would simply say, "God help me!"*

This is when I decided I needed to get some help, that I couldn't go through this grief alone, so I started going to a Christian based support group called *Grief Share*. I went to four meetings right before Christmas, then I was left alone during the last two weeks of the year to deal with my overwhelming grief. *I honestly felt like I would be consumed by my grief and sorrow, and I would drown in an ocean of tears, but Jesus rescued me before that could happen. It always amazes me how God gives me exactly what I need when I need it. I am His child and He loves me.*

I will never forget that Christmas Eve. I sat in my living room chair feeling so alone, until I finally decided to attend a Christmas Eve service down the street from me. As I was leaving the service, a young child came by me singing *Joy to the World*, which really impressed me. Something about her reminded me of myself at her age. *I believe God put her there for that purpose, and to give me hope that I would be joyful again like that little girl.*

I was told at *Grief Share* that the first holidays without your spouse are the worst, and they certainly were for me. I was never so happy to see 2019 end! As of now, it is Thanksgiving of 2020, and though I don't feel good about being alone without my husband, I don't feel devastated like I did last year at this time. I will always miss Larry, but time has made my grief more bearable.

I am so thankful for Grief Share.

A Christian Music Miracle!

I have always believed that it gets darkest before the dawn, that when we are the lowest is when God opens doors for us, and what happened in December of 2019 is a testimony to that. Right when my grief was coming out in huge waves and I felt like I could be pulled under, Jesus came out on the waves and brought me back to shore, but not in a way I would have imagined. God is always surprising me! It still amazes me when I think of the miracle God brought my way!

I like to go shopping at the *Salvation Army* a lot, and one day right before Christmas I happened to be looking through the music CD's and found an *Emmilou Harris* CD, a beautiful singer from the 1980's I was familiar with, so I bought it. About a week later I put the CD in to listen to it, but was surprised to see it wasn't *Emmilou Harris* CD, but a group called *Casting Crowns*. What is this? I noticed the name of the CD was *Lifesong*, which caught my attention, so I put it in the CD and was pleasantly surprised to find out that *Casting Crowns* is a Christian singing group! And I was blown away by how much I loved their music! Wow! And what amazed me about this CD was that one of the songs on it is called *Praise You Through the Storm*, which is exactly what I needed to hear at that time. The song says, *'though my heart if torn, I will praise You through the storm.'* What is also amazing about this CD miracle, is that it led me to get more Christian music, which has been such a huge blessing. I was amazed at all the beautiful Christian music that is available nowadays. I love having this music in my home, as it is filled with the Holy Spirit.

Though praising God was not what I felt like doing at that time, listening to that song reminded me that it was what I should at least be trying to do. But how? I was in SO much pain. "Please, God help me" was all I could seem to muster up the breath for.

God knew exactly what I needed and provided it. Although I have been a Christian for years, I had only occasionally listened to Christian music on the radio and was surprised how much I loved it! I got on Amazon and started ordering more of their CD's, along with other Christian singers, and am now so in love with Christian music that it plays in my home all the time! ***It lifts me up and makes me feel closer to the Holy Spirit. What a HUGE BLESSING He gave me that day in the Salvation Army store! The Christian music was largely how I was able to draw closer to God, Jesus, and the Holy Spirit, which was ultimately how I was able to make it to shore! Thank You SO much Lord, for Your goodness!***

Another miracle that happened around the same time was on tv. I watch very little tv since Larry passed away, but one day I happened to turn on the tv and Celine Dion was on a talk show talking about her new CD, *Courage,* that she produced after her husband passed away a few years ago. I got the CD and listen to it sometimes when I'm feeling like I need support from someone who understands. The song *Courage* says, *courage, don't you dare fail me now; you're all I have to hold on to.* Boy, can I ever relate to that! ***It has taken every bit of courage I have some days to*** *even get out of bed and face another day without my husband, but I do somehow by the Grace of God.* My heart goes out to any widow.

I often get gut feelings about things, and one day I was going by a resale shop and felt there was something important for me to find, so I went in and just started browsing around, praying for God to show me. I happened to notice a small memorial plaque for a loved one, so I picked it for Larry and placed it by my favorite picture of us when I got home. I was browsing through a box of free books they keep at the door as I was leaving, and took a book called, *On Becoming a Widow.* It was only a small and simply written paperback book, but I was impressed with what I read. She expressed so many of my thoughts and feelings about being a widow, that I thought she must have got in my head somehow! In the book she wrote about being around other widows, and how all we have to do is look at each other and we *just know.* The saying, *it takes one to know one,* certainly applies to widows.

I have a neighbor who recently lost her husband, and I remember telling her last year that she would better understand me when she loses her husband. She has admitted to me that she really didn't understand what I was going through, but she does now that her own husband is gone.

There is a reason why God says to be there for the orphans and widows; He knows how much we need help. I have been both a foster child and a widow, so I know God takes special care of me! God faithfully

states, *"I will never forsake you or leave you,"* and *I have never been so fully aware of this as I have been since Larry's passing. Thank You Lord, for being a faithful and loving Father!*

Grief Share Alone

Grief Share started meeting again around the second week of January, then the thirteen-week session ended, and I had to wait a few more weeks for another one to begin. Just when I was beginning to feel like I was getting the support I needed, everyone was on lockdown due to the Covid pandemic, and I was left alone again, this time shut in my home all alone trying to deal with all my intense emotions. The grief was coming on strong during this time and I was crying a lot. I felt like I couldn't cope with my intense grief. I was talking with a woman who is a facilitator at *Grief Share*, but she could only do so much for me. I explained to her about all the loss I had a child, but she couldn't help me because she wasn't a trained therapist. I know she felt bad for me, but just didn't know what to say or do to help me.

Because *Grief Share* is a Christian support group, it is designed to help us grow spiritually and then send us on our way. She knew how spiritual I was and thought because I was so close to God that I was doing ok and didn't need *Grief Share* anymore. Who was she to tell me what I need? When I made a comment about liking to be around other people who understand, she said, *"Grief Share* is there to help people grow through their grief with God; it isn't there for a social reason." Really? Since when aren't support groups social?! Support groups work because they are social! People are connecting with others with the same issues and therefore don't' feel so alone. That is a no brainer! I still keep in touch with this woman, but I know better than to expect her to understand where I am coming from about my deep-seated grief from my childhood. As I sit writing, *Grief Share* is still not reopened, but I am ok with that. I just kept trucking along with my grief, alone. ***"God help me!" is my continual prayer.***

I had a friend who was a support for me during this time, talking with me some. She knew my husband and me from a church we attended, so she was aware of the close relationship we shared and how devastated I was by the loss. ***Again, God knew what I needed and gave me a listening ear.*** We rarely speak anymore, but I am grateful for the time she gave me then, as I was in so much grief and pain I wondered if I could go on, and even if I wanted to. I missed my husband so very much that it felt like pure anguish.

I could say more about this person and her 'friendship' with a family member of my husband's, but it would tarnish her good reputation as a 'good Christian,' so I will be quiet and walk away gracefully, knowing that 'what goes around, comes around.' And I will more closely heed Jesus' warning, "beware of wolves in sheep's clothing."

We truly do reap what we sow. I try my best to sow good seeds in my life because I do not want bad karma! I know I have sowed exceptionally good seeds with FACT! And I pray those seeds continue to sprout and produce fruit. I always pray that FACT will bless all the foster children, past, present, and future. I pray they find hope in the words God gave me to speak to them.

Sixteen Again

As I approached the first anniversary of my husband's passing, I realized more and more how deep seated my grief was. Of course I already knew I had issues from my childhood, but what I didn't realize was that a lot of my grief hadn't been fully dealt with. For the first time I was really beginning to understand my deep seated childhood emotions about my past from an adult perspective and realized just how traumatic it was. I was looking at it through someone else's eyes. I have had people who know about my childhood say remarks like, "you come from a brutal past" and/or "you had a childhood from hell," but never agreed with them because I truly did not realize how bad it was. As a child I was not thinking about my childhood being bad; I was just trying to survive it. Being able to gain this perspective was an important turning point for me, because now the child and adult are more connected.

What impressed me the most about my deep-seated grief after Larry passed, was that I fully realized that I never grieved my father's death when I was sixteen. And when the grief surfaced, I was shocked by the amount I had. Here I was grieving the loss of my dad so many years later. I know from being in therapy that emotions bottled up for years will come out stronger if/when finally emerge. For example, anger becomes rage, fear becomes terror, etc. My unresolved grief was overwhelming, and I felt like I was regressing back to the age of sixteen, which felt strange. I realized how alone I had felt, how sad I felt, how abandoned I felt, and I was overcome with compassion for that girl who had nobody to help her through her grief. For crying out loud, I had lost my dad! I remember walking around feeling much too old for my age, but I was just surviving then and didn't realize it wasn't normal for a teenage girl to feel that way. I simply accepted my situation as a fact of life for me like I did when I was a child in foster care. It felt normal for me.

I also gained a huge insight about myself from working through this old grief, one so obvious to me that I am amazed I didn't realize it sooner. I now realize I have in many ways been emotionally stuck at sixteen, especially in my relationships with men. When my husband passed away, I felt in many ways like I did when my father passed away. I was a typical teenager who wanted the freedom to leave and still come home to the love and support of my dad, but I no longer had that comfort, which left me unable to truly become independent. I now realize why I have had such struggles in my relationships with men, wanting both freedom and independence. I was always afraid I wouldn't survive the independence if there wasn't a man in my life. My husband was in many ways like my father, always there for me and protecting me, which I miss a lot. It is why being alone has been emotionally healthy for me. It has made me realize I can be alone and independent without the comfort of a man around. Someday I may have another serious relationship, but for now I am quite comfortable on my own. Wow! This feels like nothing short of a miracle to me! It's emotional growth.

As I have been reliving my past through writing my autobiography, I see more clearly where I have been and why I ended up there. I mean really, what normal seventeen girl would get herself mixed up with a junkie who is an ex-convict? A girl who had a childhood of loss and abandonment, that's who. I can't beat myself for making a bad choice then. I was only doing what any desperate young girl might do in my vulnerable situation. I was very vulnerable and needy.

When I think back on my young adult years, I think of myself as a young sapling that was blowing in the wind. Wherever the wind took me, I went, and it took me to some bad places. I wish I had gotten the support I needed back then, but I didn't. As one therapist said, *"Carol, you fell through the cracks." I went from stepping on the cracks to falling through them!* Sad, but true. It feels like I am more deeply at the core of my childhood issues, which is both scary and freeing. One thing I do know for sure though, is that I need to *be real and feel to heal*.

As I sit editing some things in 2023, I am now in EMDR therapy and truly understanding things much more deeply. I understand dissociation from the trauma I experienced in the past. I told my therapist I thought I was crazy, but he said, "you aren't crazy, Carol; you are human. Everything you feel is normal for someone who has had trauma. What a relief it was to hear that! *Thank God for my therapist, as he really helped me understand the trauma and is helping me to heal.*

Writing my Autobiography

Speaking of my autobiography, I should mention that I did not want to do it! The publisher at *GoldTouchPress* highly encouraged me to do it, telling me that it would help the *FACT* book to sell, but I was still highly reluctant to do it. Not only did I not want to put the work into it, but I did not want to go back into my past again! I started having anxiety over the idea of writing an autobiography and was advised by friends not to do it because it would be too much for me emotionally. One friend said, "with all you are going through after losing your husband, you shouldn't do it. You aren't strong enough." I didn't think I was strong enough either, until I talked with a spiritual woman who told me, *"Carol, your sorrow is your strength."*

Although I will listen to people's input, I ultimately listen to God and use my own judgment, which is what I did in this situation. I thought about it and prayed about it, and then when I was still confused, I decided to contact a spiritual woman to help me, and what she told me convinced me to forge ahead. She told me that she understood how uneasy I was of going back into my past again because of everything I had gone through emotionally doing the *FACT* book, but that I didn't realize how much I had healed from doing the *FACT* book. That is what caught my attention more than anything, that I had healed a lot and therefore wouldn't be as traumatized this time.

Although it has been extremely emotional for me writing my autobiography, I believe I am healing more. I feel as though I am looking at my past with a whole new perspective, and the one thing I realize more than ever is that I want to live in the present today. ***Thank You God, for giving me wisdom and courage about this book! I pray it will be a living testimony of Your Love and Grace.***

When I started writing my autobiography, I thought I would be unsettled and traumatized, but what I felt more than anything was just bored. I am so tired of my past and talking about it. I would much rather listen to other people's stories than my own. Just the fact that I would rather listen than talk tells me that I am more healed. My heart has not really been into this book like it was for the **FACT** book. I was driven by such a strong sense of purpose while doing the **FACT** book that I don't have about my autobiography. I am only doing it because I believe it will help the **FACT** book to sell. Honestly, I feel like I have worked hard enough and would much rather relax and have fun in my life, but here I am again, working on another book. I am healing more though by writing my story, and I now understand why God wanted me to write my autobiography.

When I first started this book, I said, "God, do I really have to do this?" No, I don't have to do it, just like I didn't have to do the FACT book, but when God gives me something to do, I do it. I know someday I will see Jesus in Heaven, and I want him to look at me and say, "well done, my faithful servant." That is really the primary reason I have done any of this work, so here I am writing my autobiography, hoping I will do it right so it will help other former foster children to at least know they aren't alone and there is hope for them. Believe me, if there was hope for me, there is hope for others. I want so much to give hope to foster children, and that is what God wants. I am speaking of God a lot in this book because I genuinely want others to know the Love of our Heavenly Father. I hope speaking of God so much doesn't offend people, but I would rather offend people than Jesus.

As I sat taking notes in the summer of 2020 while relaxing down by the water, all I could think of was that I would rather be in the water floating around on my raft and looking at the clouds floating by than writing about my past, which I want to be in the past! I no longer want the baggage of the past. I want to live and be free today.

Will I ever get over it? I thought when my husband first passed and I realized how deeply affected I was because of my childhood, that there was no way I would ever get over my past, but as a therapist said years ago, "no, Carol, you will never get completely over it, but you can get beyond it," which I believe I have. What the therapist did not tell me though, was that the only true way to heal was by the Grace of God.

The True Healer

What I believe more than anything, is that the Holy Spirit is the Healer. He can heal us in ways that we cannot comprehend. Sometimes God helps us by leading us to the right people who can help heal us, but He can heal us through the power of the Holy Spirit if we let Him. When I am still and feel the presence of the Holy Spirit, I realize that God is much bigger than anything I have ever gone through. His Spirit can lift me up to Heavenly places that I could never go to alone without His help. His Presence transcends and lifts, but I need to be still enough to allow His Peace to enter in. I have a huge thing on my entryway wall that says, "Be Still and Know I am God."

It is only in looking back over my shoulder that I can honestly say that the Holy Spirit is the Healer, as I see the evidence of it within me. I am not the same person I was years ago, which I believe is mostly due to the wooing of the Holy Spirit. Like my husband always said, "The Holy Spirit is a gentle, wooing Spirit." Years ago, I would never have thought I would be where I am spiritually today, and I know it is only by the Grace of God and His Holy Spirit that I am. The only thing I can really take credit for is being willing and open; the rest is God. When I think back on all the time I spent going to people for advice instead of seeking God's, I am ashamed of myself for not trusting Him more. My old therapist and friend, Kim, reminded me at Larry's memorial that the strength I looked to her for years ago was already within me. I see the truth in them words now and thank her for expressing them to me.

I am at the point in my life where I am ready to fully surrender to His Powerful and Almighty Grace. Why? Because I want PEACE! The biggest motivation for this spiritual journey I am on is not because I am trying to be holy or good; the reason I want Jesus and His Holy Spirit is because I want peace in my heart and soul. I have had a very traumatic past that has left me angry, ashamed, and feeling alone like I expressed in the ...fact is...document, which I am sick and tired of! I want true healing. I do not want to carry the burden of the past anymore. I want freedom, and the only way for me to be free is to surrender my life to God and move forward, trusting that He will take me by the hand and gently and firmly guide me into greener pastures. He will lead me Home.

Jesus the Shepherd

My favorite description of Jesus is of Him as a shepherd. I have a shepherd statue of Him in my home to remind me of who He is to me. I was lost and wandering about years ago, but He found me. When I look over my shoulder today, what I see is the Hand of God. He never let go of me, even when I let go of Him. He is faithful and true. He loved me relentlessly. The day after my husband passed away, I opened the Bible and seen the verse, "I will never leave you, nor forsake you." God knew *exactly what I needed to hear that day. I held those words in my heart and mind constantly for days and weeks following his death, and I still do. My Father in Heaven loves me! And he loves all the other lost and wandering children, and I believe God has a special place in His Heart for foster children, who so desperately need to know His Love.*

FACT Meetings!

I always say that God's timing is always perfect, and He was right on time again! In May of 2020 I received a phone call from a girl who shared her story in the *FACT* book, expressing a desire to start FACT meetings on ZOOM! Wow! What a surprise! *I always say that God likes to surprise me, and He certainly did this time!* I had all but given up on the idea of any *FACT* meeting taking place. It had been twenty-one years since I had formed *FACT* and attempted to have them, and now I was miraculously surprised!

Kristina was having a difficult time in her own life and felt the need for meetings, and I most certainly did with the loss of my husband, so we both agreed to her forming *FACT* ZOOM meetings. The first one took place on May 27th, 2020, and have been taking place every other week. There are usually at least seven of us at the meeting, and hopefully it will grow. *I am sure in God's time and way it will.* I am so grateful for Kristina doing this, and I am also proud of her. She doesn't think much of it, just like I didn't think much of forming *FACT*, but the truth is we both felt a need for support and had the initiative to reach out, which not everyone will do.

*It has now been a year since the *FACT* meeting was formed, and I am happy to say it is flourishing! *Praise God! His timing couldn't have been more perfect for me and my intense grief.*

I never thought much of what I was doing years ago when I first had the idea of forming **FACT**. All I knew was that I needed support and decided that since there weren't any support group available for former foster children, I would rise to the occasion and form one myself. Kristina knows more about computers and doing ZOOM than I do, so I was happy and relieved that she did this. I also want other former foster children to be involved in **FACT**, and this was a good way for them to be involved. I let her do the **FACT** meeting the way she wanted, without any interference from me. The most important thing to me is that **FACT** reaches former foster children. It truly warms my heart to see lives being touched by **FACT**. I look forward to the meetings and the sense we all have of being a family, which is what I have always hoped for.

We truly are **together,** and not just at the meetings. We keep in touch over the phone, and one of the girls who shared a story in the **FACT** book needed help moving, so some of the other girls helped her. The girl who was moving grew up feeling very unloved by her own family, so it was important for us to reach out to her. We even read her story at the **FACT** meeting, which we were all touched by. I was reminded by reading her story that I could have had it so much worse. As I told Kristina, I had love in my childhood, but that poor girl grew up feeling unwanted and unloved by her own family. It is stories like hers that remind me why I do this work. ***The greatest blessing I could ever have in this life is to know that the words Jesus spoke to me, "be there for my children" will be a FACT.***

Losing Holden

Just when I thought I was beginning to get past at least the worst part of my grief about Larry, I had another major loss in my life, which I still have trouble talking about or writing about, as it was very traumatic for me.

My dog Holden passed away. He started having symptoms of UTI around the beginning of June, so I got some natural remedies. He started acting strange, coming over to me as if to say, "I don't feel well and I want your attention." He bit me on the wrist when I was putting on his leash, which bothered me a lot because he had never been aggressive toward me. Then one evening after coming home from a walk in the park, he refused to get out of the car and started growling at me. I knew then that something was wrong, so I took him to the vet the following day.

The vet came out to get Holden when I arrived because he wouldn't get out of the car due to being in so much pain, which I recognized at home when he wouldn't get out of the car, but I still didn't think it was serious. I thought he only had a UTI and would be ok once the vet treated him, but I was wrong. A few minutes later I received a phone call from the vet while I was outside waiting in my car (I could not go in due to Covid), informing me that Holden would have to be put down, that he had kidney cancer that had spread to his lungs, and he wouldn't even make it two weeks if I brought him home. Oh my God! NO! I went into shock and started crying immediately. I couldn't believe it! I lost my husband in April of 2019, and now here I was losing my dog too!

I went inside to talk to the vet and look at the ex-rays so I could see proof of Holden's illness, and repeatedly asked him, "are you sure? Isn't there something you can do for him? Do I have to put him down?" Then when he convinced me there was nothing that could be done and that he needed to be put down, he tried reassuring me that I was doing the humane thing by putting him down. I can tell you that I did not feel humane about it at all. I felt like I was murdering my own dog! I had never watched a pet I love be put to death right before my eyes, and I do not ever want to do it again! I have never in my whole life felt so horrible about anything as I did this.

But somehow God gave me grace to do it.

I was given the option of being present for Holden's departure or not. I wanted to leave the room because I knew how painful it would be for me to watch, but then decided I would stay with Holden, to give him comfort and love until the very end. For anyone who has loved an animal the way I loved Holden, you can understand the pain I felt. My heart was so torn apart that day. I just cried and cried the whole time, and I kept crying for at least a few days. It hurt me so much. I can't even kill a squirrel without crying, and I watched my baby Holden, the most precious and sweetest dog I have ever had, die right in front of me.

Holden was brought into the room, and we spent a few minutes alone before he was put down. I held him, looked at him, told him how much I loved him, how much joy he brought into my life, and that I would never do this if I didn't have to. They had already tranquilized him some, so he looked peaceful in our last moments together. I looked into his eyes while we were together and told him over and over how much I loved him and always would. Holden always understood when I told him that. I would always tell him while we were out walking how much I loved him, and he would always wag his tail when I said it. I believe animals understood more than we think they do, and Holden understood everything I was trying to tell him that last day together.

He was gone within a minute after he was given the injection, and I was left with nothing but memories and my grief. I took a picture of him lying on the blanket after it was all over, and I keep that picture in my phone to remind me that I was there for him until the very end.

Part of the reason I wanted to be there for Holden was because I have carried guilt for not being with Larry when he died on our couch, and I did not want to do that with Holden. In a way I was trying to say to Larry, "I am sorry. I should have stayed on the couch that night with you. You should have passed away in my arms. I should have been with you until the very end. Please forgive me." I did the brave thing and was there with Holden until the very end, which I know he appreciated. If he could have spoken to me, I am sure he would say, "thank you mommy, for being here with me. I love you." As much as it hurt me to watch Holden pass, I feel good about being able to overlook my own emotional pain to be there for him.

I struggled with some guilt about my ignorance of how ill he was, but the vet reassured me that I couldn't have known, and that there was nothing I did wrong, but it sure didn't feel that way to me. Often the hardest thing to accept is that we don't know why things happen. I kept going over in my mind about why Holden got kidney cancer. Was it the water? What did I do wrong? Why didn't I know sooner? On and on the guilt train was rolling down the tracks, and I couldn't seem to get off, until I finally realized and accepted that I am not a perfect human being, and I needed to forgive myself.

What bothered me the most about Holden is the grief he felt about my husband's passing. He was very bonded with my husband, and I know he missed him a lot. My husband and I were mommy and daddy to Holden. He still had his mommy, but with Larry gone, Holden was left without his daddy. I did everything I could to reassure him that I was there for him, but he was sad for his daddy. I have wondered if his grief affected him to the point where he got ill. I am a firm believer that our emotions affect us physically, and maybe Holden's illness was at least partially due to his own grief. I walked him all the time, we cuddled all the time, I was always telling him how sorry I was that he lost his daddy, and that I would always be there for him, that I would never abandon him, but I can't help but wonder if his grief contributed to his illness. Some people may think it's strange that I would be so tuned into Holden's pain, but I don't care. I have been told by spiritual people that I have a gift with animals, which I believe I do. I now talk with my dog Opie, and I really believe he understands me.

Holden was a rescue dog that we got after he was found out in the street after being hit by a vehicle and then taken to the vet. My husband, who never loved dogs that much, fell in love with Holden. Whenever I went for walks with Holden, he would always barge in the door to see his daddy. I felt so bad for him when Larry passed away. Whenever there was a man in my home for business Holden would want his attention because he missed his daddy, especially Alan, who was so much like Larry. It left me feeling rather helpless. What can I do to make Holden feel better? I have often said, "I don't know how mothers explain to their children that daddy isn't coming home when there is a divorce or a death. I can't even do that to my dog!" Opie is very sensitive to abandonment, as my home is the forth or fifth home he has been in, and he was also abused by one of the owners. When I first got him he was rather timid, but today he is well adjusted and so incredible lovable. Everyone loves Opie. He is without a doubt the sweetest dog I have ever had, and there is strong bond between us. Opie and I have healed each other.

This is such a precious memory of Larry and Holden. I remember taking this picture about a year before Larry passed on. He loved that do a lot. I like to think that maybe Holden is with his daddy now.

CAROL LUCAS

Hospital Drama

The trauma of losing Holden was not the only trauma I went through that day. While at the vet's, I was informed that the dog bite needed to be treated at ER. What? I didn't realize how dangerous dog bites can be. I thought using peroxide on the infection would make it heal, but I was wrong. I was told, "you have to take care of this, or it can get very serious." A woman at the vet had her own experience with this, which put enough fear in me to listen and do as I was told, so I went straight to ER afterward. The girl at the vet's offered to take me, as I was so upset about Holden's death, but I decided I would feel stronger and more in control if I took myself. It was my childhood all over again. I must be strong.

The hospital stay ended up being good for me, though it didn't feel that way initially. I hate hospitals! I went there and got one IV of antibiotics and then left against the doctor's advice. He wanted me to spend the night and I refused. I did not want to go into the hospital when I was six years old, and I did not want to go in now! I also didn't have any health insurance yet, which was a practical concern. The nurse put an ink line around the infection before I left and told me to come back for more penicillin IV's if the infection got worse.

The next day when I was on my way out of town to visit the Little Rose Chapel, I went by a friend's house to visit, and she convinced me that I should go back to ER, which I reluctantly did. The same doctor who treated me the night before chewed me out for leaving the night before and put enough fear in me to get me to stay. He told me, "worst case scenario, you could die, or you could lose your arm, and if we can't get this infection cleared up tonight with IV's, you'll have to be flown to Ann Arbor and have the hand surgeon there operate on you." Oh Lord! When he came to see me in my room and I asked him if I was going to be all right, he said, "yes, as long you stay here and get treated. I had to put fear in you to get you to stay." "I'm staying," I said. I may be stubborn, but not stupid! I explained that the main reason I didn't want to stay the first night was because I didn't have any insurance until July 1st, which was a few days away. The doctor told me not to worry about the money. My attitude is the same as my husband's—it is what it is. That is my short version for the serenity prayer—*God, grant me serenity to accept the things I cannot change, the courage to change the things I can, and the wisdom to know the difference.*

Praise be to God, I only had to pay $200 for the first ER visit on June 26th, and I never received a bill for the second visit on June 27th!

What was interesting about the second hospital visit, was my reaction to it. I realized that I didn't feel so triggered by my past as I thought I would. I even felt peaceful enough to sleep part of the night. I was crying about losing Holden and having to be in the hospital, but I made it through without having any panic attacks, and I prayed hard that I would not have to be operated on. *God answered my prayer, and I was released from the hospital in the early morning, with a prescription for more antibiotics and a follow up appointment with the hand surgeon. I could feel sorry about myself over all of this, but I decided I would trust God and move on in my life. I didn't like it, and even got angry at God about the unfairness of losing my husband and dog, but I also believe that my life is unfolding as God wanted, and I just need to go with the flow...*

Although I handled the vet and hospital all right, it was mostly because I resorted to the same coping skills I learned as a child. I was strong, but what was different in this situation was that I realized what I was doing and reminded myself that it was ok to be vulnerable. I could cry, shout, and even get angry at God, and I would not die or go crazy from it! It was OK; in fact, it was perfectly fine and normal to be human and have all my feelings! Lord, I lost my husband, and now my dog! Of course I am going to grieve and cry! I thought, what's next now? Me? At least I won't have to grieve for myself, and I can be with Jesus and Larry! Needless to say, this was a very sad time for me. But by the Grace of God I got through this time.

I wondered if I would ever feel joy or happiness again, but as I sit writing in 2023 and my life is unfolding, I am feeling joy and happiness again, *thank God!*

All Alone

I miss Holden so much. He was such a comfort for me when Larry passed away. He knew I needed comforting and would come over and lay his head on my lap whenever he heard me crying. My husband was gone, but at least I still had Holden, and now he was gone too! It wasn't fair! Holden was the last part of my husband that I had, and now he was gone.

This was like the final straw for me. I never felt so alone as I did when Holden died. I spent a lot of time away from home, going down to the beach and going out on my land, just so I wouldn't have to be in my home alone. I used to love coming home and seeing Holden's sweet face looking out the window for me or looking out the window for me when I was working in the yard.

When Holden first died it felt strange to go walking alone, but now I am adjusted to it and enjoy my walks alone, which is good for me. Just to be comfortable with myself and enjoy my own company is a healthy and wholesome feeling, which I need and want right now. I don't need to go out and get another dog right away just because I might feel like I can't stand being alone. I may have gone beyond my comfort zone by being alone, but I feel as though going beyond it ultimately took me to a *beyond* that I have never been before, which is why today I am ok without a dog or a husband. *I don't want to be alone forever, but I feel that God wants me alone during this time. Like the Bible says, there is a season for everything, and this is my season to be alone. When the time is right for me to be married and/or have another dog, then that will be another season in my life. I believe in trusting in God and going with the flow. As God spoke to me years ago in a quiet moment, GO WITH THE FLOW... THE FLOW IS LOVE. Why would I want to fight the flow of God's LOVE? It doesn't make sense to me that I would want to fight LOVE, so I am choosing to go with the flow, and even if I don't know where the flow is going, God does.*

Trusting God's timing has been the hardest part for me, but I am more patient than I ever used to be. All I have to do is look over my shoulder and I can see that God's timing is perfect. I may feel like He is too slow, but I still need to trust that.

No having control over my childhood was a scary thing, but as I look back on it I now realize that God was there all along and knew what I needed. It's when I am feeling uncertain about things in my life that I tend to want to control things too much, but I am constantly being reminded that all I have to do is trust.

He is my Heavenly Father and I am His child. It really is that simple if I let it.

"I will never leave you, nor forsake you."

Do you hear that Carol? Let it sink into your heart and soul.

At the core of these beliefs is the necessity to trust, which is difficult when your trust has been destroyed as a child by abandonment. How do you trust when you don't feel worthy?

The message my mother gave me when she abandoned me was that I wasn't worth it. Thank God my dad thought I was worth it and didn't abandon me. I learned to trust again with my dear daddy!

Going With the Flow of Life

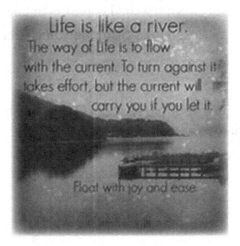

Life is like a river.
The way of life is to flow
with the current. To turn against it
takes effort, but the current will
carry you if you let it.

Float with joy and ease.

Going with the flow is the only way for me to live today. How much control do I really have anyway? I have some control over some things, like paying my bills, taking care of my body, taking care of my home, etc., but I don't have control over everything that happens in my life. I can't control the weather, and I most certainly can't control people, and I don't want to waste my time trying! The only person I can control at all is myself, and that is a big enough job for me!

No Control

Having had the unstable childhood I did, I learned at a young age that I had no control over what was happening to me when I was six years old. None. When I sat in a courtroom and had the judge slam the hammer down on my childhood, I was left feeling terrified, hopeless, helpless, and totally out of control, though at that age I couldn't recognize these emotions. I didn't walk out of the courtroom thinking that I was terrified, hopeless, helpless, and totally out of control, but that was how I was feeling. What an awful feeling it is for a young child to have no control over what is happening, especially when the child doesn't even understand what IS happening. All I understood was that I didn't understand! Petrified is what I was!

As Debra Cruz said, *"there are no words to describe what it is like to be a child and have no control over what is happening to you. It is a horror beyond words."* I could not agree with her more.

There really are no words to describe to what it is like for children who are going through foster care.

Triggered

On December 2, 2020 I started writing after I got off the phone with the **FACT** ZOOM meeting and found myself crying, and asked myself, "why are you crying?" Today it is important that I understand the why of my tears so I can work through them and heal. Without that I am just left feeling like I am an emotional basket case.

When the tears came, I immediately recalled our conversation at the end of the **FACT** meeting that we were having about foster children and school. We were discussing different topics for the **FACT** meetings, and I suggested we discuss foster children and school, since so many of us have strong issues with that. RD, an older man in the group, mentioned that I seemed like an intelligent woman, and I replied, "yes, I am an intelligent woman, but I had a big issue with school when I was a child and thought I was stupid. I flunked first grade!"

Though I had no way of understanding my problem as a child, I was so traumatized from being taken away from my family and placed in foster care that I had difficulty learning. It makes perfect sense to me now than I am an adult, but it made no sense to me as a six-year-old child. Now when I think about the situation I was in, I think, seriously, how could I learn when I was so severely emotionally messed up? I simply could not concentrate enough to learn much, as I was too busy disassociating from the emotional trauma! I could not be in two places at the same time, and I would rather be daydreaming than feeling the emotional pain I was in.

As a result of flunking first grade, I was always behind a grade throughout school, which I was not happy about! It does not matter to me now, but as a child growing up it did. I can laugh about flunking first grade now, but it was not funny as a child. I felt stupid! I like what Debra Cruz said, *"you aren't just the new kid in the class, but you are the stupid new kid."* That is how I felt. I spent years in school trying to prove that I was not stupid, and the sad part is, I never was, but what happened early on affected me and my self-esteem.

I remember the severe test anxiety I had when I was in college. **When people talk about God being taken out of school, I tell them, "as long as there are tests, God is still in school, because I prayed all the time for Him to help me pass!"** I was always so relieved when I took a test and found out I did well. I graduated with high honors, which was a huge accomplishment for me, mostly because I finally proved I was smart. I took an IQ test while I was in school and was amazed to find out my IQ was 130! What?! I cannot be that smart! I thought it must be wrong, so I took it again sometime later, and it was still 130! Wow, I do have brains! That proved to me I was not stupid, but sadly, it also showed me how emotionally messed up I was as a child in foster care.

I asked myself, why are you crying about flunking first grade and feeling stupid? What is the underlying feeling behind what happened? I sat in my living room and felt like I was six years old again, and I got in touch with the feeling I had stuffed. The feeling was shame. I never liked talking about my school handicap because I had so much shame about it. As a child I felt bad about it, but never knew I felt ashamed of myself. As a child I did not have the ability to connect the fact with the feeling, but now I can. I have such a deeper understanding about my childhood traumas since writing my autobiography. The insights I have gained are actually quite phenomenal. I have a clarity I never had before, which is amazing! I am so thankful for the **FACT** meetings! And I love the feeling of connection we have with one another. We get it! ***Thank You God, for the FACT meetings!***

Family Disconnection

As I already mentioned, there is a huge disconnect in our family. We are as scattered as we were years ago when we went into foster care. I no longer dwell on it, get upset, or blame anyone. If I were to throw blame around I would also in all honesty have to throw some at myself, as I am not any better than any of my siblings at connecting. The saying in AA, *when you are pointing a finger at someone, don't forget to point four back at yourself,* would apply in this situation. My dad did his best to fix the wreckage of the past damage, but unfortunately his best efforts were not enough to keep our family together. There had been too much emotional damage done to all of us. Our dad was the glue that held our family together, and our family went to the grave with him. Everyone went their separate ways, including me. We have not been a true family since my dad passed in 1971.

Though I was hesitant to leave Illinois and move to Michigan, over the years I realized leaving my family was the best thing for me, which is sad but true. The past is too much of a heavy burden on my heart that I do not need or want to carry. It is difficult to even have a conversation with any of my siblings without the past being brought up, which I believe is largely why we aren't comfortable talking with each other. The only sibling I talk with regularly is my sister who was in the children's home with me. We have fun talking and laughing on the phone, and we both keep a sense of humor about our family, which is nice. She once said, "considering what we all went through, we didn't turn out too bad. At least we didn't end up murderers or anything like that." True. When I told my brother what she said, he joked and said, "at least they haven't found the bodies yet!" I find that having a sense of humor about my family helps a lot. I can even find the humor in in how my younger brother went through our family like a tornado going down the train track in 2011, which is amazing.

I have learned to accept my family for what it is. A lot of families are disconnected, but I believe ours is more so due to the past disconnection. There are long term consequences to foster care, and family disconnection is one of them. For anyone who thinks it is simple to *just go on from here*, which were famous words of my mom, think again. It is not that simple or easy. We have too much emotional baggage. You cannot take emotionally damaged siblings and expect them to *just forget about the past*.

My dad had our family in counseling at one point when he first got us, apparently because he understood we were all emotionally messed up. We were all very emotionally needy, especially the younger ones, which I am one of. It seems the older siblings are not quite as insecure as the younger ones, but we all have our emotional baggage that we carry. We all have our issues.

I am so grateful my dad understood this and got us some therapy, though I do not know how much good it really did. At least he cared enough to try, which is more than most parents would do. He did his best to heal our family, but unfortunately his best was not enough to completely fix the wreckage of the past. It was no small task that my dad took on, of getting his children out of foster care and trying to mend the emotional damage that had been done to all of us individually, and as a family. When I think about the overwhelming task he had doing this, it humbles me and makes me feel so blessed that I had a father who loved his children enough to face the challenge. Thank you, dad, for all your loving kindness! *And thank you God, for giving me such a loving dad!*

A Family Healing?

I always say that God works in surprising and mysterious ways, and a pleasant surprise came my way in the summer of 2020. I decided that I would contact my niece on Facebook, the one I had a difficult time with in 2011 when I wrote the **FACT** book, to let her know that I had decided to edit the material about her dad that had been put in the first **FACT** book publication when I republished the book in 2020.

I thought when I contacted her that there would be no further communication between us. Afterall, there was so much anger and bad vibes between us. There had been some mean and nasty things said to each other that I thought neither one of us could just forgive and forget. Some things are harder to forgive, and attacking my character is one of those for me, which she did. I thought there was no hope for any relationship between us, nor did I even really care. I never even knew her until 2011 when my two brothers contacted her on Facebook and let me know about her. We had talked twice on the phone briefly, then after my younger brother stirred up trouble between us, it was over. So much for family, I thought. With the sad and sorry shape of my family, I was not surprised this happened, nor did I have any expectations of anything better. I did not see the sense of being upset over a niece I had no history with, and let it go. All that was important for me was to make amends and be at peace with myself.

Apparently, it was important to my niece, as she contacted me and asked if we could talk! Wow! Was I ever surprised, and pleasantly! We ended up talking on the phone for about four hours, having a heart-to-heart talk about everything that had happened years ago. We shared our hurts and misunderstandings and came to the conclusion that the reason we butted heads was because we are so much alike! We laughed a lot!

I went to my niece with a humble heart. I sincerely wanted to make amends for any hurt I caused her and explained that at the time I sincerely thought I was doing the right thing by writing the content in the **FACT** book, but now felt it was best to respectively remove it for all concerned, including myself. There was a common connection and understanding between us because we had both suffered the tragic loss of our dads at a young age. I was sixteen when I lost my dad, and she was thirteen.

Losing my husband has been a very humbling experience, which has made me more fully realize the importance of making amends. I decided I did not want to leave this earth without making this right with my niece. Life is too short and precious for that. She is my brother's daughter, who suffered a terrible tragedy at a very young age, and my heart truly went out to her while we were talking on the phone. I know she can't understand my foster care experience, and I told her "thank God you can't! I am glad you didn't have to go through what I did." Although she does not understand my foster care experience, she commends me for the work I have done for foster children and would love to read both of my books. I am not sure if I will ever meet my niece in person, but it is nice to be on friendly terms with her. I made peace with her and her dad.

I told my niece that I wish I had been there for her when her dad died. I also apologized on behalf of my whole family for not acknowledging her while she was growing up and explained to her how dysfunctional and disconnected our family is, that we don't even connect with each other, but I still feel bad about it. She is a grown woman with a family of her own, and I tell her to cherish her family, which she does. I told her I do not have a family, and she tells me that I do have a family with her family, which makes me feel good. The sad part is that I have spent so many years without family connection that it feels strange. I also do not completely trust it. Is something going to happen to mess it up? Will I do something to mess it up? I see other people interact with their family members like it is no big deal, and for me it is an emotional battle because of my childhood and all the turmoil in our family. I always feel like I am walking on eggshells with my family. To my niece it is no big deal. You are family! Wow, that was easy! Nothing in my family has ever been that easy before! I remember my therapist Frank saying, *"if something sounds too good to be true, it probably is."*

I have learned not to have high expectations in my family, that way it doesn't hurt so much when things go bad, which they often have in my family. My attitude is that I will have a relationship with anyone who is open to one, if I feel emotionally safe, but I back right off and crawl into my safe shell when I feel unsafe. I have been that way all my life, and it is not going to change. I have very healthy boundaries today with my family because I know how messed up I can get without them. I have just been through too much in my life and I can't and don't want to take any more. It may sound cold to some people, but I am far from being cold; I am just protecting myself. It is because I am so big hearted, sensitive, and caring that I have a difficult time with my family. And I often say, "if a boundary doesn't work, a wall will!" And a wall is what I have with my older brother, who is a narcissist. It would take pages to explain all of our history together and everything that has happened, so all I will say is that the dynamics between us are not healthy at all, for sure not me, and really not for him either, though he isn't wise enough to know this. All I know is I can not and will not tolerate him in my life anymore. He is so unhealthy for me that I have anxiety even writing about him. A boundary didn't work, but a wall will!

Boundaries with my Brother

When my brother went through our family like a tornado on a train track, I was the only one who forgave him, because I am loving, forgiving, and understanding of the deep emotional pain behind all his evil actions. I have a sister who claims to be a Christian and yet still will not forgive my brother. Being Christian means being Christlike, which means being loving, and to love others we need to look at the heart of people. That is what Jesus did, and it is what I strive to do.

I admit it was not initially easy to forgive my brother for what he did, but I did. I told him that I forgave him, but I do not trust him, which is true. He stole about a $1,000 worth of goods from our home, and the only financial restitution was $20. My husband never wanted anything to do with my brother after what he did, and although I still love him and care about him, I would never be comfortable having him in my home again. I must have safe boundaries. My husband admitted to me after my brother was gone from our home after the brief visit in 2011, that he never left me alone with my brother because he was concerned for my safety. Knowing what my brother's issues are from the past, I am so thankful that Larry was so protective of me. I took what Larry said to heart. I have found out the hard way that you can never be too careful in this world. And I can never be too careful in my family!

Understanding Foster Children

One thing I have learned, and learned the hard way, is that I can't expect someone who hasn't gone through my experience to understand me. It used to bother me that people didn't understand, until I finally realized it was not realistic for them to be able to. It doesn't mean people don't care, though I am sure they often don't; it means they don't have the experience to understand. Whether they can't or don't want to understand doesn't affect me today, as I have no expectation of it anymore. All that matters to me today is that I understand, and that there are other former foster children who understand. I often remind myself that this work I have done is for foster children, not the entire population. It doesn't matter to me what other people think of it, because I didn't do it for them. Whether they approve or disapprove is irrelevant to me. *I did this work for foster children because God wanted me to. His approval is the only one I care about.*

When I do mention my childhood, people either act uneasy, like they don't know what to say, or they say things like, "well, nobody has a perfect childhood," as if I am looking for pity, which is not the case. Empathy is one thing, but pity is another. All the former foster children I have been in touch with while doing the book and through the *FACT* support group only want validation and compassion, not pity.

Today I just don't expect anyone to understand. I understand that they can't understand and leave it at that. I am not angry or frustrated that they can't understand. It is what it is. The only thing that matters is that I do understand.

Emotional Baggage from Foster Care

I know everyone has their struggles, but I believe former foster children really do have more emotional baggage to deal with than the average person. We obviously come into foster care already emotionally damaged, or we wouldn't be in foster care to begin with. Then we have all the emotional baggage from being put in foster care, then depending on what kind of foster home we have, there is the likelihood of more emotional baggage. We at least deserve some validation for that so we can begin to heal from our foster care experience. There is never any healing from anything in life, whether it is alcohol, drugs, addictions, or dysfunctional behaviors, unless we first recognize it.

In 1982 when I finally decided to get sober, I first had to recognize that I was an alcoholic, then from there I could recover. I worked through the 12 steps of AA and did an inventory of my past behavior while drinking to discover the root cause, which for me was mostly emotional issues. The same is true for former foster children. *Yes, I have problems from having been in foster care," and I need to do an emotional inventory to find out the nature of the damage.* My AA inventory was only the tip of the iceberg; the iceberg was my inventory of emotional baggage from having come from such a dysfunction childhood and being in foster care. It was through doing my AA inventory that I realized I had deeper issues than just drinking, which led me to form **FACT**.

As stated in the **First Stepping Stone,** *'we recognize we have been injured from our foster care experience, that we are powerless over our past and our lives are unmanageable.'* We must understand that we have issues with our past before we can move forward and heal from them. **The Fourth Stepping Stone states,** *'make a searching and fearless emotional inventory of our foster care experience to discover the nature of the damage,'* which is so important for our recovery.

I know for myself that without discovering the nature of the damage, I am left wondering why I am damaged, with my unconscious mind trying to work things out, which in my past caused me SO much pain! I began to truly heal when I allowed my conscious mind to deal with my unconscious trauma and pain. I need to express that if I make this sound easy, simple, and/or straightforward, it was anything but that. It has been a messy thing for me. I have often gone two steps forward and two steps back, which left me wondering if I would ever heal, but I did the best I could. This stuff is not easy stuff to deal with. It takes time. I have learned to be gentle with myself, and I have also learned not to take myself too seriously, to have a sense of humor! *I am sure God has a sense of humor!*

Grieving

It is now December 2020, my husband has been gone one year and eight months, and Holden has been gone for four and a half months, and I am not sure what to think or feel about that. My happy life that I had with my husband is gone, and all the joy I had with Larry and Holden has disappeared into thin air. It feels like I will never really be happy or joyful again. Sometimes I sit in my home remembering all the happy times we shared and imagine them here with me, only to be sadly reminded that they are never coming back. I was sitting in my living room one day looking over at my couch and had a pleasant memory of watching Larry sitting on the couch petting Holden as he was nuzzled up to him, and a deep feeling of sadness came over me that that made me cry. I miss them both so much. Sometimes I feel like my heart is beyond broken; it is shattered. Will I ever be happy again? *Only God knows my deep pain, and only He can truly heal it.*

While chatting with a friend of mine today about how much I miss Holden, he suggested I get another dog, but I told him I am not ready yet. I cannot put my heart into another dog right now any more than I can put my heart into another man. I am just not ready. I woke up the other day on the pity pot, feeling sorry about losing Larry, losing Holden, health issues, medical bills, no real family around me, etc., but it did not take long for me long to get off the pity pot. It is not a comfortable place for me to be. I want to happy and joyful, and I can't be that way when I'm not counting my blessings. *I keep a gratitude journal to remind myself of all my blessings, and the biggest blessing I have is the Love of my Heavenly Father!*

One thing I have learned about grief through the Grief Share support group, is that I need to find my new normal, whatever that is. The reality is, that my husband and dog are not coming back. I am alone without them, and I must find a way to go on without them. Do I like it? NO! But I have no choice, other than offing myself, which I would never do. Losing my husband and grieving is without a doubt the hardest thing I have faced, and I faced it without drinking or doing drugs, which is a miracle considering my past. I have heard stories in AA about people who relapsed after a spouse died, and although I have never had the thought of drinking, I do understand how that could happen. Grief has taken me places I have never been before, which are not all bad. I feel that my grief has helped me grow in ways I never have before. The onion is being peeled to deeper levels, which ultimately is helping me to heal more from my past. Of course it has been painful, but *no pain, no gain.*

Grief took me places in my childhood also, but the difference between now and then is that I know I am grieving today, whereas I didn't have any understanding or words for the way I felt in my childhood. Today I know what I am feeling and why. Is it any wonder that as a young child

I wanted to escape in the classroom, play like a maniac, and then drink and drug myself into oblivion as a young adult? It would have made a huge difference had I understood what was going on and gotten the support I needed, but I didn't realize all this until after the fact, when I was wondering why I was in AA and therapy. What am I doing here? I asked myself. They have a saying in AA, *'I'm here because I'm not all there!'* Yep, that's me! I can relate to that saying!

That is why it is so important for young people who are aging out of the foster care system to get the help they need, hopefully before they wander down a dark road like I did and end up incarcerated, homeless, or dead. The streets are filled with former foster children who have aged out, and these are the ones who most need **FACT**. For any of you who happen to read the **FACT** book or my autobiography, please know this: YOU ARE NOT ALONE. It should at least be a comfort to know you are not alone in your circumstances, or your feelings. Foster children do have some unique issues in comparison with the general population, but not between themselves. We get it. Like I stated in the *...fact is...document, we may appear we walk the same roads as everyone else, but our shoes show the difference.* For anyone out there who thinks otherwise, try walking in our shoes...

As I continue this grief journey I am reminded of my early losses, which I decided to make a list of:

Losses I suffered before in my childhood before I went into foster care:

I lost trust when I was sexually abused.

I lost my innocence when I was sexually abused.

I lost my health due to poor nutrition.

Because my mother favored me, I lost some food sibling connections.

When my mother left to work, I lost her.

I lost a sense of security and safety when she was gone, when older
  siblings were abusive toward me.

I lost my sense of safety.

I lost my happiness and joy that I believe I had when I was a toddler

I lost *me.*

Now here is list of losses I suffered when I entered foster care:

I lost my mom.

I lost my dad, whatever was and could have been.

I lost my home.

I lost my siblings.

I lost my sense of security and stability.

I more trust due to the abusive foster home I was in.

I lost my connection to earth due to spacing out in the heavens.

I lost my ability to learn in school.

I lost my sense of identity.

I lost my sense of pride, of being a special child deserving of love.

I lost *me.*

Now here is a list of losses I suffered as a teenager after my dad died:

I lost my dad, who rescued me from foster care.

I lost my sense of security and stability, again.

I lost the ability to connect with my classmates, due to emotional
  issues.

I lost my education.

I lost my family, due to dad being there. We all scattered.

I lost whatever emotional stability I received from my dad.

I lost my sense of self, which is so important for teens.

I lost my morals some, due to being vulnerable and needy.

I lost my tenderness because I was so angry.

I lost more trust, due to my stepmom being abusive.

I lost my sense of self-esteem and self-worth.

I lost my trust in God.

I lost *me*.

Now here is a list of losses I suffered as a young adult:

I lost my sense of self-esteem and self-worth even more.

I lost my sobriety, staying drunk and high for seven years.

I lost my connection to God.

I lost my trust in God.

I lost trust in men, due to being with abusive ones.

I lost whatever good sense I had, due to being so vulnerable and needy
with men.

I lost my morals and values to some degree.

I lost most family connection.

I lost stability, living like a gypsy at times.

I lost my independence, due to being with controlling men who
wanted to keep me down.

I lost the ability to be a mother due to my own insecurity about being
a mom because of my own lack of mothering.

I lost my emotional maturity.

I lost decent jobs because I was too unstable and lacked education.

I lost any sense of direction.

I lost *me*.

I wrote '*I lost me*' at the end of each list, because that is ultimately
what I did lose. How sad to be walking around without yourself. You are
in your body, but there is nobody home. No wonder I drank and drugged!
It may sound strange to some people, but I believe part of the reason

I started drinking was to find *me*. I certainly began drinking to come out of my shell. I believe I was an extremely sweet and lovable young child, a beautiful little girl who loved everyone, who trusted, who wasn't emotionally damaged. Then came the sexual abuse, and my trust was destroyed. Then came foster care, and my trust was further destroyed. Then came my dad, who bless his heart, did everything he could to repair the damage that had been done to me. Then came his death, and I was left with an abusive stepmom who became even more abusive toward me than she had been when he was alive. Then came my young adult years when I just copped out to cope. I had had enough and all I wanted was to self-destruct, or at least self-medicate. I couldn't take the hurt and pain any longer. I was grieving and didn't even know it.

Unstable Past

It was not until I seen the way other people lived that I realized how unstable my life was in the past. Seriously, I don't know anyone who has moved around like me. I thought it was important to make a list in order to see the instability. I have learned to have a sense of humor about this now, thank God!

> I was moved from the country into Mattoon, Illinois right after I was born in 1955.
> I lived in a house in Mattoon, IL from 1955-1961.
> I went into my first foster home in August 1961.
> I went into my second foster home in Rose Hill in August 1961.
> I went into ISSCS children's home in September 1961.
> I went to live with my Aunt Norma and Uncle George in June 1963.
> I went to live with my dad in Decatur IL in 1965.

I moved to Hammond IL in August 1968.

I moved to Sullivan IL in June 1972.

I moved in with my brother in January 1973.

I moved into an apartment with Dale in April 1973.

I moved into another apartment in August 1973.

I moved to Bozeman, Montana in September 1973.

I went into State Hospital in October 1973.

I went into a half-way house in Decatur IL in December 1973.

I moved into a trailer with Dale in May 1974.

I lived in motel for a short time in May 1974.

I moved into a house in Alabama in June 1974.

I moved to Santa Fe, New Mexico in July 1974.

I moved into a country house in IL in August 1974.

I moved in with Dale's sister in Delaware in December 1974.

I took a job as a live-in nanny in January 1975.

I lived with Dale's friends for a short time in April 1975.

I moved to Alabama in April 1975, living at fruit stand.

I moved into a trailer with Dale in Montgomery, AL in May 1975.

I left Dale and stayed with my sister in Hammond IL in June 1975.

I married and moved into apartment in Decatur IL in August 1975.

I moved into house with Dale in Decatur IL around October 1975.

I moved into an apartment by myself in Decatur IL in May 1977.

I moved into a house with Dale in Decatur IL in July 1977.

I moved into a beach house on Sanibel Island, Fla in Dec. 1977.

I moved into an apartment on Sanibel Island, Fla in Jan. 1978.

I moved in with Jim on Sanibel Island, Fla in February 1978.

I moved into an apartment in Fort Myers, Fla in March 1978.

I lived with Jim's friends for a short time in Michigan in April 1978.

I moved into an apartment in Decatur IL in May 1978.

I moved into an apartment with Jim in Decatur IL in Sept. 1978.

I moved into an apartment with Jim in Decatur IL in Feb. 1979.

I moved into a motel in Fort Myers, Fla in March 1979.

I moved into an apartment in Fort Myers, Fla in April 1979.

I lived in various motels on the way to New Orleans in Sept. 1979.

I lived in the Salvation Army in New Orleans in Sept. 1979.

I lived in apartment briefly in Decatur IL in October 1979.

I moved into an apartment in Decatur IL in October 1979.

I moved into an apartment in Decatur IL in March 1981.

I moved into an apartment in River Rouge, MI in May 1981.

I moved in a house with Jim's dad in Detroit MI in August 1981.

I moved into an apartment in Albuquerque, NM in Dec. 1985.

I moved back home to Detroit n Jan. 1986.

I moved into an apartment in IL August 1986.

I moved back home to Detroit in September 1986.

I moved in with a friend around Detroit, MI in January 1989.

I moved into an apartment in Detroit, MI in May 1989.

I moved into an apartment in Dearborn, MI in May 1990.

I moved into a flat in Dearborn, MI in September 1990.

I moved into an efficiency apartment in Dearborn MI in April 1992.

I moved in with a friend in MI in May 1992.

I moved into an apartment in Detroit, MI in June 1992.

I moved into an apartment in Detroit, MI in August 1992.

I moved into a house in Detroit, MI in December 1993.

I got married and moved into a house in Howell, MI in March 1996!

And I might be adding to this list in the not too distant future if I
    move out of the home I am living in to a smaller home.

I moved around so much that I lived in the same apartment twice!
The apartment I had on my own in May 1977 was the same apartment
I had in March-May 1981. What are the odds of that happening? I guess

with a life like mine, the odds were pretty good. Maybe God was trying to tell me something, but if He was, I wasn't listening to Him at the time. I think it's funny now.

I was also in a few hospital psych wards—one in Bozeman, Montana in October 1973, one in April 1977 in Decatur, IL, and one in Chelsea, MI in August 2011. I was also in jail for a short time in March 1977.

Judging by what I have seen in other people's lives, I would say I lived a very unstable life until I met my husband. I feel like I was a young sapling blowing in the wind when I was young, with very few roots, and as a young adult girl, l I was like a leaf blowing around in the wind, going in every direction. I just went wherever the wind blew me.

ME!

In the process of all this crap I went through, I lost the most important in the world to me—*me!* What a tragic loss! ***It has taken me years of AA, support groups, including the FACT support group, a lot of therapy, and eventually a loving husband, and last but certainly not least, God, to find the 'me' I lost so many years ago.***

It has been almost thirty-nine years since I began this journey of sobriety and recovery, and although it has been a bumpy ride at times, especially with the loss of my husband, I feel as though I am finally coming to a place of complete wholeness within myself, a place where I can just be ok with *me* and my past. I feel as though I am truly healing for the first time in my life. I know my husband healed me tremendously, but due to the lack of his presence and comfort in my life, I am healing even more emotionally, and growing spiritually by leaps and bounds.

It is such a wholesome feeling to finally have *me.* The journey was worth it. I encourage anyone who has had the same struggles as I have had to not give up. *Most importantly, hold on to God's hand, for He will love, guide, and heal you in ways that only He can. He is the ultimate Healer.*

Gratitude

I started keeping a gratitude journal not long after Larry passed away, and I continue to keep one because I know how easy it can be for me to feel sorry for myself. *When I get in these moods, which usually don't last long, I get on my knees and beg God for help. "Please, Lord, help me to surrender everything to YOU, and trust that everything is divinely orchestrated, even if it doesn't make any sense to me." I need to remind myself that God's ways are much deeper and higher than my ways, and that He sees the beginning and the end. I don't know what God has for me in the future, and I don't need to know. All I need to do right now is stay focused on doing this autobiography and drawing closer to the Holy Spirit. That's all I know. God will work out the rest of my life if I just GO WITH THE FLOW. There is no sense in me fighting the flow, even if it takes me along some rocky spots. One thing I have learned is that with great pain comes great gain.*

Some people believe that being a Christian means having a blessed life, with everything materially and otherwise being perfect. They go to God as if He is Santa Clause, looking for the blessings of God, instead of seeking Him. *He is the ultimate blessing! I seek Him, and whatever God decides to bless me with is His business. I have learned the hard way that I don't always know what is best for me anyway, so I need to step out of the way and let God do His thing. The biggest blessing is His Love.*

I read a lot of Oswald Chambers, and he talks a lot about God being the blessing. I love it when God blesses me with things I want, such as beautiful dress at a cheap cost, but the reason I love getting these blessings is not so much for the blessing itself, but because it brings me so much joy to know that my Heavenly Father loves me. To me, it a way to draw closer to God Himself. Oh, how I do love Him. He is a good, good Daddy! And I am His child! What an amazing thing to know. And it should be an amazing thing for any former foster child who has struggled with feelings of abandonment to know this. In Psalm 27 it says, "when my father and my mother forsake me, then the Lord will take me up." These are not just words; they are a living reality to those who will open their hearts to His abundant love. This should be a great comfort for all foster children.

Our Heavenly Father's Love

My biggest hope and desire for former foster children who read the FACT book and my autobiography is to know the love of God. I want them to know they are His children, and just as precious and beautiful in His sight as any other child. No child should ever have to endure what foster children have, and I refuse to believe it is the will of a loving Father to see any of his children suffer, but we live in an imperfect world with imperfect people, who for whatever reason could not or would not take care of their children, and these are the foster children. It isn't fair, and it stinks to high heaven that we have gone through what we have. The sense of abandonment that we all suffered with from having been in foster care is the most brutal form of abuse any child could suffer. The worst thing that could have ever happened in my childhood was being abandoned by my mom when I was at my most vulnerable in foster care. It was a loud and clear statement of my worth to her, which obviously was not much, but the most damaging of all was overall sense of worth to even God.

A lot of foster children have problems believing and/or trusting in God because of their abandonment issues. The very first role model we should have for God are our parents, and if we are being abandoned by our own parents, what does that say about God? That He will abandon us too? I know for myself that I struggled with this very issue, not that I didn't believe in God, but questioning my worth to him and whether he would be there for me. As children we want so much to believe we are loved and cared for by our parents, and when they let us down, we are left questioning our worth. If we aren't worth anything to our own parents, it is difficult to believe we are worth anything to anybody, including God. And if we aren't feeling worthy, how can we believe and trust in a Heavenly Father? How can we trust in Him when all else has failed?

I have always been too trusting, especially when things are unstable in my life, and I believe part of the reason for that is that I feel so vulnerable and needy that I desperately need to trust. I found myself being too trusting of people around me when my husband died because I so much needed to trust. *I always say that God had to prove His love for me, and thank God He did, but I find it sad that it ever had to come to that. God, how my heart goes out to foster children.* I have always said that I will spend my last dying breath speaking out the behalf of foster children. I can't change my past or anybody else's, but I can at least do my part by showing love and compassion *by being a voice for the unheard millions.* Hopefully, I can at least give them some hope.

I like what my younger brother shared in his excerpt in the **FACT** book: "*for all of us who have been foster children, for those who are now, and for those who will be—we must remember that these trials produce perseverance, and perseverance produces character, and character produces hope. And hope does not fail.*"

Here is another excerpt from the **FACT** book, that should help someone: "*Being bounced around in foster care made me feel very abandoned, and I always felt like I was a puzzle piece that didn't fit in the puzzle anywhere. I had a lot of anger, resentment, and shame about being in foster care, and I grabbed onto everything I could to try to overcome my past, which often was not good for me. I tried so hard to fit into the puzzle, but it seemed to no avail was another fail, until I finally surrendered my life to God, Who will never abandon me.*

This could be an excerpt for many other foster children, summing up the feeling of never fitting in anywhere, the anger, resentment, and shame attached to feeling unwanted and abandoned. When I was first putting some material together for FACT years ago, I had this very concept in my mind. *I felt I kept trying to fit into the puzzle, until I finally found a path of my own choosing, and surrendered my life to God, Who will never abandon me. I know I may sound like a broken record, writing so much about the love of God, but it truly was the only way out of my*

darkness. I came to God with a broken heart and spirit, desperately in need of love and guidance. He was and still is my only hope. I don't want foster children reading this book to think I am preaching at them. I am not. I am speaking from experience. I only want Love for them.

Would I wish my past on anybody else? Never! Am I glad I went through all the crap I went through in my life? No way! But I am glad that because I went through all my trials and tribulations, I have character and integrity. One thing people who know me well say is that I have integrity. I am a caring human being. I have compassion and empathy. I may not enjoy adversity when it is happening, but it does build character, and without character, what am I worth as a human being? Not much. It really is all about love.

Only people who have gone through the fires of suffering can truly be compassionate and loving. Only people who have seen tragedy in their life will take the time out to listen with empathy to other people's suffering.

A New Beginning with Opie

As I sat writing on January 21, 2021 about grieving the loss of my dog Holden, I began wondering when or if I would ever be ready to get another dog. I happened to talk with a friend that night about not feeling as safe without a dog, and she encouraged me to get another one. It had been seven months since I lost Holden, so I thought maybe I should at least be open to the idea, especially since I love to walk so much, so I got online and looked at adoptable dogs at the nearby shelter, and there was *Opie*! Surprise, surprise! *I always say God loves to surprise me, and He did it again!* I went there the next day to look at him and knew right away he was right for me. I was amazed to find out Opie had the same background as me. He was abused some and moved around. This is the fourth home he has been in, and it will be his last. I reassured Opie I will never abandon him. I was wanting a Golden Lab, which is what he is. I took him for a walk and adopted him that day! That was easy! *I know from experience that when something happens that easy in my life, it is a God thing! And 'God' is 'dog' spelled backward!*

I brought Opie home and he made himself at home right away! So sweet! I love Opie so very much. He is my fur baby and I hope and pray God will keep him with me more many more years. All I want to do is love Opie.

I have been told I have a gift with abused and/or neglected animals, which does seem to be true. Animals come up to me all the time because they feel safe with me and know I love them. Opie knew he was safe with me and responded to my love for him without hesitation. He snuggled with me on the couch the first night, and kept me awake some because he was snoring, but I was happy to have him with me, and he was obviously happy to be with me, as he practically wanted to lay on top of me!

God never ceases to amaze me in the ways He works! I now have a dog with a similar childhood of mine! Because I understand his issues so well, I am the perfect pet mama for him! What a blessing to give Opie a loving home! I am not only giving Opie all the love he needs, but I also feel like I am giving myself love because our backgrounds are so similar. I am extremely sensitive to his feelings. When I first got Opie, he was very timid, but with a lot of love and reassurance from me, he is now very mellow and very comfortable with me. It has been such a joy to watch Opie heal as I am healing.

On June 28, 2021, I went to Walmart, and while shopping heard a voice over the intercom say, "there is a tornado warning; please go to the back of the store." I dropped everything and rushed out the door to go to my car instead. Opie was in the car with the windows rolled down, and NO WAY was I going to leave him like that! I got in my car and drove home in the pouring rain, praying the whole time for God's protection and we arrived safely at home. I wouldn't abandon a dog, let alone a child. My mother should have been ashamed for abandoning her own children, but she wasn't. How pathetic and sad.

A Miracle Letter!

On January 29th, 2021, I received a letter that has left me even more amazed at the power of God. I was so blown away by it that I feel compelled to share it:

> *1-25-2021*
>
> *Dear Carol,*
>
> *First, I hope this letter finds you well and that you are the Carol Lucas that wrote the book for former foster children. Secondly, praise be to God, if you are, for all*

of the hard work you must have done to make that book happen and for surviving through the foster care system yourself! In my careers, I've had the pleasure of working with many foster children and I've often wondered what they are doing now and how they are.

Now, Carol, I know this letter might come as a shock or seem weird. Believe me, it does to me too! I am a Christ follower and I try my best to always do what I believe God is asking me to do. For whatever reason a few days back, your name came to mind while I was praying. Of course, we do not know each other so I did what anyone else would do, I Googled you. LOL! I was immediately drawn to your work with foster children. One of those careers of mine that I mentioned was a child maltreatment investigator and foster care worker.

There are no telling how many people you have helped and continue to help by sharing your story.

Sometimes our work doesn't come to fruition until many years later and sometimes we don't even get to see it play out. Never the less, God uses it to touch the ones it is supposed to touch. So, never doubt you have changed lives!

If you are not Carol at all or the Carol Lucas who wrote a book about foster children, there is some reason you are receiving this letter. Try to figure out the reason why. Maybe it's your turn to encourage someone or maybe it's time to purchase and read the Bible. It's a fascinating book, just as I'm sure Carol's is as well.

Well, my work here is done for today. Whomever is reading this letter, I pray that God will shine bright in

your life and that you will know your value in this world
because it is just wouldn't be the same without you. You
have a story to share that someone else needs to hear.

With much love and respect because of Him,
AA

I was so overwhelmed by this letter that it moved me to tears. That
Almighty God would speak my name to this woman who has never
known or heard of me is SO amazing! That she would take the time to
contact me is also amazing! It is a true testimony to the Love of God,
which I took personally. I believe it was a message of hope for me to keep
forging ahead with this autobiography. God understands how difficult
it has been for me to write my story and wanted to remind me that the
work I put into was worth it, that it would help others.

Thank You God, for your awesome and wonderful love!

I responded to AA's letter by writing her one, which I felt very much
led to do. On February 11th, 2021, I received an email from her, which I
was even more amazed by than the letter, as she described in detail how
God spoke to her. Here is the email she wrote:

Hey, Carol!

I cannot begin to tell you how relieved I was to get
your letter. You are so right....God is full of surprises.
Yep, smack dab in the middle of my prayers one night,
your name popped into my mind. I'd love to say that I
immediately said "Ok, God, let's go! What do you want
me to do?" But, no...I struggle with wondering "Is that
God talking to me or is that just me making up stuff in
my mind?" So, instead, when your name popped in my

mind, I said to God.. "Huh, God? I don't even know anyone named Carol Lucas." And true to God's nature, He just kept on and on with Carol Lucas...Carol Lucas... all through the night. It went like this...

God: Carol Lucas

Me: But God, I really don't know anyone named Carol Lucas.

God: Carol Lucas

Me: I think that's just me making up a name. Maybe I read it somewhere.

God: Carol Lucas

Me: Come on, God, really? What am I supposed to do with that?

God: Carol Lucas

Me: OK, God. If I remember her name in the morning, I will try to figure something out.

God: silent...nothing...yikes

Next morning...

God: Carol Lucas

Me: You got it, God. Tell me what to do.

God: Google

Me: This is nuts but you are God!

Crazy, right, Carol? I don't know why I am so hard headed. The good news is that 99% of the time, I will follow through with what He is asking me to do. I've often said to my friends that I know God just laughs and shakes His head at me sometimes. :) Well, I Googled Carol Lucas and a bunch of you popped up. I started reading through anything about the Carols that struck *my mind and you were the only one that I could relate to or had something in common with. Here is the super fun part for me. As soon as I started reading about you, Carol, as clear as the clearest ocean where you can perfectly see the fish swimming (know what I am talking about?), I KNEW you were the right Carol Lucas. God said, "That's THE one!" I read about your foster care work and found that you had authored a book. The book told me you were from Howell. Next came the search to try to find some way to contact you. God, led me to your husband's obituary. Oh, Carol, I am so, so sorry for your loss. The article in the newspaper helped me tie back to Howell.*

I fervently prayed while writing the letter to you that I was doing the right thing, that you were the right person, that I would use the right words, and that you wouldn't be spooked that someone had looked you up. Even writing to you now, I get teary eyed because of the great love of our Lord. You said it....He is so loving and so gracious. I am amazed at how He can use us to encourage each other, to spread His love, and to move His work further down the road.

Sweet lady, I don't even begin to know the reason or claim to understand why, but God did a whole lot of moving me to get to you. You are special to Him. You are valued, needed, loved, worthy. This autobiography you are writing must be powerful. No doubt God has something up His sleeve and a person in mind that needs to read it. So, write it for all you are worth. Pour everything into it. You must.

I'd love to stay in contact with you and just so you know, I have great listening ears. I completely understand the part about not sharing so much anymore with your friends; although, I bet they would be more willing to listen than you think. :)

No Facebook...I try to stay away from social media as much as I can.

I wish you the best of luck in your endeavors with the book and will definitely be praying for you. I'm forever grateful to have crossed your path because this wonderfulness has given me validation that I AM hearing from God and need to keep on trusting His words to me.

In it with God to see where we go next,
AA

Talking with AA

Within a week of getting the letter we were texting each other and made a date to talk on the phone. Wow! She told me everything that was in the letter—how she was in prayer one evening and kept hearing my name, how the Lord persisted the next morning when she woke up, and that she was told to Google me. It was one thing to receive an email about this, but to hear her speak about it on the phone was even more awesome! We both wondered why God did this, and figured it was for both of us. *I believe God was giving me a loud and clear message to forge ahead with my story, that my work would help many former foster children, and she believes it was done for her own spiritual growth. I know God can do all things, but for God to speak my name to a stranger is awesome beyond words! GOD IS AWESOME!*

As AA said at the end of her last email to me, "*in it with God to see where we go next.*"

I am not sure where God is taking this, but I am certain He does. I am not sure what the future holds for me, but I am sure of the One Who holds it in His Hands, so I will hold on tightly to His Hand and GO WITH THE FLOW...THE FLOW IS LOVE....

This picture reminds me of my work for foster children, and amazingly, the little girl he is holding looks like me as a young child!

JESUS, PLEASE BLESS EACH AND EVERY FOSTER CHILD— PAST, PRESENT, AND FUTURE, WITH YOUR WONDROUS LOVE!

CAROL LUCAS

Acknowledgements

My deepest gratitude toward the ones who helped me in writing my autobiography is for God, as I know it was ultimately Him who gave me the courage, strength, perseverance, and grace to do it. It was His Hand that guided mine in writing a living testimony of His Love in my life.

I am grateful for the ones who encouraged me to write my story. Had it not been for them telling me it would help my other book *Fostered Adult Children Together On the Bridge to Healing* sell better, I would never have done it. I had no desire to *go back there* again, nor did I want to put the work into it, but I forged ahead because I knew I had a calling from God and want the FACT book to reach former foster children.

I am so blessed to have Angel Paulson, my publishing consultant from IUniverse. He truly has been an angel!

I am also grateful for God leading me to a spiritual mentor who reassured me I would not only be strong enough to write an in-depth story, but it would also be more healing for me.

I am so very grateful for Ashelyn, a Christian woman who contacted me to let me know God kept speaking my name to her while in prayer, which happened when I was emotionally struggling about sharing my deepest and most shameful parts of my past. She helped me over that hurdle and made me realize *I must tell the truth and nothing but the truth.* I always say "be real to heal," and God forbid I be a hypocrite, so I told the whole truth. Most importantly, speaking my own truth frees other former foster children to speak theirs and reassures them they aren't alone in their struggles and suffering. I want to be a voice for them.

Last but not least, I am beyond words in expressing my gratitude for my late husband Larry, whose love motivated me. My sorrow truly was my strength.

Printed in the United States
by Baker & Taylor Publisher Services